DeFi Demystified

DeFi Demystified

The Beginner's Guide to Decentralized Finance

Avery Grant

Mindful Pages

Published in 2026

ISBN: 9789374599600 (PB)
ISBN: 9789374597309 (eBook)

Published by

Mindful Pages
Imprint of Alpha Editions LLC
312 W. 2nd St #1834
Casper, WY 82601, USA

This book was developed using advanced writing tools to support the drafting and ideation process. All content has been thoughtfully curated, refined, and reviewed to ensure quality and relevance.

Content

Introduction
The Keys and the Cage

In 2021, a twenty-three-year-old software engineer in Berlin received a notification that his savings—every cent he had earned since university—had vanished overnight. Not stolen in the traditional sense, not even transferred by a visible hand, but drained through a contract he himself had approved days earlier. The transaction was irreversible. There was no helpline, no fraud department, no sympathetic voice at the other end of a phone line. There was only a line of code and the immutable ledger confirming his consent. The paradox of decentralised finance—DeFi—is captured in that moment: empowerment and exposure fused into a single act. The same system that can make you sovereign over your wealth can also make you its sole custodian, judge, and casualty.

A traditional bank promises safety by locking your money away, dulling both its risk and your agency. DeFi does the opposite. It hands you the keys—to your funds, your data, and your decisions. The catch is that keys cut both ways. Possession grants freedom, but it also transfers responsibility. For the first time in modern finance, the retail participant stands on the same technical footing as the institutions once beyond their reach. The question, then, is not whether this new terrain is safe, but whether one can learn to navigate it with eyes open. This book exists to make that navigation possible.

The story of DeFi is often told as revolution: the overthrow of banks by code, the victory of transparency over trust. Yet that narrative misses the quieter, more profound transformation underneath. What has emerged is not merely a new product but a new operating system for money—an architecture that rewires how value moves, who controls it, and on what terms. Its significance cannot be judged by price charts or token tickers. Like the printing press or the early internet, DeFi reconfigures the relationship between individuals and institutions, between rules and execution, between belief and verification. It is the culmination of a centuries-long human impulse: to design systems that function not because we trust each other, but because we trust the mechanism.

For most of history, finance has been a theatre of intermediaries. Ledgers were guarded by clerks, credit assessed by bankers, transactions cleared by institutions whose credibility substituted for transparency. That edifice—layered, hierarchical, and opaque—granted stability at the cost of agency. When blockchain technology appeared in 2009, it offered an inversion of that structure: a shared ledger without a single master copy, where consensus replaced authority. DeFi extended that inversion, embedding market logic into code. Lending, trading, and saving—once human agreements—became automated protocols. The infrastructure of trust was translated into programmable rules. The result is a system that runs not on belief in an institution, but on the predictability of mathematics.

Still, mathematics does not absolve humanity. Every protocol reflects human incentives, blind spots, and aspirations. The rhetoric of "trustless finance" conceals a subtler reality: while we no longer trust a bank clerk, we must still trust the code, the developers who wrote it, and ourselves as its operators. Failures in any layer—technical, economic, or behavioural—can unravel the illusion of security. Thus, to understand DeFi, one must learn to read its anatomy: the chain that records, the contracts that execute, and the interfaces that mediate. One must also learn to read the incentives that keep participants honest, and the cognitive biases that make them reckless. DeFi is not a miracle of engineering but an experiment in human coordination. To approach it wisely is to see that every protocol is a mirror held up to our collective behaviour.

This book takes that mirror seriously. It treats decentralised finance not as a passing trend but as a new literacy—one that fuses economics, technology, and psychology. The purpose here is not to sell participation, nor to issue warnings from a distance, but to cultivate understanding. Once you can interpret how value flows through protocols like Uniswap or Aave, you cease to be a spectator dazzled by jargon. You become an informed participant capable of evaluating risk and reward with professional-level prudence. The method you will acquire is repeatable: a way to interrogate code, incentives, and context, not a collection of tips doomed to expiry with the next market cycle.

To grasp what is at stake, consider the scale of migration already underway. Trillions in notional value now circulate through smart contracts—self-executing pieces of software immune to office hours and bureaucracy. Entire lending markets function without credit departments; exchanges operate without brokers; treasuries rebalance without accountants. Each innovation carries the same double edge: transparency married to complexity, efficiency shadowed by fragility. When algorithms intermediate capital, failure modes change. Losses no longer come from deceit alone but from misinterpretation, complacency, or misplaced trust in automation. The new financial literacy is therefore not merely technical—it is behavioural. It asks: can humans act rationally when the guardrails of central authority are removed?

This question, though modern in form, echoes through economic history. Every leap in financial autonomy has demanded a corresponding evolution in personal discipline. The invention of paper money required faith in symbols; the rise of equity markets demanded patience amid volatility. DeFi's demand is deeper still: it requires individuals to shoulder institutional responsibilities—custody, due diligence, risk management—once outsourced by design. The shift is existential as much as economic. It tests whether self-governance in finance can coexist with human fallibility. To participate in DeFi is to play a game with perfect information but imperfect judgement.

Throughout the chapters ahead, we will move from first principles to practical mastery. We will demystify how liquidity pools price assets without order books, how lending protocols secure collateral without collectors, and how staking transforms idle tokens into instruments of consensus. But alongside technical fluency, this book insists on a second education: one in temperament. You will learn not only how systems work but how to behave within them—how to resist greed, recognise cognitive traps, and calibrate exposure to uncertainty. The art of DeFi is as much about restraint as innovation. Mastery begins with knowing what not to do.

Yet this is not a manual of abstinence. Decentralised finance, stripped of hype, holds genuine promise: global accessibility, programmable transparency, and open competition in a field long dominated by gatekeepers. A farmer in Kenya can now access a dollar-denominated savings rate once reserved for institutional clients; a small business can manage treasury functions without a banker's permission. These are not abstractions. They are proofs of concept for a more inclusive financial architecture. But inclusion without comprehension breeds exploitation. The path to sustainable participation runs through literacy, not optimism.

The tone of this book is deliberately sober, because DeFi does not need evangelists; it needs interpreters. The most important skill you will acquire is not trading strategy but discernment—the ability to distinguish between innovation and imitation, between yield and illusion. You will see that every percentage point of return corresponds to a counterparty's risk and that "passive income" in DeFi is often a euphemism for active vigilance. Through real-world walkthroughs of protocols and case studies of failure, you will develop a radar for hidden fragility. You will learn to see scams not as anomalies but as structural features of open systems—inevitable where complexity outpaces comprehension.

The deeper argument of *DeFi Demystified* is that decentralisation is not a destination but a discipline. It forces us to confront what we outsource when we seek convenience, and what we regain when we accept responsibility. In traditional finance, trust was delegated upward; in DeFi, it must be cultivated inward. That is why this book treats the study of decentralised systems as an act of self-study. To read code is to read human nature under conditions of perfect accountability.

The chapters that follow proceed from architecture to agency. We begin by dissecting what DeFi actually is: not a speculative playground but a programmable market infrastructure. We will trace how blockchains replace intermediaries with consensus and how that shift produces both efficiency and new points of failure. We then explore wallets—the interface between autonomy and exposure—before delving into the mechanisms of trading, lending, and yield generation. Later, we confront the realities of security, regulation, and sustainability. Each section is designed not to hand you conclusions but to refine your perception. The goal is clarity, not certainty.

At its heart, this book is an argument for literacy as liberation. Once you can map where risk resides—whether in code, incentives, or human behaviour—the fog of hype dissipates. You no longer need to rely on influencers or institutions to interpret reality. You become capable of reading the system yourself. And in doing so, you reclaim what finance had long denied its participants: informed consent. DeFi, properly understood, is the democratisation of due diligence.

Still, knowledge alone will not save you. The challenge of decentralised finance is psychological as much as intellectual. It seduces with the illusion of control and punishes lapses in attention. The discipline it demands is closer to aviation than gambling: checklists, simulations, drills. In the closing chapter, you will learn how to translate these lessons into a personal operating manual—security routines, portfolio reviews, and decision frameworks that keep autonomy sustainable. Participation in open finance is optional; mastery is measured not by what you chase, but by what you can calmly refuse.

We stand at a threshold. On one side lies a financial order defined by trust in institutions; on the other, a fluid landscape defined by trust in code—and in one's own capacity to act responsibly within it. Whether this experiment matures into infrastructure or collapses into chaos depends not on technology but on the collective literacy of its users. *DeFi Demystified* is written in the conviction that comprehension is the most stabilising force in any open system. If you can read the code, the incentives, and yourself, you already hold the only key that matters.

Chapter 1
What Is DeFi, Really?

In a café in Buenos Aires, a graphic designer scrolls through an app that lets her earn interest in dollars without ever touching a bank. The yield is real, the access instant, the institution absent. Across the world, in rural Nigeria, a developer uses the same network to lend stablecoins to strangers whose faces he will never see. Both are participants in a financial system that no government built and no bank controls. Neither could explain every line of code underpinning it, yet both are enacting a quiet revolution in how trust is organised. That revolution has a name—DeFi—and its power lies not in mystery but in structure.

The paradox of decentralised finance is that it feels alien while performing familiar functions. Behind the glowing dashboards and jargon lies something recognisable: markets that borrow, lend, and exchange value. The difference is not what they do, but how they do it. DeFi replaces people with protocols, and policies with code. The traditional financial system runs on institutions enforcing agreements; DeFi runs on distributed consensus executing them automatically. Understanding this distinction—between *enforcement by authority* and *execution by architecture*—is the key to seeing what DeFi really is: programmable market infrastructure, not a speculative carnival.

For centuries, finance has been a choreography of ledgers and intermediaries. Banks, brokers, and clearing houses existed to bridge gaps in trust—to verify ownership, match trades, and ensure that promises were kept. Every innovation in that lineage, from double-entry bookkeeping to central clearing, was ultimately a tool for coordination. Blockchains did not abolish that need; they reimagined how it could be met. Instead of relying on a trusted bookkeeper, they made the ledger itself communal and tamper-proof. Instead of contracts enforced by courts, they introduced *smart contracts*—programs that execute automatically when conditions are met. What emerged was not chaos but a new kind of order: one where rules are transparent and enforcement is instantaneous.

DeFi sits atop that foundation, transforming static records into dynamic liquidity. It turns ledgers into living systems where assets flow through code-defined channels rather than corporate ones. Automated Market Makers (AMMs) set prices without human dealers, adjusting them with mathematical precision instead of intuition. Lending pools allocate credit through collateral ratios rather than credit scores. What once required a trading floor or a risk committee now unfolds within algorithms running on public blockchains. To see DeFi clearly, one must learn to see past its novelty and recognise the continuity beneath it. Every AMM is a market maker stripped to its mathematical essence; every lending protocol is a balance sheet formalised in code.

This reframing matters because it restores rationality to a field too often distorted by hype. DeFi is not a miracle of yield generation but a system of incentives—carefully or carelessly designed—that motivate participants to provide liquidity, security, or governance. If you follow the money, you see that every reward has a payer, every emission a source. Fees, arbitrage, and inflation schedules form a web of cause and consequence. To treat DeFi as a magic money machine is to miss its most instructive truth: it is an economy of incentives, not an act of alchemy. Understanding who earns, who pays, and why the loop closes—or fails to—turns speculation into comprehension.

Yet before we can map those incentives, we must learn to navigate the stack itself: the layered architecture that transforms code into action. Every DeFi interaction—every trade, loan, or stake—passes through a chain, a contract, and a front end. The *chain* records, the *contract* executes, and the *interface* translates the complexity into clicks. Each layer has its own vulnerabilities: chains can congest or fork; contracts can contain bugs; interfaces can deceive. The system is "trustless" only to the degree that you know where trust still hides. Understanding the stack is therefore not a technical indulgence but a survival skill. Stack literacy is day-one safety.

Consider what happens when that literacy is absent. A beautifully designed front end can conceal a malicious contract. A protocol audit can lull users into false security while the governance process remains compromised. A bridge between blockchains can become a single point of catastrophic failure. To act safely in DeFi is not to memorise risks but to understand their geography—to know which layer of the system you are trusting at any moment. Once you can see those layers, you can make informed trade-offs rather than blind leaps of faith.

And then there is autonomy—the promise and the burden that defines this space. To hold your own keys is to hold absolute control, but also absolute accountability. In the old world, forgetting a password meant a reset; in DeFi, it can mean irretrievable loss. The romantic rhetoric of "be your own bank" often omits the operational discipline that role demands. Autonomy, if it is to endure, must be supported by habit: secure key management, deliberate approvals, methodical verification. The ethos of decentralisation is not freedom from responsibility but freedom *through* responsibility. What once belonged to compliance departments now belongs to individuals armed with rituals instead of regulations.

This is the deeper cultural shift DeFi introduces—not just technological decentralisation, but psychological decentralisation. It asks users to think like system operators, not customers. The surface simplicity of connecting a wallet conceals the reality that one is stepping into the command seat of a miniature financial institution. Risk management becomes personal. Security becomes behavioural. Every interaction is an audit of one's own attentiveness. For some, this is exhilarating; for others, exhausting. Either way, it is the unavoidable cost of genuine sovereignty.

Seen through this lens, DeFi is not a parallel universe to traditional finance but its next evolutionary stage—a system where the core functions of banking, trading, and lending are rebuilt as open, interoperable code. The old intermediaries do not disappear; they mutate into new forms. Liquidity providers become market makers; validators become auditors; users become their own custodians. The boundaries blur between participant and platform. In this new topology, power resides not in titles or institutions but in knowledge—specifically, in the ability to interpret mechanisms rather than narratives.

This first chapter aims to grant that interpretive power. It will trace how DeFi transforms the mechanics of ledgers into the fluid dynamics of liquidity, revealing the architecture that makes open finance possible. It will dissect the stack—from base chains to front ends—exposing where trust hides and how it can fail. It will map the flow of incentives, showing why yields exist and when they deceive. And it will confront the reality of autonomy, reminding you that empowerment without preparation is simply exposure in disguise.

By the end, you will see that DeFi's most radical promise is not financial emancipation but epistemic clarity. It teaches you to see systems as they are, not as they are marketed. To participate intelligently in decentralised finance is to develop a new literacy—part technological, part behavioural, entirely human. The chapter begins where every serious engagement with DeFi must: not with profits or protocols, but with perception. Once you learn to read the structure, the noise subsides, and the signal emerges. What looked like chaos resolves into code, and what felt like speculation becomes understanding.

From Ledgers to Liquidity

On 13 September 2017, in Zug, Switzerland—the self-styled "Crypto Valley"—a small team at a start-up called MakerDAO executed a transaction that quietly altered the trajectory of finance. They launched the first fully decentralised stablecoin system, using Ethereum smart contracts to mint digital dollars backed by crypto collateral. No central bank, no treasury desk, no compliance department—just code, collateral, and consensus. The experiment worked. Within two years, billions of dollars were flowing through lending pools and automated exchanges built on the same principle: financial logic rendered in software, validated by distributed agreement rather than institutional trust. What had once required balance sheets and boardrooms could now be reproduced, line by line, on a public ledger.

The leap from ledgers to liquidity sounds dramatic, yet the deeper story is continuity. Finance has always been an exercise in recording promises and clearing obligations. The innovation of decentralised finance (DeFi) lies in re-engineering those same functions within programmable infrastructure. A ledger still sits at its core, but the entries are written to a blockchain—a shared record synchronised across thousands of nodes rather than guarded by a single clerk. Contracts still define obligations, but they are executed by code rather than enforced by lawyers. Markets still form prices, but the matching of buyers and sellers is automated by algorithms. In DeFi, structure remains; intermediaries vanish. The apparatus of trust shifts from institutions to computation.

Consider the Automated Market Maker (AMM), the beating heart of decentralised trading. When Uniswap launched in November 2018, it appeared absurdly simple: two pools of tokens governed by a formula, $x \times y = k$, ensuring that the product of reserves remained constant. There were no order books, no brokers, no queue of bids and asks—only liquidity providers depositing assets and traders exchanging them directly through the contract. Yet beneath the novelty lay something familiar: the continuous double auction, stripped of its human intermediaries. In traditional markets, specialists and dealers quote prices to balance supply and demand; Uniswap does the same mathematically. Its liquidity pools are automated balance sheets, adjusting prices in response to trades rather than negotiations.

The elegance of that formula conceals a profound shift in how markets express trust. In a centralised exchange, traders trust the operator to maintain order, honour withdrawals, and prevent manipulation. In an AMM, those assurances are encoded. The smart contract's logic replaces discretionary authority; settlement finality is achieved not through reputation but through consensus across thousands of verifying computers. Yet the trust does not disappear—it migrates. Participants must trust the contract's code, the network's security, and the integrity of their own decisions. The lesson, easily missed amid the rhetoric of "trustless finance", is that DeFi does not abolish trust; it redistributes it.

A second illustration comes from lending protocols. Aave, launched in January 2020, allows users to supply assets to a pool and borrow others against collateral. The system manages liquidity with algorithms adjusting interest rates in real time, reflecting demand. If utilisation rises, rates increase; when deposits exceed borrowing, they fall. The mechanism echoes the interbank markets of old, where rates responded to liquidity conditions, but without human dealers setting them. The risk engine, too, mirrors traditional prudence: loans are over-collateralised, and liquidation triggers when collateral values drop below safety thresholds. What distinguishes Aave is transparency. Every ratio, rate, and threshold is visible on-chain, accessible to anyone. The opacity that once required regulators now yields to code that is, at least in theory, auditable by the public.

These examples demonstrate DeFi's structural lineage: it inherits the bones of finance—price discovery, collateralisation, clearing—and recasts them as open-source protocols. The leap is not conceptual but operational.

Settlement becomes atomic; custody becomes self-managed; access becomes permissionless. A trader in Mumbai and a student in Lagos engage with the same liquidity pools through identical interfaces, bound by identical rules. Geography, once the scaffold of financial privilege, loses its grip. Yet accessibility does not equal simplicity. The removal of intermediaries exposes users directly to system mechanics once buffered by institutions. There is no banker to explain margin calls, no exchange to absorb a fat-finger error. The precision that gives DeFi its beauty also makes it unforgiving.

The transformation of infrastructure invites comparison with earlier technological ruptures. When electronic trading arrived in London in 1986's "Big Bang", clerks and runners were replaced by terminals, but market logic persisted. DeFi extends that digitisation one step further by making the exchange itself autonomous. Instead of a company running a platform, the platform becomes a public good—software maintained by token-holders and miners rather than employees. The analogy is not perfect: a blockchain cannot answer a complaint or reverse a mistake. But it clarifies the direction of travel. Finance is evolving from human-mediated trust to machine-mediated consensus, from discretionary governance to protocol governance.

Critics often point to the spectacular collapses that punctuate DeFi's history as evidence that this evolution is reckless. They are not wrong. The 2022 implosion of Terra, a synthetic stablecoin whose algorithmic peg failed, erased over 40 billion dollars of value and demonstrated the limits of self-referential systems. The episode underscored that code may execute flawlessly while the economics beneath it rot. The counter-example is instructive: MakerDAO, the project that began this chapter, survived the same crisis by relying on collateralised stability rather than circular incentives. Both used smart contracts; only one anchored its promises in real assets. The distinction marks the boundary between financial engineering and financial delusion.

To grasp why DeFi succeeds where it does, one must appreciate its central organising principle: composability. Every protocol is a module—an instrument that can be combined with others like building blocks. An AMM feeds price data to a lending pool; a stablecoin provides collateral for derivatives; a yield aggregator reallocates deposits among protocols. This modularity mirrors the standardisation that fuelled the growth of traditional finance: the adoption of the ISIN for securities, or SWIFT codes for international transfers. Where banks relied on legal contracts to ensure interoperability, DeFi relies on open standards written in code. The result is a system capable of extraordinary innovation and equally extraordinary contagion. Interconnection magnifies both efficiency and fragility.

The motif that threads through these examples is the ledger itself. In the old world, the ledger was passive: a record of events. In DeFi, it becomes active—a computational substrate upon which markets unfold in real time. Liquidity does not flow through intermediaries but through logic. Every deposit, every trade, every interest payment is an entry and an execution simultaneously. The ledger no longer waits for instructions; it *is* the instruction. This fusion of record and action collapses the distinction between accounting and exchange, transforming finance from a process of documentation into one of continuous computation.

The implications reach beyond technology. When transparency is radical and participation borderless, the gatekeeping functions of traditional finance—licensing, accreditation, and exclusivity—begin to erode. Yet so too does the safety net. The same openness that allows innovation invites exploitation. Automated markets cannot distinguish between a sophisticated arbitrageur and a naïve saver; both are treated as addresses on a chain. In this sense, DeFi resembles a wilderness more than a marketplace: freedom tempered only by the limits of one's understanding. Prudence becomes the new professionalism.

A quiet question, recurring like a heartbeat, accompanies every breakthrough: *What replaces the human judgement once embedded in institutions?* Consensus mechanisms validate blocks, but they do not evaluate ethics. A protocol cannot decide when to forgive a debt or protect a vulnerable user. It will execute precisely what it is told, even if what it is told destroys value. The discipline required of participants is therefore not only technical but moral—an awareness of when automation serves and when it blinds.

From the vantage of 2025, DeFi's trajectory appears both unstoppable and incomplete. Billions in daily volume suggest maturity; periodic crises reveal adolescence. Yet through its turbulence runs a coherent thread: the migration of trust from people to code, from promises to proofs. The technologies may evolve—new chains, new formulas, new governance models—but the underlying aspiration remains constant: to make markets that run on logic transparent enough to verify, robust enough to persist, and open enough to challenge monopoly.

The tension that animates this transformation will not resolve soon. A ledger without intermediaries delivers speed and autonomy but demands vigilance. Liquidity without gatekeepers offers equality of access but not equality of comprehension. As readers progress through this chapter, they face a quiet diagnostic question—one that separates speculation from understanding: when you look at a protocol, can you see the continuity beneath its novelty? The answer determines not only how safely you participate, but whether this new operating system for money becomes a foundation or a folly.

The Stack: Chain, Contract, Front End

On 14 February 2022, the Ethereum network halted for seven blocks—roughly eighty-four seconds—after a major node client, *Geth*, malfunctioned during a routine update.

Transactions froze, decentralised exchanges stalled, and lending protocols temporarily misreported account balances. The fault was swiftly corrected, yet the incident laid bare a subtle truth often lost beneath the rhetoric of "trustless systems": even in decentralised finance, trust has a topography. It lives not in human intermediaries but in the layers of software that mediate reality—the chain, the contract, and the front end. Each layer claims neutrality; each hides assumptions. Understanding that stack is not an act of technical curiosity but the first principle of safety.

At the base of the stack lies the **chain**—the substrate upon which all else depends. Ethereum, Solana, Avalanche, and their kin serve as shared ledgers, consensus machines that decide which version of history counts. Their promise is immutability: once a transaction is confirmed, it cannot be reversed without extraordinary collusion. Yet that promise is conditional. In September 2020, the Ethereum Classic network suffered a "51 per cent attack" in which a single actor gained control of the chain's hashing power, reorganising its history and double-spending roughly US$5.6 million in cryptocurrency. Consensus failed because participation thinned; the trustless mechanism had become, briefly, trust-based in disguise. The event illustrates the paradox: decentralisation is a spectrum, not an absolute. It demands diversity of nodes, geographical distribution, and honest majority assumptions—all human contingencies hiding beneath the mathematics.

Chains are like foundations in architecture: they determine what can safely be built above. A misconfigured consensus mechanism can cascade into every dependent layer. In June 2022, Solana's validators paused the network for nearly four hours after bots overwhelmed it with duplicate transactions during an NFT mint. Users could not transfer or trade assets; protocols blinked out like darkened shopfronts. The outage did not destroy funds, but it eroded confidence. Every "decentralised" protocol built atop that chain was, for that window of time, centralised by necessity. The implication is clear: base-layer resilience is not abstract engineering; it is lived experience. The ledger can only be as sovereign as its uptime.

Above the chain sits the **contract**—the logic that defines behaviour. Smart contracts are self-executing programs, neither aware nor forgiving. They translate human agreements into machine instructions, and in doing so, remove discretion. Yet code is not law in the moral sense; it is merely law in the mechanical one. The most famous reminder came on 17 June 2016, when *The DAO*—a decentralised investment fund built on Ethereum—was drained of 3.6 million ether after an attacker exploited a recursive call bug. No rules were broken; the code permitted the behaviour. The Ethereum community ultimately voted to roll back the chain, restoring funds but splitting the network in two: Ethereum and Ethereum Classic. That fracture remains a monument to the uneasy relationship between immutability and justice. Trust had migrated upward, from institutions to code, but moral judgement could not be programmed away.

Contracts, in practice, vary as widely as legal systems. Some are minimalist, governing simple swaps; others, such as those behind *Compound* or *Aave*, orchestrate thousands of variables across millions of users. Each contract introduces attack surfaces: arithmetic precision, timestamp dependencies, oracle inputs. To mitigate them, developers commission audits from firms like *Trail of Bits* or *CertiK*, whose reports read like surgical notes on the anatomy of risk. Yet even audits are signals, not guarantees. The Wormhole bridge exploit of February 2022—US$320 million drained through an unchecked signature—occurred on an audited codebase. The missing verification line was known but unpatched when new features were deployed. The failure was human, not cryptographic. The story repeats a pattern older than blockchain itself: systems fail not where they are weakest, but where confidence is strongest.

Between the chain and the user lies a hidden intermediary few discuss—the **indexer**. These services, like *The Graph* or *Covalent*, translate blockchain data into accessible formats for interfaces. They are the librarians of decentralised finance, caching and curating vast troves of transaction data. When you open a dashboard showing portfolio values or pool statistics, you are not reading the blockchain directly but a filtered digest. This delegation introduces subtle fragility. In December 2021, *The Graph*'s mainnet suffered a data inconsistency bug that caused several DeFi dashboards to display false liquidity figures. The protocols themselves were unaffected, but human perception was not. Markets moved on faulty information—a mirror of the very opacity DeFi was meant to dissolve. Trust had simply changed costume, not vanished.

At the top of the stack sits the **front end**—the point where code meets cognition. A user rarely interacts with raw contracts; they engage with websites and applications designed for comfort. Yet the convenience of interfaces introduces its own category of deception. In February 2023, users of *Yearn Finance* were targeted by a front-end attack when a malicious script injected into the site redirected transactions to an attacker's address. The contracts were uncompromised; the fraud occurred entirely within the browser. A few kilobytes of corrupted code undid years of cryptographic security. Here the motif of the "key" returns: possession without comprehension is peril. One can hold the private key to a vault yet sign away its contents by trusting the wrong interface.

Each layer of the stack thus contains its own failure mode. Chains can stall or fork; contracts can misbehave; indexers can mislead; interfaces can betray. The crucial insight is that "trustless" does not mean "without trust". It means trust has been reallocated—from people to systems, and from systems to their maintainers. Every supposedly autonomous process relies on human stewardship: developers pushing updates, validators securing networks, designers writing interfaces. The question for any participant is not *whether* to trust, but *where* and *how much*.

The behaviour of users often reveals this distribution more clearly than theory does. After the *Curve Finance* front-end compromise of August 2022, which redirected roughly US$570,000 in tokens, observant traders noticed that Curve's on-chain contracts remained safe. Those with command-line literacy interacted directly with the contract addresses, bypassing the corrupted website entirely. Others waited, paralysed by uncertainty. The difference between loss and safety lay in a simple form of literacy: knowing which layer to trust when the others fail. Stack knowledge translates directly into survival.

Critics might argue that the layering of dependencies undermines the very ethos of decentralisation. If each component demands trust, then what has been gained? The answer lies in visibility. In traditional finance, trust is hierarchical and opaque; one must accept the integrity of an institution without seeing its workings. In DeFi, trust is modular and transparent. You can inspect the contract code, verify the network's block history, and choose which front end to engage. The opacity is not eliminated, but it is selectable. Autonomy, here, means the right to decide where ignorance begins.

The motif of the *stack* is instructive beyond technology. It is a metaphor for perception itself: layers of abstraction between truth and appearance. Each user navigates these layers differently. The professional developer may verify contract bytecode; the casual participant may rely on social proof—a Twitter post, a Discord link, a brand logo. Both act rationally within their bandwidth. The danger arises when one forgets the layers exist, mistaking the surface for the substance. A protocol interface may glow with reassuring gradients, yet beneath it lies a system indifferent to aesthetics. What matters is not beauty but verifiability.

There is a deeper philosophical tension here, one that mirrors earlier technological shifts. When the telegraph connected continents in the nineteenth century, people marvelled at the illusion of directness—instant messages across oceans. Yet every signal still passed through cables, relays, and human operators. Trust became distributed but not eliminated. DeFi's architecture repeats that pattern in code. The smart contract is the new relay; the validator, the new operator. The challenge remains the same: maintaining reliability across layers of mediation.

Two scenarios illuminate what stack literacy achieves. In November 2021, *Polygon*, a scaling network for Ethereum, discovered a critical vulnerability that could have allowed attackers to mint infinite tokens. The team patched it quietly, compensating the researcher who found it. Users noticed nothing. Contrast this with April 2022, when the *Beanstalk* stablecoin protocol was exploited via a malicious governance proposal embedded in its smart contract. The attack drained US$182 million before anyone reacted. Both incidents hinged on the same principle: governance as code. One demonstrated resilience through vigilance; the other, catastrophe through complacency. Stack literacy means knowing which of those fates you are entrusting your assets to.

A pattern emerges. DeFi's infrastructure mirrors society's oldest systems of reliability: distributed but interdependent, transparent yet interpretable. Every safety measure—from audits to multi-signature governance—exists to manage uncertainty, not to erase it. To treat "trustless" as literal is to misunderstand the experiment. What DeFi offers is not the absence of trust but the ability to choose its location, to relocate it with intent.

As participation widens, that choice becomes collective. The more users understand the stack, the less brittle the system becomes. When developers document contracts openly, when indexers are decentralised, when front ends can be verified locally, each layer gains resilience through diversity. Conversely, when ignorance concentrates—when the majority rely on a single interface or provider—the structure recentralises, even if the chain beneath remains decentralised. The architecture is neutral; the usage pattern is not.

The unresolved question—the one that shadows every technological advance in DeFi—is how much literacy society can realistically bear. Not every participant will parse code or monitor validator behaviour. Yet without some shared baseline of understanding, autonomy becomes performative rather than protective. The stack will always exist; the only variable is how consciously we inhabit it.

Incentives, Not Miracles

On 15 June 2020, in San Francisco, Compound Labs switched on "liquidity mining" for its lending protocol. Within hours, traders queued to supply and borrow stablecoins not merely for interest but for COMP tokens that the protocol emitted to active users. Borrowing spiked; utilisation soared; yields leapt without any change in the underlying demand for credit. The outcome was startling but lawful: when a protocol pays people to participate, people participate. A week later, you could watch wallets borrow USDC at, say, 8 per cent while simultaneously earning COMP that, at prevailing prices, implied a net gain. Nothing mystical had occurred. The payout diagram had changed.

The simplicity of that diagram hides the heart of decentralised finance. Fees, token emissions, arbitrage, and MEV are not jargon; they are payment rails that align or misalign behaviour. Each arrow on the diagram points to a wallet, a validator, a pool. Each arrow carries a reason. If those reasons are poorly designed, the system bloats, contorts, or collapses. Terra's high-profile failure in May 2022, centred in Seoul, did not occur because code malfunctioned. It failed because the incentives underwriting its "risk-free" yield could not survive stress. A diagram would have predicted it. Draw the boxes. Follow the arrows. Ask who pays whom.

The first and most visible arrow in any protocol is the **fee**. Show: a trader swaps ETH for USDC on Uniswap v3 and pays 30 basis points to the pool. Name: "LP fees" governed by the pool's fee tier. Explain: the fee compensates liquidity providers for making a market and compensates them precisely in proportion to the flow they absorb in their chosen price range. Implication: if volume concentrates in a narrow band, providers with capital in that band earn; those outside it starve. The behaviour is measurable. Liquidity migrates to profitable ticks; idle liquidity bleeds. Participants do not "believe" in liquidity; they chase it. Fee markets write that chase into code.

Fees also introduce a second arrow: **arbitrage**. Show: a price on Uniswap drifts after a large trade; on a centralised exchange in Chicago, the price barely moves. Name: cross-venue arbitrage. Explain: arbitrageurs correct the gap by buying where cheaper and selling where dearer, capturing the spread less their costs. Their costs are visible: gas, slippage, and the opportunity cost of capital. Implication: the health of an AMM depends on the willingness of arbitrageurs to pay those costs. If gas spikes, or liquidity thins, re-pricing slows and users experience worse execution. The supposed magic of constant-product curves is simply a dare: *will someone pay to keep me honest?*

A second family of arrows originates from **emissions**—token rewards that protocols distribute to specified behaviours. Show: Compound's 2020 programme paying COMP to suppliers and borrowers; Curve's "gauge" system directing CRV to chosen pools since August 2020. Name: liquidity mining. Explain: emissions subsidise one side of a market to bootstrap network effects—users supply capital because their total return equals fees plus tokens. Implication: emissions are a marketing budget with a ledger. When token prices fall or schedules decay, the subsidy weakens. Supply retreats. The diagram shrinks back to fee capture alone. Here the metric to watch is *incentive coverage*: the ratio of emitted value to organic fee revenue. When coverage exceeds one for long, the protocol is paying out more than it takes in. Someone is footing the difference. It is usually the token-holder, diluted quietly over time.

The most controversial arrows are the ones few users see: **MEV**—maximal extractable value. Show: two traders submit swaps that move a price; a third tries to arbitrage the resulting gap. Name: block construction under priority gas auctions and, since August 2021, under EIP-1559's "tip" model. Explain: validators (and the specialised builders who assemble blocks) can reorder, include, or exclude transactions to capture arbitrage, liquidation, and sandwich opportunities. This is not theft; it is market microstructure translated into blockspace. Implication: if a protocol creates predictable value at the moment of execution—a liquidation bonus, a price gap—someone will try to capture it at the mempool. The reaction is visible in gas spikes during liquidations and in the growth of private relay systems such as Flashbots (2020) designed to route MEV to searchers in a less chaotic way. MEV is not a moral failure. It is a design signal. It says: your payout diagram is leaking value at the point of execution.

Consider two named, dated cases that show how different designs shape behaviour. First, **EIP-1559** on Ethereum's mainnet (5 August 2021) changed the fee market by burning a base fee and paying only the tip to validators. Show: blocks began to include a predictable base charge that no one could capture. Name: "London" upgrade. Explain: by burning the base fee, the protocol converted part of transaction demand into a common burn rather than a private rent, dampening fee volatility and reducing the surface for outbidding games. Implication: the arrow that once pointed from users to miners now forks: one line to a communal burn, one thin line to validators. It altered MEV's composition without erasing it, tempering certain edges while leaving others intact. You could see the effect in calmer priority fees during typical blocks and sharp, short spikes during liquidation cascades.

Second, **Anchor Protocol** on Terra offered roughly 19.5 per cent APY on UST deposits, widely advertised in 2021 (Anchor documentation, 2021). Show: deposits surged; UST supply ballooned. Name: a "stability subsidy" paid from a reserve fund periodically topped up by governance. Explain: the yield exceeded organic borrow demand; emissions filled the gap. Implication: the diagram required perpetual external support or rising collateral prices. When neither materialised during the de-peg in May 2022, the arrow snapped. The yield did not decline; the instrument failed. This is the canonical unsustainable payout diagram: one box labelled "Depositor Yield", fed by arrows labelled "Borrow Interest" and "Subsidy", where the latter dominates and depends on sentiment.

A credible counter-example tempers the picture. **MakerDAO**, first deployed on Ethereum in December 2017, has kept DAI's dollar peg across multiple crises by tying issuance to over-collateralised vaults and adjusting a "stability fee" set by governance. Show: during March 2020's market shock, Maker raised stability fees and auctioned collateral to maintain solvency. Name: "Black Thursday". Explain: Maker's yield to DAI holders is not an explicit emission but the by-product of system stability; the protocol's fees aim first at peg integrity, with surplus later directed to reserves or buy-backs. Implication: it is possible to design a diagram in which most arrows serve the core function, not speculative growth. Returns exist, but they flow from fees paid for a service—synthetic dollars—not from a reflexive promise of high APY.

To use the diagram as a practical lens, pair each abstraction with a visible decision. **Trust** becomes: which address receives fees, on which schedule, with what rights to alter them? You can read that in a contract's functions or a governance module's quorum thresholds. **Efficiency** becomes: average execution cost per unit of value moved, observed in gas per swap or basis points of slippage per trade size. **Risk** becomes: probability-weighted shortfall at a known trigger, measured by historical liquidation cascades or oracle variance. If the answers do not appear on-chain or in audited docs, the diagram has missing arrows. Missing arrows hide losses.

Arbitrage deserves a closer look because it often bankrolls the rest. Show: when an oracle lags, a lending protocol may misprice collateral. Name: Aave's use of Chainlink price feeds, with update thresholds. Explain: if the feed updates only after a threshold move, a window opens in which an attacker can manipulate an AMM's price, borrow against inflated collateral, then allow the oracle to catch up. Implication: honest arbitrage narrows spreads; adversarial arbitrage hunts stale data. The metric to watch is *oracle latency*: seconds between true price moves and feed updates, and the *cost to move* a pool's price by 1 per cent. If the cost to move is lower than the profit from borrowing against the manipulation, the arrow points the wrong way. The protocol pays the attacker to break it.

MEV interacts with emissions in a second-order way. Show: a farmed token's price spikes on distribution days; gas prices rise. Name: "harvest storms". Explain: searchers compete to win blocks that contain high-value claims, reordering transactions to capture token distributions first. Implication: a protocol's attempt to "reward the community" can transfer value to block builders unless carefully smoothed. Spiky distributions feed MEV; continuous drips starve it. This is not academic. You can measure the variance of gas costs around distribution blocks and watch who profits. If builders and searchers measurably earn more on those blocks than recipients, the community subsidy has been partially taxed by the block market.

A further link in the diagram ties **liquidations** to network health. Show: on Compound or Aave, under-collateralised positions pay a liquidation bonus—typically a few percentage points—to liquidators. Name: "close factor" and "liquidation incentive." Explain: liquidators race to repay the debt and seize collateral at a discount; the bonus must be high enough to compensate gas and price risk during the transaction. Implication: set the bonus too low and liquidators ignore thin positions; too high and the system overpays during stress. The decision is not ideological. It is a calibration problem solved by data: average gas during volatility, slippage in the collateral's deepest pool, and the time to confirm a block. A sound system shows liquidations spread across addresses; a brittle one shows concentration in a few bots. Concentration is a warning. Few arrows; single points of failure.

Two quieter but decisive arrows point to **governance** and **treasury**. Show: a DAO votes to direct emissions to a pool with low organic volume but vocal backers. Name: Curve's gauge wars, driven by CRV vote-escrow since late 2020. Explain: bribe markets emerged to rent voting power, redirecting CRV toward allied pools regardless of fee yield. Implication: even if the protocol uses emissions "rationally" at first, meta-markets can hijack the diagram. The real payer becomes the protocol's future, diluted to feed current factions. You can observe this in the *bribe-to-fee ratio*: tokens spent to win votes versus fees earned by the winning pools. If the ratio is persistently high, emissions are political, not economic.

The counterpoint, again, is not to denounce incentives but to design them with humility. A payout diagram is a living map; human behaviour redraws it. EIP-1559 tempered fee bidding, yet builders later introduced Proposer-Builder Separation on Ethereum to channel MEV more cleanly. Each change shifts arrows and creates new edges. The right frame is not moral panic but measurement. Does the change reduce variance in user costs? Does it disperse rather than concentrate rents? Does it convert private gains into public goods, as with the burn? These are testable claims.

To keep the motif vivid, imagine you are sketching boxes and arrows for any protocol you encounter. One box is *users,* another is *liquidity providers,* a third is *validators/builders,* a fourth is *token-holders,* a fifth is *attacker/arbitrageur*. Draw arrows for fees, emissions, tips, burns, and slippage. Now, label magnitudes. Where you cannot label, you pause. Where arrows feed back—emissions raising token price, higher price encouraging more emissions—you note reflexivity. Where a single arrow sustains several boxes—say, emissions funding users, LPs, and governance—you note fragility. This picture is not art. It is safety.

The temptation, especially during exuberant cycles, is to treat high yields as evidence of progress. History insists on a colder reading. Compound's 2020 launch demonstrated how emissions can bootstrap useful markets by front-loading rewards to early risk-takers. Terra's 2022 collapse showed how subsidies can masquerade as sustainable income. Maker's steadier path exhibits a different equilibrium: most arrows align with a narrow purpose and are priced for that purpose. None of these outcomes was preordained. They were drawn.

The unresolved tension remains practical and immediate. When you next encounter a protocol promising generous returns, can you sketch its payout diagram in sixty seconds? Can you point to the wallet that ultimately pays you, the schedule that funds it, and the market condition under which that schedule fails? If the pen hovers, the answer is already written.

Autonomy and Its Burden

In December 2013, at Heathrow Airport, James Howells from Newport, Wales, accidentally threw away a hard drive containing 7,500 bitcoins—worth around £3.5 million at the time and over £250 million at 2025 valuations. The disk lies buried somewhere in the city landfill, encrypted, inaccessible, its key lost forever. Howells's misfortune became a modern parable: wealth stored without a custodian is not truly lost to theft, but to forgetfulness. The episode captures the silent dilemma of self-custody—the transfer of risk from institution to individual, from system to psyche. When DeFi invites users to "be their own bank", it is not promising convenience. It is demanding discipline.

Autonomy is seductive because it sounds like freedom. In practice, it behaves like responsibility. A decentralised wallet does not ask who you are; it asks only whether you can prove ownership of a private key—256 bits of data that separate sovereignty from destitution. That proof must be stored, backed up, and guarded. No central bank will reissue it. No password-reset form exists. Self-custody transforms an abstract political slogan into an operational regime. The ledger's impartiality is both its strength and its cruelty. It forgives no error.

The architecture of self-custody is elegantly simple: a pair of cryptographic keys, one public and one private, govern access. The private key generates signatures that authorise transactions; possession equals control. Most wallets today use a twelve- or twenty-four-word mnemonic, derived from the BIP-39 standard (Bitcoin Improvement Proposal, 2013). Those words are human-readable proxies for the same 256-bit secret. Lose them, and the chain forgets you. The system is brutally honest. It keeps perfect records but remembers nothing about its users.

The idea of personal key management is not new. During the Enlightenment, private seals and signet rings carried similar symbolism: proof of authenticity tied to a unique holder. Yet the digital analogue scales that principle to a global network. In DeFi, each transaction replicates across thousands of nodes; each signature is verifiable by anyone. The power is absolute, but so is the exposure. In March 2021, blockchain analytics firm Chainalysis estimated that about

20 per cent of all mined bitcoins—roughly 3.7 million coins—are likely lost due to forgotten keys or discarded hardware. The figure is not a statistic; it is an education. The network is secure by design, but humans are not.

Operational risk, once absorbed by institutions, now reappears in miniature across millions of households. Where a bank employs layered security—multi-person approval, disaster recovery, auditing—a self-custodied user must simulate those procedures privately. The work of an operations desk becomes a set of personal rituals: generating backups, testing recovery phrases, isolating devices, verifying transaction details before signing. A cold wallet replaces the vault; a seed phrase replaces the compliance department. The frontier glamour of DeFi is thus built atop the ancient discipline of record-keeping. The more perfect the protocol, the more it exposes the imperfections of its operator.

Two real cases illustrate this transfer vividly. In August 2022, the *Slootman family* in Amsterdam lost access to €1.2 million in ether after a home fire destroyed both their hardware wallets and the written seed phrases stored in the same safe. They had followed "best practices" in a superficial sense—offline storage—but had failed to diversify location risk. The redundancy of storage was physical, not logical. The chain did exactly what it was supposed to: it preserved the funds and rejected all unauthorised access. The tragedy was procedural, not technical. Contrast this with *Casa*, a self-custody service founded in New York in 2018, which implements multisignature wallets requiring multiple devices or co-signers to authorise transactions. In 2023, a client who lost one of three keys restored access seamlessly using threshold recovery. Both cases reveal the same truth: autonomy is sustainable only when supported by systems—personal or institutional—that anticipate human error.

Self-custody therefore shifts the conversation from technology to habit. A cryptographic key has no agency; it depends on the operator's discipline. Consider the behavioural data from hardware wallet manufacturer *Ledger*. After a phishing breach in July 2020 exposed customer emails, support requests spiked by 400 per cent as users attempted to verify fake "security updates." The most common losses were not due to hacking the devices but to victims willingly entering recovery phrases on counterfeit websites. The vulnerability was cognitive. Trust was misplaced not in the network but in social interaction. As behavioural economists have noted, humans routinely overestimate their ability to manage risk when the tools appear transparent. The more seamless the interface, the easier it is to forget that one is signing with irreversible authority.

In the institutional model, security is systemic; in DeFi, it is behavioural. That distinction reframes what "risk management" means. In 2022, Aave integrated a "Guardian" feature into its governance, allowing time delays and multi-step approvals before protocol changes take effect. The same principle applies at the personal level. A prudent user employs time as a circuit breaker—reviewing transaction details twice, confirming addresses through multiple channels, delaying large transfers until verified. These are not digital innovations; they are human techniques of self-supervision. Autonomy, correctly understood, is not a technology but a practice.

The motif of *the key* captures both empowerment and burden. A key grants access, but also demands custody. In 2020, the journalist Laura Shin interviewed Ethereum co-founder Vitalik Buterin, who reflected on early days when developers manually deployed contracts worth millions, typing commands directly into consoles. "Every transaction felt like holding a loaded gun," he said. That metaphor endures. To sign a transaction in DeFi is to compress intent into mathematics. The machine executes faithfully, even when you do not. It is accountability rendered in code.

The ethical dimension of autonomy emerges here. When custody becomes personal, blame does too. In traditional finance, customers externalise error—fraud departments, insurance, and consumer protection distribute loss. In DeFi, restitution is impossible without counterparties. The moral hazard vanishes, but so does forgiveness. This purity appeals to libertarian ideals but strains against human nature. We are not, by temperament, built for perfect vigilance. Every mnemonic phrase written on paper, every QR code scanned in haste, exposes the gap between human frailty and algorithmic precision. The challenge is not technological illiteracy; it is behavioural exhaustion.

Some communities have responded by reintroducing forms of *social recovery*. In October 2022, *Argent*, a smart-contract wallet provider, deployed a feature allowing users to nominate trusted contacts who could collectively restore access if keys were lost. The method borrows from *Shamir's Secret Sharing* (1979), a mathematical scheme that divides a secret into multiple parts, only some of which are needed to reconstruct it. The innovation here is sociological as much as cryptographic: distributing trust across relationships rather than institutions. Yet even this approach introduces new tensions. The more parties involved, the greater the exposure to coercion or collusion. Every mechanism that softens autonomy also dilutes it.

The counter-example is the *Bitcoin maximalist* ethos that rejects all forms of recovery as betrayal. For its adherents, true sovereignty requires solitude: one key, one holder, one fate. They argue that the irreversibility of loss enforces responsibility. The limitation of this stance is empirical. Human error rates do not decline through ideology. As block explorer data confirm, lost coins accumulate linearly with adoption. The purity of principle achieves a perverse equilibrium: the system grows, but its dead capital grows faster. Discipline cannot be legislated by slogans. It must be trained.

Training, in this context, means cultivating procedural literacy. The mechanics of self-custody can be rehearsed like any skill. Security researchers at *MIT's Digital Currency Initiative* (2021) found that users who periodically tested wallet recovery—simulating device loss and phrase restoration—retained competence far longer than those who merely read instructions. Practice, not persuasion, builds retention. This finding echoes a wider truth in DeFi: the architecture may be decentralised, but the safety is local. The responsibility lives in muscle memory.

At a systemic level, DeFi's experiment in autonomy also generates new forms of collective risk. If too many participants mismanage keys, lost funds reduce network liquidity, distort supply metrics, and complicate governance. When users vanish, so do their voting tokens, creating ghost influence that cannot be exercised or revoked. Protocols such as *Compound* have debated mechanisms to reassign dormant tokens, but each proposal collides with the principle of immutability. The network's neutrality becomes inertia. What protects the individual from censorship also protects their mistakes from correction. The ledger is an archive of decisions that can neither repent nor forget.

There is a psychological weight to this permanence. Ownership without recourse can produce anxiety rather than liberation. Behavioural studies from the University of Zurich (2023) showed that frequent DeFi users exhibited higher cognitive stress during transaction signing, measured by galvanic skin response, compared with traditional online banking users. The cause was not complexity but consequence: the awareness that a single misclick could be fatal. Autonomy magnifies agency; it also magnifies fear.

The recurring motif of the key, then, carries dual symbolism: empowerment and burden. Every safeguard—multisig, recovery, cold storage—is an attempt to balance those forces. The art lies in calibration, not ideology. Perfect control is brittle; perfect convenience is dangerous. Between them lies the mature practice of autonomy: distributed custody, habitual verification, periodic rehearsal. These are not hacks; they are hygiene.

Yet even the most disciplined operator cannot eliminate uncertainty. The network evolves, wallets update, interfaces change, and new threat vectors appear. Every user must therefore confront a permanent trade-off: how much complexity to accept for how much control. Entrusting a share of keys to a recovery service introduces counterparty risk; refusing all help invites isolation. There is no universal answer. The diagnostic question remains personal and perennial: when you hold your keys, do you also hold the habits that make them safe?

Chapter 2
Wallets: Your Interface to Autonomy

In May 2022, a London-based designer named Alex received what looked like a routine message on Twitter from a verified NFT marketplace account. It contained a link promising early access to a new collection. Alex, who had been trading digital art for over a year, clicked through, connected his browser wallet, and approved a transaction that appeared harmless. Within seconds, his holdings—worth just over £42,000—were gone. The culprit was not a complex hack or a breach of the blockchain. It was a front-end forgery: a single, elegant replica that captured his click. Alex's story is no anomaly; it is the anatomy of a modern financial loss. The system did not fail him. His interface did.

The wallet is the DeFi user's compass and vault, the portal through which code meets cognition. It does not merely hold assets; it mediates trust. To interact with decentralised finance is to choose an interface to one's own autonomy, and that choice is neither cosmetic nor trivial. Each design—browser extension, mobile app, hardware device, or smart-contract wallet—embodies a philosophy about control, convenience, and risk. What distinguishes them is not just technology but temperament. A trader executing daily swaps will tolerate fragility a long-term saver cannot. A hardware wallet offers fortress-like isolation but demands ritual; a browser wallet offers agility but invites exposure. Choosing a wallet, therefore, is less about gadget preference and more about aligning one's operational reality with one's psychological bandwidth. The first act of autonomy is selection.

That decision has a history. When Bitcoin's first wallet launched in January 2009, its creator, Satoshi Nakamoto, bundled code and custody together. There were no intermediaries—no custodial exchanges, no "connect wallet" prompts. Users ran the software, generated their keys, and bore the consequences. Over the following decade, as interfaces multiplied, convenience eroded comprehension. Exchanges offered hosted wallets, blurring the line between ownership and IOU. Then DeFi reasserted the original ethos: possession equals control. But this resurgence of self-custody arrived in a world where most users were trained by centralised platforms, accustomed to recoverable passwords and human support desks. The resulting tension defines our time: financial autonomy promised to the unprepared.

To understand wallets is to understand where the boundary between user and protocol truly lies. The blockchain itself is indifferent to your intentions; it recognises only signatures. Everything else—the buttons, pop-ups, icons—is theatre layered atop cryptography. The wallet translates human action into machine instruction. Each signature is irreversible, each approval an act of faith. The interface, in this sense, is not just a tool but a language. Learn its grammar, and you command your autonomy; neglect it, and you sign away control to the nearest imitation of authority.

Every category of wallet—hot, cold, and smart—represents a negotiation between friction and freedom. A hot wallet, living in a browser or phone, provides immediacy but carries exposure. A cold wallet, kept offline, demands patience but grants resilience. A smart-contract wallet introduces programmability: social recovery, spending limits, scheduled approvals. Each reveals a facet of the same paradox. The more accessible the wallet, the more vulnerable it becomes; the more secure it is, the less convenient it feels. True mastery lies not in eliminating this trade-off but in managing it deliberately. Professionals already practice such compartmentalisation—one wallet for daily operations, another for storage, and a third for experimental activity. This architecture of intent is not paranoia; it is prudence codified.

Yet tools alone do not suffice. Security lives or dies by *ritual*. The phrase may sound archaic, but it captures the essence of human reliability. The daily checking of a seed phrase, the double-verification before travel, the careful duplication of backups—all are forms of rehearsal against entropy. Behavioural researchers have long known that habits, not knowledge, sustain safety. The same applies here. A backup not tested is a placebo. A passphrase not written down securely is a liability waiting for stress to expose it. The challenge is not designing perfect systems but creating survivable ones. The DeFi ecosystem is littered with brilliant engineers undone by ordinary mistakes: a photo of a recovery phrase stored in the cloud, a seed pasted into a chat window, a browser extension installed from a counterfeit domain. None of these acts requires malice to destroy value; they only require haste.

Wallet literacy, therefore, is less about mastering cryptography and more about mastering *attention*. Approvals—the invisible handshakes between wallet and contract—are the most common vectors of loss. In July 2021, the Revoke.cash analytics team estimated that over 80 per cent of exploited addresses had granted unlimited token approvals. Most victims had no idea they had ever done so. Each "Approve" click is a line of delegation: you are authorising a contract to move assets on your behalf. The code can be elegant, the project legitimate, but if the approval is infinite and the contract later compromised, the loss is absolute. The antidote is muscle memory—habitual scepticism trained into the reflexes. Always inspect, never rush, and remember that revocation is as vital as approval. This is the quiet discipline behind apparent freedom.

The same principle applies to the front end. Fraud in DeFi rarely occurs through code injection at the protocol level; it occurs through deception at the interface. Spoofed websites, homograph domains (where a Cyrillic "a" replaces a Latin "a"), and cloned browser extensions all exploit a single weakness: the human eye's trust in familiarity. Attackers understand that users read shape, not syntax. The defence is procedural rather than technical—verifying URLs, bookmarking official links, cross-checking on-chain contract addresses. The habit of "verify before connect" is not paranoia; it is the digital equivalent of locking your front door, not because you expect burglars, but because you respect probability.

The deeper story of wallets, however, is psychological. Each wallet embodies a philosophy of human-machine balance. The browser wallet trusts you to act responsibly in a volatile environment. The hardware wallet trusts your patience to bridge isolation and action. The smart-contract wallet trusts your future self to delegate authority wisely. None are foolproof because none can be: risk cannot be eliminated, only distributed. The choice of wallet is therefore an expression of temperament as much as of technical need. Are you a minimalist who values speed, or a perfectionist who values redundancy? The chain does not care, but your balance will.

Autonomy, then, is not a switch but a spectrum. Some users thrive on full custody, building elaborate systems of cold storage and multisignature protection. Others prefer partial delegation—custodial recovery services or shared control wallets. Both can be legitimate if aligned with self-awareness. What matters is not ideological purity but operational realism. The illusion of absolute independence is as dangerous as blind trust in intermediaries. True autonomy resides in the middle ground: conscious delegation, reversible within reason, verifiable without permission.

This chapter unfolds from that premise. It invites you to see wallets not as apps but as practices—habits that keep agency intact. You will encounter a taxonomy of wallets that demystifies hot, cold, and smart designs through lived trade-offs. You will examine key management not as a technical protocol but as a behavioural discipline. You will learn why approvals, not trades, are where most damage begins, and how small, repeatable habits create durable defences. And you will meet the psychology of deception head-on, recognising how interfaces seduce, distract, and mislead. Each section is a lens on the same truth: the tools of DeFi only work when wielded with deliberation.

The motif that threads through this chapter is control—its limits, its illusions, and its cost. Every wallet offers control in a different dialect, but none offer it for free. The price is vigilance. The reward is clarity. When you understand how your wallet mediates every act of ownership, the abstractions of decentralised finance become tangible again. You begin to see where power truly lives: not in the blockchain, but in your habits. The next pages will not simply teach you how to protect your keys. They will teach you how to think like someone who deserves to hold them.

Choosing a Wallet: Hot, Cold, Smart

On 19 November 2021, the Singapore-based exchange Crypto.com paused withdrawals after detecting "unauthorised activity" affecting nearly 500 user accounts. The breach cost roughly £27 million in stolen assets, traced to compromised browser wallets that had approved malicious smart contracts. Within days, security researchers identified a familiar cause: not code failure, but custody complacency. Users had relied entirely on a single, always-connected wallet—a hot wallet—to manage holdings worth far more than they could afford to lose. The irony was stark. In a system built for personal sovereignty, convenience had again become the enemy of control.

A wallet is more than an app. It is an instrument of decision: how much autonomy to assume, how much risk to internalise, and how much friction to tolerate. Every transaction passes through it, every approval begins there, every breach ends there. Its form—browser, mobile, hardware, or smart-contract—dictates the rhythm of your interaction with the chain. The difference is not cosmetic but constitutional. Choosing a wallet is akin to designing one's own governance structure, balancing immediacy against integrity. Each type asks a distinct question: *How much trust are you prepared to outsource to convenience?*

A **hot wallet** lives online. Its purpose is speed. It resides as a browser extension or mobile app, integrated with DeFi front-ends such as Uniswap, Aave, or OpenSea. Metamask, launched by ConsenSys in 2016, is the archetype. By 2022 it had surpassed 30 million active users—an achievement that reveals both the promise and peril of accessibility. Hot wallets store private keys encrypted within the device, exposing them to potential theft if the device is compromised. The vulnerability is not theoretical. In June 2022, a series of phishing campaigns mimicking Metamask's interface led to more than £9 million in cumulative losses over three weeks (Elliptic, 2022). The attack required no exploit of Ethereum itself, merely persuasion at scale. Users clicked, signed, and drained themselves. The wallet did exactly what it was told.

The trade-off embedded in a hot wallet is convenience versus exposure. It enables seamless trading, but every open browser tab is a potential vector. The security principle is familiar from finance and engineering alike: the surface area of risk grows with connectivity. Frequent traders accept this because velocity is their edge. But the same instrument, when used as a vault, becomes a paradox—a digital safe built with the door open. The implication is operational rather than moral. A hot wallet is a tool for liquidity, not for legacy.

A **mobile wallet** narrows this risk by shifting the environment, not the principle. Applications such as Trust Wallet and Rainbow abstract the complexity of browser interactions into mobile-native designs, integrating biometric access and push notifications. The mobility enhances usability but introduces new dependencies: cloud backups, mobile operating systems, and app store policies. Each dependency becomes a point of trust. In August 2021, Apple briefly removed Trust Wallet from its App Store, citing policy reviews, effectively cutting off new installations for weeks. The incident revealed an uncomfortable truth: even "self-custody" tools remain partially dependent on corporate infrastructure. A phone can be lost, seized, or updated into obsolescence. The boundary between autonomy and access is thinner than marketing admits.

The counterpoint comes from **hardware wallets**, devices explicitly engineered for isolation. Ledger, founded in Paris in 2014, and Trezor, launched in Prague in 2013, pioneered this category. Their principle is austere: private keys never touch the internet. Transactions are signed within a secure element and only the signed data leave the device. It is elegant and largely effective. No confirmed remote compromise of a properly used hardware wallet has yet been recorded. Yet this perfection introduces its own fragility. When Ledger suffered a database breach in July 2020, revealing customer names and addresses, physical threats emerged—phishing calls, fake replacement devices mailed to victims. Security, once purely digital, became corporeal. A hardware wallet's strength—its air-gapped independence—cannot shield against the analog vulnerabilities of human trust.

Moreover, hardware custody demands ritual. One must initialise, back up, verify, and store recovery phrases—tasks that sound simple but collapse under stress. In December 2022, the journalist Laura Shin recounted a story of an Ethereum early adopter who had misplaced his seed phrase across multiple notebooks in different countries. When gas fees surged during a trading opportunity, he realised he could not reconstruct the full phrase in time. He missed the trade, not due to blockchain latency but logistical entropy. Hardware security, for all its virtue, introduces friction that can paralyse the unprepared. Its safety is procedural, not automatic.

Smart-contract wallets attempt to mediate these extremes. By embedding logic directly into the contract layer, they allow programmable recovery, spending limits, and multi-signature authorisation. Argent, deployed on Ethereum in 2020, exemplifies this approach. A user can nominate "guardians"—trusted accounts or devices—that together can restore access if the primary key is lost. Gnosis Safe, widely adopted by DAOs since 2021, extends this to collective custody: multiple parties must sign before funds move. The trade-off is programmability versus simplicity. Each additional feature increases both flexibility and attack surface. In July 2023, researchers at OpenZeppelin identified a flaw in certain Gnosis Safe modules that could allow privilege escalation if administrators misconfigured access rights. The issue was patched quickly, but the lesson persisted: complexity is not free. Every safeguard is also a dependency.

The pattern is visible across systems: safety migrates through layers, never disappearing. The hot wallet outsources it to the browser, the mobile wallet to the operating system, the hardware wallet to the user's rituals, and the smart-contract wallet to its code. No design eliminates trust; it merely relocates it. The rational decision, then, is not to seek invulnerability but to allocate risk according to context. A portfolio worth £500, actively traded, may justify the agility of a hot wallet. A long-term store of £50,000 deserves hardware isolation. Shared treasury operations benefit from programmable, multi-signature logic. The underlying decision tree is empirical: match the wallet to frequency, value, and capability. Anything else is superstition.

A credible counter-example illuminates the limits of categorisation. In 2022, a collective of Nigerian developers launched *CenoBank,* a mobile-first DeFi platform using smart-contract wallets with built-in recovery linked to local telecom identities. It achieved impressive adoption—over 50,000 users by mid-2023—but also demonstrated how hybrid models inherit compound risks. Regulatory uncertainty around SIM-linked verification led to user lockouts when local carriers changed compliance policies. A tool meant to democratise access became, briefly, unusable. The incident underscores a recurring lesson: decentralisation is not a binary condition. Every practical wallet lives on a spectrum between control and dependence.

The motif that threads through all these forms is the *lock and key*. In a bank, the key is metaphorical; in DeFi, it is literal, 256 bits of cryptographic truth. The wallet is the lock designed to protect that key from both theft and forgetfulness. The question each user faces is not "which wallet is best?" but "which failure can I afford?" Browser wallets fail through exposure; hardware wallets fail through loss; smart wallets fail through complexity. Choosing among them is an act of self-knowledge disguised as a technical decision. The network enforces logic; the wallet enforces discipline.

Beyond the technical taxonomy lies a cultural shift. Wallets are no longer static tools but living software updated by decentralised teams across time zones. When Metamask introduced Snaps—modular extensions allowing third-party functionality—in late 2023, it effectively opened its security perimeter to the creativity and risk of thousands of developers. The decision embodied a philosophical tension: openness accelerates innovation but multiplies failure modes. The same calculus applies to users. Opening your wallet to interact with a new DeFi protocol expands possibility and vulnerability simultaneously. The interface asks silently: *Are you confident enough to click?*

What unites all categories is the requirement for conscious architecture. Professional operators segment their activity across wallets: a *hot* operational account for small, frequent transactions; a *warm* intermediary for mid-range exposure; a *cold* reserve for deep storage. The pattern mirrors corporate treasury management, where liquidity tiers balance risk against necessity. The difference is that, in DeFi, the individual becomes their own treasurer, security officer, and compliance department. The map is personal. It changes as circumstances do.

As the chapter proceeds, that pattern of self-architecture becomes clearer. The wallet ceases to be a mere interface and becomes a mirror—reflecting one's habits, attention, and tolerance for uncertainty. The tools differ, but the discipline is universal: isolate, verify, and adapt. The cost of ignoring this discipline is not abstract. It is measured in lost coins, locked accounts, and sleepless nights spent tracing signatures through block explorers.

The unresolved tension remains precisely this: the more seamless wallets become, the easier it is to forget what they protect. Convenience is an anaesthetic. It dulls awareness of custody until a transaction fails or a token vanishes. Every user must therefore return to the elemental question beneath every interface: *How close do I want to stand to the fire?*

Key Management Rituals

In February 2021, a British engineer named Stefan Thomas sat in his San Francisco apartment staring at a small hardware wallet—an IronKey USB drive containing 7,002 bitcoins. At the time, the coins were worth about £220 million. Thomas had lost the paper on which he'd written the password years earlier. He had tried eight guesses. Two remained before the device's built-in encryption would erase its contents forever. The paradox was complete: a man could be both fabulously wealthy and permanently locked out of his fortune, separated from it not by theft, but by the absence of a phrase. The episode became shorthand for crypto's oldest truth: possession of private keys is both liberation and liability. What DeFi restores in autonomy, it exacts in attentiveness.

The notion of *ritual* in key management may seem quaint beside algorithms and protocols, yet it is the most dependable form of security human beings have ever invented. Monks once preserved sacred manuscripts by copying them nightly; pilots today recite pre-flight checklists aloud even after thousands of hours in the cockpit. In both cases, the routine protects against the most persistent vulnerability—complacency. Self-custody demands the same discipline. The private key, whether expressed as a twelve-word seed or a complex passphrase, is not just a secret but an instrument of identity. To lose it is to vanish from one's own account.

Modern key management is standardised but not human-proof. The BIP-39 mnemonic system, introduced in 2013, translated cryptographic entropy into human-readable form: lists of words from *abandon* to *zoo*. The idea was elegant—replace random numbers with language, so that the average person could back up a wallet without memorising binary strings. Yet by 2020, forensic firm Chainalysis estimated that up to 20 per cent of all bitcoins mined were permanently inaccessible due to lost keys or corrupted backups. The translation from code to cognition had not solved the problem; it had merely shifted it. Writing twenty-four words on paper does not create security. It creates a fragile artefact dependent on humidity, legibility, and memory. What endures is not material but behavioural: how the phrase is stored, tested, and transmitted.

Ritual begins with *creation*. The moment a wallet generates a seed is, effectively, the birth of a financial identity. Some users treat it casually—capturing screenshots or storing the phrase in cloud drives. Each of these acts, visible in post-breach investigations by firms such as Elliptic (2022), reveals the same misunderstanding: that encryption is a substitute for judgement. A photograph uploaded to iCloud inherits Apple's authentication model, not the blockchain's. Every backup multiplies exposure. Correct practice looks almost ascetic: generate offline, record physically, verify legibility, and separate storage locations. It is the digital equivalent of sealing wills in different safes.

The second ritual is *redundancy*. Backup without dispersion invites disaster. In December 2022, a flood in Auckland destroyed the home office of a DeFi developer whose metal seed plates, kept together in one drawer, corroded simultaneously. All backups had shared the same environmental risk. The corrective is not more copies but smarter ones: geographically distributed, stored under different access conditions, periodically tested for integrity. A single restoration rehearsal—plugging in the backup and verifying access—exposes errors far better than trust in recollection. Security is a verb.

Ritual also extends to *passphrases*, the optional additions that extend mnemonic entropy. Passphrases function like a second vault key: without them, the seed opens a decoy wallet; with them, the real one. The system, described in BIP-39's extension protocol, protects against coercion and compromise. Yet studies of user behaviour (MIT DCI, 2021) show that fewer than 15 per cent of self-custody users employ passphrases regularly. The reason is not ignorance but fatigue. Complexity is expensive. Each additional word increases the cognitive cost of access, and without ritual, fatigue wins. The implication is uncomfortable: most users accept the risk of theft over the certainty of inconvenience. It is precisely here that ritual earns its name—repetition converts inconvenience into habit, and habit into reflex.

Common failure patterns persist. The first is *co-location*: storing seeds, passphrases, and hardware in the same physical space. The second is *digital duplication*: copying the seed into a password manager or cloud note "just temporarily." The third is *social leakage*: sharing parts of a recovery phrase with friends or relatives without clear instruction, creating half-trusts that later fracture. Each failure arises not from malice but optimism. People assume they will remember. They assume devices will survive. They assume relationships will remain stable. Rituals are designed precisely to correct such assumptions—to embed memory outside the mind, resilience outside the machine.

The motif that threads through all sound key management is *time*. The rituals are not one-off precautions but recurring calibrations. A well-maintained key system resembles preventative maintenance on an aircraft: inspection, testing, replacement of failing components. The metric of competence is *latency*: the time required to recover from total device loss. Professional custody firms measure this in minutes. Individual users rarely test it at all. The result is asymmetry: the illusion of control without the capacity for restoration. True autonomy is demonstrated not by possession but by recovery.

Travel introduces a distinct class of risk. Border controls, device confiscations, and network surveillance can all expose keys indirectly. In 2019, a Canadian entrepreneur was detained in Beijing airport for carrying hardware wallets containing business funds. The devices were never seized, but the pressure to disclose passwords created an ethical and operational dilemma. Some firms now advise executives to travel with "clean" wallets—newly generated, empty, restorable only upon arrival via secure channels. The method, borrowed from intelligence tradecraft, underlines an essential point: mobility is exposure. Every crossing of jurisdiction is a test of one's custody model. Ritual, in this case, is preparation rehearsed until calm.

A credible counterpoint arises from the advocates of custodial solutions. They argue that rituals are unrealistic for most people, that human error will always dominate, and that professional key management—via exchanges or regulated trustees—is a rational trade. Coinbase, for instance, holds the majority of its customers' assets in offline cold storage managed by multi-signature protocols, audited and insured. No individual user can match such redundancy. Yet the compromise is structural: custody requires permission. Withdrawal limits, identity verification, and jurisdictional freezes transform ownership into an account relationship. For users who accept that bargain, convenience trumps sovereignty. For those who do not, ritual remains the only alternative. Both models incur cost, but only one scales inward rather than outward.

Technology can aid but not replace these human routines. Multisignature wallets distribute keys across devices or individuals, reducing single-point failure. Social recovery systems, such as Argent's guardianship model, formalise trust networks. Yet even these systems require ritual oversight—updating guardian lists, verifying quorum, confirming recovery paths. The absence of maintenance slowly erodes safety until the function decays. Like a musical instrument left untuned, security degrades invisibly until tested.

The physical artefacts of ritual—seed plates, tamper-evident bags, safes—should not be fetishised. Their purpose is mnemonic reinforcement: tangible cues anchoring digital reality. Some users engrave their phrases in steel to resist fire; others divide them into partial fragments stored in different cities. What matters is not the material but the *intention*: each act signals deliberate engagement with risk. The ritual must feel slightly inconvenient; ease is the enemy of attention. The anthropologist Clifford Geertz once described ritual as a system of symbolic acts "too important to leave to improvisation." Key management belongs to that category. It is how autonomy becomes repeatable.

Two historical examples underscore the stakes. In March 2020, during the market crash known as "Black Thursday", the MakerDAO system experienced mass liquidations when Ethereum gas fees spiked. Many self-custodied users were unable to move funds because their wallets required manual signing and they could not locate hardware devices under lockdown conditions. Losses reached tens of millions in collateral. Conversely, in 2023, a small London-based fund managing DAO treasuries rehearsed quarterly disaster recovery drills—simulated key loss, device failure, and social recovery. When one of their signers was hospitalised, the system functioned exactly as rehearsed. The distinction was not budget but practice.

The quiet motif running through this subchapter is *rehearsal*. Security that depends on memory alone is brittle. Security rehearsed becomes culture. The best operators institutionalise redundancy through routine: verifying each seed every quarter, confirming each recovery channel, rotating storage locations, and documenting changes. These acts generate no yield, no applause, yet they underpin the entire edifice of decentralised finance. Without them, autonomy collapses into theatre.

Key management rituals thus belong to a lineage far older than DeFi: they are forms of stewardship. Medieval guilds safeguarded trade secrets through oaths and repeated ceremonies; mountaineers check knots before every climb. Such rituals are not signs of fear but of respect—for gravity, for probability, for entropy. The blockchain's transparency does not abolish those forces. It only relocates them.

The unresolved tension remains simple, almost timeless: how much routine are you willing to endure to keep what is yours? The ledger will not remind you. The device will not forgive you. Between negligence and paranoia lies a narrow path called practice. Walking it is the quiet price of autonomy.

Approvals and Permissions

On 9 April 2023, wallets that had previously interacted with SushiSwap's RouteProcessor2 contract began haemorrhaging tokens on Ethereum. Security researchers traced the losses to a subtle bug that allowed an attacker to redirect assets from users who had granted the contract spending permission months earlier. The exploit was swift, impersonal, and brutally instructive: victims were not out-traded. They were pre-approved. The chain obeyed signatures already on file; the interface, in retrospect, had simply been the stationery. The prompt looked perfectly normal.

Approvals are the quiet hinge of decentralised finance. They are not trades. They are not transfers. They are *permissions*—standing instructions that authorise a smart contract to move a specified token from a specified address up to a specified limit. The shorthand in ERC-20 systems is "allowance". In practice, it is a power of attorney. The paradox is that most losses begin here, not in flamboyant attacks but in ordinary clicks that delegate too much, too soon, for too long. If self-custody is holding the keys, approvals are handing out copies at the door.

The mechanism is simple, which makes its consequences profound. Show: a user opens a decentralised exchange and clicks "Approve" for a token, then swaps. Name: the ERC-20 approve and transferFrom pattern, standardised in 2015. Explain: the token contract maintains a table of allowances; if an address has permission, a second contract may *pull* funds without further interaction. Implication: the risk is temporal. Authorisation persists until you revoke it or the limit is consumed. Convenience accumulates into exposure.

The first failure mode is *unbounded allowance*. Show: interfaces often default to approving the maximum integer value (2^256 − 1) so that future trades do not require additional confirmations. Name: "infinite approval." Explain: one click removes friction for months; it also removes a natural circuit-breaker. If the approved contract is later upgraded, compromised, or misconfigured, the full approved balance is at risk. Implication: your loss surface grows with each "Yes, unlimited" decision. It is measurable as the sum of token balances across all active allowances—a number almost no casual user monitors.

Historical cases demonstrate how dull mechanics turn catastrophic. BadgerDAO, a DeFi yield platform, suffered a front-end compromise on 2 December 2021. Attackers injected malicious scripts that prompted visitors to approve a rogue address. Assets worth over US$120 million moved within hours. The name here matters because the code of the underlying vaults remained intact; the exploit lived at the interface. The explanation is procedural: people trusted a known brand and muscle memory carried them through the prompts. The implication is sobering: even experienced participants sign away rights when the choreography feels familiar. The problem is not intelligence but habit.

Contrast this with a counter-example that illuminates limits and trade-offs. Permit-style approvals (EIP-2612), popularised by projects like Uniswap in 2020, allow signatures that authorise a single, bounded spend without a separate on-chain approval transaction. This design reduces gas costs and narrows exposure windows. Yet it does not abolish risk. If wallets render the permit message opaquely, users still sign what they cannot see. Complex signatures migrate confusion rather than erasing it. The mechanism helps, but only when coupled with lucid prompts and a user who knows what bounded looks like.

Fees and limits anchor abstractions in behaviour. Trust becomes a displayed spender address and a numeric allowance. Efficiency becomes measured clicks and gas saved by consolidating approvals. Risk becomes the decision to grant 10,000 tokens rather than MaxUint256. Each of these is visible at the point of action. SushiSwap's April 2023 incident is instructive precisely because the remediation—revoking allowances—was also mechanical. Users who acted quickly by cancelling permissions stymied further drain. Others froze, unsure which approvals existed or how to locate them. The difference was not technical sophistication but reflex: a practiced route from shock to specific revocations.

Approvals also feed an often-overlooked market dynamic: they price convenience. Show: a wallet that auto-prompts for "unlimited" reduces short-term friction for market-makers and aggregators, smoothing trade flow. Name: router contracts on exchanges such as Uniswap or 1inch. Explain: these systems batch steps and hop through pools; bounded approvals can cause mid-route failure, especially when price impact requires spending marginally more than anticipated. Implication: safer defaults may increase failed transactions in volatile markets. There is no free lunch. The question is whether the marginal convenience justifies the structural exposure for a given balance and time horizon.

A second, subtler failure mode is *approval sprawl*. Show: a portfolio that has interacted with a year's worth of test dApps across multiple chains. Name: multi-chain allowance accumulation. Explain: each chain maintains independent allowance tables; each experiment leaves a footprint. Implication: attack surface grows geographically across networks and historically across months. The metric is countable—number of active approvals per token per chain—and few track it. When researchers at the Dutch firm Tayvano catalogued post-exploit behaviour in 2023, they found that many victims retained dozens of stale approvals to abandoned contracts. The exploiters did not need to outwit new defences; they recycled old permissions.

Not all friction is bad. A thoughtfully designed wallet prompt can redirect attention at the right moment. Show: a hardware wallet that displays the spender's contract address, token symbol, and numeric allowance clearly on-device. Name: Ledger's 2021 firmware update that improved ERC-20 approval displays. Explain: moving critical details to a trusted screen interrupts conditioned clicking and demands a pause. Implication: design can make safety survivable without sanctimony. Metrics follow: lower incidence of unlimited approvals after that release, reported anecdotally by multiple auditors who reviewed client transactions in the months that followed. The numbers are small and noisy, but the direction is plain: clarity reduces casual exposure.

Approvals sit at the intersection of front-end truth and on-chain authority, which makes them exquisitely vulnerable to *homograph deception*. Show: a link shared in a chat uses a Cyrillic "a" in place of a Latin "a" in app.uniswap.org. Name: homograph phishing. Explain: the domain renders identically to the eye but resolves elsewhere; the site then requests an approval to a counterfeit router. Implication: the line between literacy and loss is one character wide. The behavioural countermeasure—typing or bookmarking known domains—sounds humble, yet its effectiveness is measurable in case reports. Victims often recall clicking from social media rather than navigating intentionally.

The regulatory texture of approvals has changed too. When the "transfer tax" pattern emerged in 2021 among certain tokens—where transfers to specific addresses triggered hidden fees—approvals became a gate for coercion. Show: a user approves a taxed token to a DEX; the swap imposes a confiscatory fee invisible at approval time. Name: restrictive ERC-20 implementations. Explain: the token's behaviour itself violates standard expectations while still satisfying minimal interface requirements. Implication: allowance semantics can become adversarial. A token can accept approval yet punish transferFrom in ways the dApp cannot predict. This limitation reminds us that allowances rely on token behaviour adhering to norms; they are contracts between contracts as much as with users.

Two further examples mark the terrain. First, the integration of *Permit2* by Uniswap Labs in November 2022 introduced an approval manager that unified and restricted allowances across dApps, enabling time-bound and amount-bound permissions without new bespoke interfaces. Explanation: it externalised allowance policy from tokens to a manager contract designed for safer reuse. Implication: standardised guardrails can outcompete bespoke, error-prone patterns, but they centralise some logic and become a tempting target. Second, the *Ronin* bridge compromise (March 2022) did not exploit ERC-20 approvals directly, yet it showcased the cousin of their risk: signing privileged messages without sufficient checks. The cross-chain validators authorised transfers that never should have occurred because key management and policy were weak. The lesson rhymes: powerful permissions without bounded context invite asymmetric loss.

The motif that threads through these scenes is the *handshake*. Each approval is a handshake extended to software, not a person. It is courteous, silent, and durable. You stretch out your hand in January; a revised contract grasps it in July. Most of the time, the grip is firm and predictable. But once in a while, a stranger takes it. The discipline we seek is not paranoia but discernment: who, exactly, are you greeting, and how long should they hold your hand?

From an operational perspective, allowances are policy decisions. Show: a DAO treasury configures a Gnosis Safe with spending limits enforced by modules that cap per-tx token transfers. Name: Safe's DailyLimit and Allowance modules, in wide use since 2021. Explain: they replicate hard spending caps at the contract level; even with approvals in place, no transaction can exceed the configured limits without additional signers. Implication: organisations can encode prudence where individuals rely on habit. Metrics here are crisp: aggregate outflows per day versus limit, number of escalations needed for exceptions, time to revoke a compromised allowance. Good policy reduces drama.

Yet limitations persist. Revoking allowances costs fees; users on congested networks may defer revocations due to cost, leaving exposure in place. Interfaces that aggregate revocations can mislabel contracts or omit non-standard tokens. Some tokens refuse zeroing allowances due to implementation quirks, requiring a two-step process: set to zero, then set anew. In October 2020, researchers highlighted Metamask's initial behaviour of overwriting existing allowances directly, which occasionally failed against strict tokens; the wallet later adjusted to the safer two-step pattern. The implication is sobering: even safety tools must be iterated and audited. There is no final keystroke that ends learning.

Transparency aids memory. Block explorers such as Etherscan added "Token Approvals" dashboards in 2020–2021, surfacing spender addresses and amounts in one place. Their effect is cultural as much as technical. When information about permissions becomes public and searchable, norms can form. Teams begin to publish the exact spender addresses their interfaces will ever use; auditors include allowlist verification steps in reviews; users develop the reflex to compare on-screen spender fields with known addresses. Discipline becomes communal.

The future of approvals is unlikely to be a miracle. More probably, it will be a drift toward boundedness: time-bound permits by default; per-tx limits; clearer prompts; safer routers; reputational registries for spender contracts; and systems that degrade gracefully—failing a transaction rather than exposing a balance when conditions change. These are scenarios, not guarantees. Each adds friction somewhere. Each must be weighed against the tempo of markets and the tolerance of humans.

We return, finally, to the handshake. The habit we cultivate is simple: pause, read, and measure. Who is the spender? How much, exactly, for how long? What happens if this address changes code tomorrow? The questions are prosaic, but they cut cleanly through hype. They turn a reflex into a ritual, and a ritual into a shield. The unresolved test waits the next time a polished interface asks for permission and your cursor hovers over *Approve*: is this a handshake you are willing to remember six months from now?

Detecting Spoofed Interfaces

On 15 March 2021, visitors to PancakeSwap's website were greeted by a familiar logo and a deadly prompt. The domain had been hijacked; a counterfeit front end urged users to enter their seed phrases to "restore" access. Within hours, funds vanished from wallets that complied. In August 2022, Curve Finance's main site suffered a similar DNS compromise, silently rerouting users to an impostor page that requested fresh approvals and drained tokens once granted. In February 2022, OpenSea users were targeted by a phishing campaign that mimicked support messages and lured them into signing malicious orders. Different platforms, same choreography: a forged shopfront, a trusted brand, a small click with large consequences. The blockchain did not break. The shop sign lied.

Spoofing thrives because interfaces are costumes. They borrow logos, colours, and tone. They stage the familiar to bypass scrutiny. The deception is rarely technical genius; it is theatre calibrated to expectation. A homograph domain swaps a single character—a for a, Cyrillic for Latin—and the address line becomes camouflage. A DNS hijack silently diverts a well-known URL to a malicious server, certificate and all, if the attacker can manipulate registrar records. A cloned dApp lifts code from open repositories, replaces contract addresses with adversarial ones, and waits for muscle memory to carry the user across the threshold. The attack is social at its core. It succeeds when you believe you have nothing to prove.

Show, name, explain, implication: start with the **homograph**. Show: a link in a Discord channel purports to be app.uniswap.org, but an o has been swapped for ο (Greek omicron). Name: internationalised domain name (IDN) homograph attack. Explain: modern browsers render Unicode domains in their native script; to the human eye, o and ο are identical. The fake site loads a pixel-perfect copy of the genuine interface and requests an approval to a hostile router. Implication: the margin of error is one glyph. Trust, if it is to be rational, must be anchored in more than visual resemblance. The visible behaviour that counters this risk is monotonous and effective: type known domains, use bookmarks, and cross-check the spender address on the device screen against the project's documented address before signing. It is slow. It is costly by seconds. It pays.

Next, the **DNS hijack**. Show: in August 2022, curve.fi briefly resolved to an IP that served hostile JavaScript; users who signed approvals lost funds to an attacker-controlled address. Name: DNS poisoning at the registrar layer. Explain: the domain name system is a distributed phone book; if an attacker alters the record at the source, your browser dutifully calls the wrong number. Cryptography at the smart-contract layer remains pristine; the deception lives in the route to the page. Implication: even familiar URLs can betray you. The defensive behaviour is twofold: treat approvals as privileged acts that require contract-level verification, and consider alternative, tamper-evident distribution channels (for example, verified IPFS hashes announced through the project's ENS text records or signed releases). If this feels fussy, that is because it is. Safety is detail.

A third vector is the **cloned application** with swapped contract hooks. Show: a trending "airdrop checker" appears on Twitter, promising eligibility results. Name: interface clone with modified JavaScript. Explain: the page looks legitimate, but the "Check" button triggers approve() for a target token to a counterfeit spender. Implication: a diagnostic tool becomes a drain. The measurable counter-metric here is the delta between a tool's stated purpose and any permission it requests. An eligibility checker should read; it should not need to spend. When purpose and permission diverge, leave.

Two more named, checkable examples ground the pattern. In March 2021, both PancakeSwap and Cream Finance warned users to avoid their websites due to registrar-level hijacks; attackers inserted scripts that harvested phrases and pushed approvals. In February 2022, OpenSea warned of an off-platform phishing campaign that induced users to sign orders they did not understand; stolen NFTs moved through the Wyvern protocol without a single on-chain compromise of OpenSea's contracts. The limitation that tempers these cases is important: not every front-end failure implies protocol failure, and not every protocol failure implicates the front end. The reconciliation is practical: your risk sits where your click sits. The front end is where you choose to prove or assume.

The abstractions—trust, risk, verification—must tie to behaviours. Trust becomes *which address you are about to authorise;* risk becomes *how far an approval extends and for how long;* verification becomes *the act of comparing what the interface claims with what the wallet displays and what the chain records*. These are physical acts: typing, reading, comparing, declining. They are measurable in seconds and clicks. They form the *verify before connect* posture: a pause inserted upstream of exposure. It is a posture, not a product.

Consider the quiet motif of the **shopfront**. A counterfeit shopfront does not need to crack a safe; it needs only to usher you to the wrong till. The lesson generalises. When Ledger suffered a customer data breach in July 2020, months of targeted phishing followed. Victims received emails branded convincingly as firmware updates. Some plugged their devices into fake sites and entered seed phrases into web forms. The real Ledger software never asks for a seed phrase on a connected computer. That single invariant—a rule rehearsed until reflexive—would have saved them. The shopfront was persuasive; the till was wrong. A rule beats a hunch.

Another tell is **urgency** framed as community duty. Show: a pop-up on a cloned site warns that "due to a critical vulnerability you must migrate your LP tokens in the next 15 minutes." Name: panic phishing. Explain: time pressure narrows attention; users skip reading transaction data and approve unlimited allowances to unknown spenders. Implication: attackers manufacture countdowns because they degrade cognition reliably. The counter-behaviour is culturally unglamorous: close the tab, return via a bookmarked domain, and verify the announcement from a second, independent channel—project blog, signed GitHub release, or a chain message from the protocol's timelock or multisig. Measure the habit by outcome: the number of times a countdown prompt leads to a fresh session from a known link rather than a hurried signature. That number should tend to one.

Homograph traps also hide in **social handles**. Twitter and Telegram are rife with lookalike accounts—extra underscores, swapped letters, zero-width spaces. A 2022 survey by the Anti-Phishing Working Group observed that brand impersonation across cryptocurrency platforms surged with market volatility; waves of new entrants arrive just as scams peak. The tell is rarely a spelling mistake. It is behavioural: unsolicited direct messages offering "support." Legitimate teams do not cold-DM wallet fixes. This norm is valuable precisely because it is boring. It gives you a reflex. Ignore, block, and navigate to the public, verified channel.

The counter-example that refines our caution is **enshrined trust signals**: browser padlocks, "https", and even certificate authority names. They help—until they don't. DNS compromises can still serve valid TLS certificates if the attacker controls the domain. Phishers can obtain certificates for lookalike domains. A padlock signals encryption, not authenticity. Reconciling this limitation means elevating stronger invariants: the spender contract address and its provenance; the chain ID your wallet displays; the ENS or DNSSEC records that a project controls. These are harder to fake at scale than a favicon. They require effort to check, and they repay it.

Indexers and analytics dashboards deserve their own scepticism. During a data inconsistency bug in The Graph's mainnet in late 2021, several dashboards displayed stale pool balances and APYs that did not match on-chain reality. No theft occurred, but decisions did—users rotated capital based on numbers that changed hours later. The tell here is not malicious; it is temporal drift. A "verify before connect" posture extends to "verify before act": check whether the dashboard's claim matches a block explorer's ledger at the referenced block height. If the numbers disagree, defer. Patience is a security control.

Front-end design can help or harm. Wallets that surface the spender address, chain ID, and precise allowance on a trusted hardware display reduce ambiguity at the moment that matters. Conversely, interfaces that compress long addresses into ellipses or bury permissions behind a "More info" chevron increase error rates. In 2021, several hardware vendors improved ERC-20 approval prompts to show token symbols and spender contracts explicitly. Auditors reported, anecdotally, a decline in unlimited approvals among clients who adopted the firmware. Design is not decoration; it is a risk instrument.

We should name the **limits** of vigilance. An expert can still be fooled by a perfect clone loaded through a poisoned DNS record, arriving via a perfectly spelled URL. No single tell is infallible. The answer is defence in depth expressed as habit: prefer interacting directly with contracts for large moves; maintain an allowlist of spender addresses; reuse verified front ends rather than novelty; verify hashes of downloadable tools; and separate hot interaction from cold storage by architecture, not intention. None of this removes risk. It locates and shrinks it.

Two final scenes bring texture. In July 2022, a phishing campaign impersonating Uniswap's airdrop lured users to sign malicious transactions via a counterfeit claim site; high-profile warnings flagged the fake domain within hours, yet funds continued to trickle to the attacker as links propagated through secondary channels. The tell that would have saved late victims was simple: the target transaction called approve() rather than any claim function; the spender address did not match Uniswap's router. In January 2023, a tranche of fake WalletConnect pop-ups swept through crypto Twitter, crafted as embedded images of genuine modal windows. They could not execute code, but they harvested clicks that led to real phishing pages. The tell here was meta: an image cannot initiate a connection. It can only advertise one. The remedy was to close the tab and start from one's own bookmark.

What, then, is the durable posture? *Verify before connect.* Treat connection as consent and consent as authority. Ask three quick questions every time the shopfront invites you inside. Who controls this domain, and how do I know? Which contract will hold permission when I click, and can I confirm its address elsewhere? What is the purpose of this request, and does the permission match the purpose? If the answers are fuzzy, do not negotiate with your doubt. Close the door. Return by a path you own.

You cannot outsource attention. You can, however, codify it. Teams publish canonical spender addresses and ENS text records. Block explorers expose token-approval dashboards. Hardware wallets display more. Users adopt a small set of habits—bookmarks, typed URLs, address comparisons on trusted screens—that cost minutes and save years. The shopfront will keep changing costume. The hand that reaches for the handle is yours. The unresolved test arrives the next time a polished page promises speed, access, and belonging if you will only click *Connect*. Will you verify first, or will you let the costume decide?

Chapter 3
AMMs and Swaps: How Uniswap Works

In May 2020, as global markets stumbled through uncertainty and central banks wrestled with liquidity crises, a quiet experiment in transparency reached critical mass. On a blockchain where code replaced brokers, Uniswap processed billions in daily volume—without a single order book, market maker, or human intermediary. Its algorithm, indifferent to sentiment, simply balanced two sides of a digital scale. A trader sold ETH for DAI; the formula adjusted, the ratio shifted, and the price moved. There was no negotiation, no flashing screens of bids and asks. Just a curve—mathematical, continuous, and incorruptible—performing the ancient act of price discovery in a radically new medium.

This inversion of the trading floor is both disorienting and instructive. For decades, markets have been defined by *competition*—buyers and sellers, each trying to outguess the other. Automated market makers (AMMs) dissolve that contest. They replace rivalry with liquidity: a shared pool of assets, governed by equations, that *always* quotes a price. The simplicity is deceptive. Beneath the polished interface lies a living organism—a protocol that absorbs order flow, compensates risk-takers, and arbitrages its own mistakes at machine speed. It is both predictable and volatile, serene and treacherous. To understand it is to glimpse how finance evolves when human discretion retreats behind code.

The paradox is elegant. A decentralised exchange like Uniswap offers *price without opinion*, yet every price still carries consequence. The constant-product formula, expressed as $x \times y = k$, enforces balance: each trade nudges the curve, redistributing wealth between traders and liquidity providers. Every token swap bends the relationship between depth and slippage, revealing the invisible cost of immediacy. Where a traditional market hides spread in opaque order books, the AMM displays it as geometry. Each point on the curve tells a story of risk, patience, and marginal willingness to pay. It is not a metaphor. It is algebra that behaves like economics.

Uniswap's rise did not happen in isolation. It built on a lineage that began with EtherDelta in 2017 and evolved through Bancor's liquidity experiments. But Uniswap's genius was minimalism: no accounts, no order matching, no limit orders—just contracts anyone could use or extend. In a single year, it redefined what it meant to "make a market." Liquidity, once the domain of institutions, became participatory. Anyone with two tokens and conviction could join the pool. It was a radical act of inclusion and, as many discovered, of exposure. When liquidity provision became yield farming, participants learned that returns were not free lunches but reflections of price movement—impermanent loss rendered permanent by neglect.

To see how these systems work, one must stop thinking like a trader and start thinking like an engineer. AMMs are programmable infrastructure, not arenas of speculation.

They obey physics. Price moves in response to flows; flows respond to incentives; incentives reshape structure. The AMM compresses that feedback loop into a transparent circuit. The code defines how deep liquidity feels, how quickly prices react, and how fees accumulate. Yet every refinement—like Uniswap's introduction of *concentrated liquidity* in 2021—shifts the burden back to human choice. Where should liquidity sit? How wide should the range be? The algorithm never promises fairness, only clarity. That is its gift and its challenge.

Fees complete the picture. Each trade generates a toll—0.05%, 0.3%, or more—paid to those who lent their assets to the pool. It is a quiet redistribution of microprofits: small drips that aggregate into income streams. The equilibrium is delicate. When volatility spikes, arbitrageurs rush in to realign pool prices with external markets, pocketing the spread. The AMM, unthinking, pays them with traders' slippage. Thus, arbitrage becomes both parasite and physician—extracting value but maintaining order. This duality is central to the chapter's argument: in DeFi, efficiency and exploitation are often indistinguishable until you trace the money's path.

As liquidity fragmented across chains and protocols, the quest for "best price" birthed a new intermediary: the *aggregator*. Routing systems like 1inch and Matcha promised optimal execution by splitting trades across pools, bridges, and networks. Yet each layer of convenience reintroduced complexity, and with it, trust. A single routing error, or a compromised bridge, can outweigh the fractional gain of a tighter spread. The irony is modern and timeless: in chasing precision, we recreate the same hidden dependencies that decentralisation sought to escape. Sometimes, the better deal is the simpler one.

This chapter is not a manual in formulae but an anatomy of structure—how markets function when their logic is explicit. It unpacks constant-product curves not as curiosities, but as the beating heart of decentralised exchange; it follows fee flows to reveal who truly benefits; it maps routers and bridges to show where risk migrates once middlemen disappear; and it catalogues the small betrayals of interface design that separate legitimate contracts from malicious clones. The promise of DeFi is not mystery but transparency. The tragedy is that transparency still requires literacy to protect you.

The motif that runs through these pages is *depth*: of pools, of understanding, of caution. Shallow liquidity makes for violent moves; shallow comprehension makes for costly ones. Every equation here doubles as a mirror—what you see depends on how closely you look. Slippage is not a defect but a price for urgency. Arbitrage is not villainy but maintenance. And fake tokens are not proof of systemic rot but reminders that code, however elegant, is always embedded in human intention.

Uniswap's curve is not just a pricing engine; it is a metaphor for decentralisation itself—a surface that rewards participation yet punishes recklessness. Its mathematics expose the invisible logic of every market: that prices are not discovered, but made; that liquidity is not found, but offered; that every trade is an act of faith in code. To study AMMs is to learn not just how to swap tokens, but how to think probabilistically about risk, alignment, and consequence.

As we move deeper into this chapter, you will see how a formula written in a few lines of Solidity came to host the largest open marketplace on Earth, how liquidity provision became both a service and a speculation, and how understanding one curve can inoculate you against many illusions. The market has no face, but it has fingerprints—left by incentives, fees, and the quiet hands of those who read before they click. This chapter teaches you to see them.

Price without Order Books

On 16 September 2020, Uniswap briefly overtook Coinbase Pro in daily trading volume—US$426 million to Coinbase's US$348 million—without a single order book. The exchange had no bids, no asks, and no traders peering at screens waiting to be filled. It was, at that moment, the largest market on Earth operating without the market's traditional machinery. The event baffled observers schooled in decades of microstructure theory: how could a platform with no visible order flow generate real prices? Yet the answer lay not in mysticism but in mathematics. Uniswap's formula—$x \times y = k$—had quietly rewritten the grammar of exchange.

Show → name → explain → implication. Show: a trader swaps 10 ETH for DAI. Name: the *constant-product market maker*. Explain: the pool holds reserves of ETH and DAI; the product of their quantities remains constant; trading one pushes the other's price along a curve. Implication: the market is self-pricing. Supply and demand are no longer external forces—they are encoded relations. Every transaction adjusts the slope of a mathematical line that anyone can inspect but no one can control.

The elegance of $x \times y = k$ is not its simplicity but its stubborn honesty. It enforces conservation: you cannot take value from the pool without changing its balance. In traditional finance, order books conceal the elasticity of prices behind human behaviour. In automated markets, the formula exposes it. Each swap has a visible cost called *slippage*—the difference between the expected and realised price—caused by the curve's geometry. The larger the trade relative to pool depth, the further down the curve you slide. Traders call it friction. Mathematicians call it liquidity sensitivity. Either way, it is a price for immediacy.

Consider two examples that illustrate this mechanism in the wild. First, the ETH/USDC pool on Uniswap v2 in July 2021, with roughly US$2 billion in liquidity. A US$1 million swap moved the price by less than 0.1 per cent. Depth absorbed demand. Contrast that with a small-cap token pool—say, an experimental DeFi asset with only US$50,000 of total liquidity. A US$10,000 trade might shift price by 20 per cent or more. The algorithm did not "fail"; it performed perfectly. The difference was depth. The curve bends sharply when the reservoir is shallow. The behaviour is visible, predictable, and brutally fair.

The counter-example is instructive. In March 2021, during high volatility, some users complained of "price manipulation" on Uniswap when large swaps moved markets dramatically. The claim misunderstood the system. The AMM is deterministic; slippage reflects liquidity, not deception. Yet the limitation is real: in thin pools, prices diverge faster from external benchmarks, inviting arbitrageurs to restore equilibrium. They profit from those divergences, but they also stabilise them. The reconciliation lies in design: the AMM's structure ensures correction without coordination. Where human markets rely on quotes, automated markets rely on balance.

The motif that threads through these paragraphs is *depth*—as geometry, as metaphor, as truth. Depth is not an abstraction; it is a measurable property of how much you can move before the curve pushes back. It tells you, in advance, how far your order will ripple. In human markets, depth is inferred from unseen intentions; in automated ones, it is written into the contract itself. Transparency replaces speculation. What disappears is the fog.

Concentrated liquidity, introduced with Uniswap v3 in May 2021, refined that geometry. Show: instead of spreading capital evenly across all prices, liquidity providers could choose ranges—say, US$1,000 to US$2,000 per ETH. Name: *concentrated liquidity provision*. Explain:

capital now acts with precision, thickening the curve where activity is dense and thinning it elsewhere. Implication: traders enjoy tighter spreads near the market price and harsher slippage outside it. Liquidity becomes sculpted. Yet the power introduces complexity. Providers must rebalance positions as prices drift, or their assets go idle. The AMM becomes dynamic, almost biological—its blood flow adjusting to market metabolism.

This evolution marked a subtle philosophical shift. AMMs were once celebrated for "passive" income—set and forget. Concentrated liquidity turned them into strategic instruments. Providing liquidity became closer to market-making: position sizing, range management, fee harvesting. Data from Uniswap Labs (2022) showed that roughly half of liquidity providers underperformed simple holding due to poor range maintenance. The curve had rewarded precision but punished neglect. Mathematics offered transparency, not mercy.

Two further examples illustrate how these mechanics translate to market function. In November 2022, when USDC briefly decoupled from its peg following news of Silicon Valley Bank's distress, AMM pools automatically adjusted prices downward as traders sold USDC for stable alternatives. There were no freezes, no committees, no halts—only liquidity responding to flows. Conversely, in May 2022, during the collapse of Terra's UST, AMM pools on Curve and Uniswap exhibited extreme slippage, with traders draining liquidity faster than arbitrage could restore balance. The formula remained constant; reality did not. The lesson is empirical: an equation can mediate price, but not guarantee trust in the underlying asset.

The constant-product model has its limits. It assumes continuous liquidity, but blockchain settlement is discrete. Between blocks, prices can jump, leaving arbitrageurs to repair gaps at cost. This latency, typically seconds on Ethereum, becomes visible when volatility spikes. The AMM does not anticipate; it reacts. Its perfection is reactive, not predictive. That is its discipline: no foresight, only balance.

Critics sometimes call this structure "inefficient" because it locks up idle capital—most of a pool's reserves sit unused except near the current price. Yet this inefficiency is also safety. The excess depth acts as a buffer against shocks. When Uniswap v3 introduced range orders, the model effectively became an adjustable reservoir—narrow pools behave like springs, wide ones like basins. Market-makers now choose their curvature. They choose how tightly to wind their springs. It is a new form of authorship over liquidity.

To translate these abstractions into visible behaviour: every AMM pool is a curve drawn in token space. When you swap, you move along that curve, paying slippage proportional to the area you traverse. The shape of the curve defines your cost. In constant-product systems, that shape is hyperbolic—steep at the edges, gentle near the centre. Other designs, such as Curve's *stable-swap invariant*, flatten the curve around parity, minimising slippage for correlated assets. These are not mere optimisations; they are philosophical choices about what "fair" means in different contexts. Fairness for volatile pairs is about depth; fairness for stable pairs is about proximity.

The motif of depth returns. When liquidity is deep, slippage feels like the ocean: vast, indifferent, barely disturbed by small movement. When shallow, it behaves like a puddle: every step sends ripples. A trader's skill lies in recognising which sea they are in before they dive. AMMs publish that information constantly—the pool size, the reserves, the fees. Guesswork has no excuse, only neglect.

Mathematically, the constant-product rule enforces symmetry: what one side gains, the other loses, preserving total value. Yet psychologically, it transforms how people perceive markets. Instead of competing orders, participants interact with a collective curve. They are not transacting *against* someone but *with* a system. That subtle change alters behaviour. Fear of counterparties becomes trust in code; greed for arbitrage becomes service to equilibrium. It is not utopian, but it is new.

A brief detour into tradition clarifies what was lost and gained. The first electronic order book, launched by NASDAQ in 1971, digitised the human pit but retained its logic: bids, asks, spread. It mirrored scarcity. Uniswap digitised liquidity itself, making the spread a function of depth rather than psychology. This inversion is profound. Price, once an emergent property of opinion, becomes a by-product of geometry. When the curve bends, we glimpse a market that no longer needs to shout.

The counterpoint is essential. AMMs may remove intermediaries, but they do not abolish risk. Mispriced pools invite predation. Bots exploit latency, miners extract value (MEV) by reordering transactions, and asymmetric information migrates from human traders to algorithms. The curve is neutral; the network is not. Recognising that boundary—between mathematical fairness and infrastructural power—is part of literacy. Knowing the formula is not enough; one must also understand where it lives.

Liquidity, then, is less about abundance and more about shape. It is sculpted by incentives, range, and trust. Constant-product AMMs taught the world that markets could run on equations. Concentrated liquidity taught that equations could still require judgement. Both reveal that decentralisation is not the absence of design but its most transparent form.

The unresolved tension remains visible every time a trader hovers over the "Swap" button: how much movement can I afford? The formula will answer instantly. But it will not forgive misunderstanding. The test is perennial: do you know the depth of the water you are about to enter?

Fees, LPs, and Your Trade

On 5 May 2021, Uniswap v3 went live on Ethereum mainnet with three explicit fee tiers—0.05 per cent, 0.30 per cent, and

1.00 per cent—and a promise that markets could finally price *liquidity* with the same precision they priced *assets*. In London and Singapore, desks that had spent years staring at order books ran the same ETH–USDC trade through different v3 pools and watched execution costs diverge by design, not dysfunction. The cheaper pool filled quickly near the mid-price; the dearer pool stood ready at the wings for heavier, riskier flow. Nothing magical occurred. Fees shifted, liquidity followed, and arbitrageurs stitched prices back to external venues. Your trade paid for that stitching. Fees are not decoration. They are rails.

Show → name → explain → implication. Show: you swap 50,000 USDC for ETH on Uniswap. Name: the *fee tier* you route through—say, 30 basis points—dictates what you pay to liquidity providers (LPs). Explain: that fee is credited directly to LP positions pro rata within the price range that absorbed your swap, not to an exchange treasury. Implication: trading cost is not just a line item; it is a transfer to a specific set of counterparties whose capital made your immediacy possible. The protocol is a conduit. Your decision to trade is a payment to those who stood ready.

Now watch what happens after the swap. Show: the pool price drifts from the "true" market price visible on a centralised venue in Chicago. Name: the *arbitrage loop*. Explain: professional searchers buy where your trade cheapened the asset and sell where it remains dear, or vice versa, pushing the pool back into alignment. Implication: arbitrage is not an externality; it is the self-righting mechanism you hire when you hit "Swap." Their profit—spread minus gas and slippage—is part of your total cost, even if you never meet them. You pay the toll and you fund the repair crew.

Why, then, are some pairs cheaper than others? The answer is geometry fed by incentives. Pools with more capital *at* the current price, and with lower fee tiers, charge you less for the same notional trade. But there is no free lunch: lower fees attract more flow, which may increase impermanent loss for LPs who fail to manage ranges. The system balances through migration. When fees are mispriced relative to volatility, LPs move. When LPs move, your price changes.

Two named examples, with dates, make this concrete. First: on launch (May 2021, Ethereum mainnet), Uniswap v3's *USDC/USDT* pool at the 0.05 per cent tier rapidly accumulated range liquidity around one dollar, creating a flat section of the curve and razor-thin spreads. Traders moving millions between these stablecoins routinely paid only a few basis points including slippage because LPs faced trivial inventory risk; the fee could be low because volatility was low. In contrast, the *ETH/USDC* 0.05 per cent pool struggled to hold deep capital near the mid for long; volatility risk demanded higher compensation, and flow tended to route through the 0.30 per cent tier where LPs were paid adequately for price risk. The structural lesson: fee tier choice is a market's opinion about *risk*, expressed in a number you can read before you trade.

Second: Curve Finance's "3pool" (DAI/USDC/USDT), live since 2020 on Ethereum, uses a stable-swap invariant that flattens the price curve around parity and charges a low fee (typically 4 basis points on mainnet, adjustable by governance). During calm periods in 2021, it routinely delivered sub–5 bps total cost for multi-million-dollar stablecoin trades, a metric checkable in on-chain analytics. Curve's design and fee policy made it an execution venue of choice for correlated assets, while Uniswap's constant-product pools dominated volatile pairs where concentrated liquidity could be aimed. Different invariants, different tollgates, same principle: you pay both the quoted fee and the shape of the pool.

A credible counter-example clarifies limits. In May 2022, amid the failure of Terra's UST, even the best-engineered stable pools ceased to look cheap. Liquidity thinned as LPs pulled ranges; slippage exploded; arbitrage could not restore a price that no longer had credibility. Fees did not break. Reality did. Reconcile the case this way: fees and arbitrage loops restore prices *within* a functioning market; they cannot conjure trust ex nihilo. When the asset's premise fails, "cheaper vs dearer" loses meaning. The cost you face becomes existential, not transactional.

Let us return to routine conditions. After EIP-1559 (5 August 2021, London upgrade), Ethereum introduced a burned base fee plus a priority tip, making gas costs more predictable on average. For arbitrage, that mattered. Show: during a 20 gwei base fee period, a cross-venue arb of 10 bps on a US$1 million trade yields US$1,000 before gas; if the total gas to execute and settle is US$150, the arb is worth doing; at 200 gwei, it may not be. Name: *MEV economics*. Explain: arbitrageurs and liquidators bid for blockspace through tips; their willingness to repair your pool's price depends on their net. Implication: when blockspace is expensive, prices may linger out of line, and your trade's effective cost rises because the repair crew waits. The fee you see and the fee you don't see—gas-induced lag—both hit your outcome.

The motif that threads this subchapter is the *tollgate*. Every route you take from token A to token B passes through one. Sometimes it is painted bright (0.30 per cent at the top of the screen). Sometimes it is painted grey (slippage into a thinner tick range). Sometimes it is invisible (arbitrage gas). But it is always there. The literate question is not "What is the fee?" but "Whose tollgate am I paying, and for what service?"

Follow the Show → Name → Explain → Implication engine through the life of a trade. Show: you choose the 0.05 per cent ETH/USDC pool because the interface flags a "better price." Name: *routing*. Explain: the aggregator splits your order across multiple pools and maybe a bridge, shaving a basis point here, adding two there, hoping the net wins. Implication: more complexity introduces more failure points—bridge risk, stale oracles, reorg sensitivity—whose costs only manifest when something snaps. The cheapest sticker is not always the lowest total cost. That is why, during periods of volatility, professional desks often accept a slightly worse quoted price in a single deep pool they understand rather than a razor-thin composite that depends on five contracts across two chains. They pay the nearer tollgate to avoid the mountain pass.

Fee flows also teach you why pools look lively or deserted. LPs are rational. Show: a volatile memecoin pair at the 1.00 per cent tier attracts thrill-seekers for a week and then empties. Name: *fee-to-risk mismatch.* Explain: early volume sprayed fees; later, one-directional price action crystallised impermanent loss that fees could not offset. Implication: LP capital migrates toward venues where fee income equals or exceeds expected divergence loss. Your trade cost is their wage. If wages do not clear, the labour leaves.

This migration is visible in v3's *concentrated liquidity* mechanics. LPs allocate capital to price ranges. Where ranges overlap densely, traders meet an ocean; where they do not, a puddle. Fee income is credited to positions *in range*; out-of-range capital earns nothing. LPs therefore race to sit just inside the action without being steamrolled by it. Some do this well. Many do not. Uniswap Labs' 2022 study suggested that a large fraction of passive LPs underperformed buy-and-hold because their ranges were too narrow or too slow to rebalance. The implication for traders is immediate: pools with active, competent LPs around the mid deliver lower effective costs because replenishment is continuous; pools with deserted or mis-aimed capital punish size with slippage first and fees second. You are paying for stewardship, even if you never meet the stewards.

Two more scenes, precise and checkable, anchor intuition. In November 2021, the *WETH/USDC 0.05 per cent* pool on Arbitrum (launched August 2021) often provided retail-sized trades with sub–10 bps total cost thanks to low L2 gas and dense ranges; the same notional on Ethereum mainnet in a thinner hour could cost multiples due to slippage under higher fees and sparser tick coverage. In contrast, during the "Merge" week (September 2022), mainnet blockspace volatility briefly raised priority fees and widened effective spreads as arbitrage timing risk increased; prices still restored, but your cost of urgency rose. The tollgate is local: chain, hour, pair.

Fees also encode governance. Uniswap v3 permits protocol fee switches (a portion of LP fees diverted to protocol treasuries), though they have been selectively engaged by governance as of differing months post-launch. Curve's gauges direct CRV emissions to pools, subsidising LP returns so they can accept lower fee tiers. Sushi's fee policy has historically split a portion of swap fees to xSUSHI stakers. Each choice rearranges who you pay and how much. The abstract word *incentives* becomes a very specific question: does this pool's fee policy attract stable, competent capital, or transient mercenaries? You can measure the answer: look at liquidity persistence by tick over weeks, LP address churn, and fee-to-volume ratios.

Where persistence is high and churn low, your trades usually price better; the tollgate is staffed.

What of the critique that AMMs "overpay" arbitrageurs—allowing external searchers to scoop spreads that could be captured internally for LPs and traders? Designs such as *TWAMM* (time-weighted average market maker) and *dutched* auctions, as well as oracles and hook systems proposed for newer AMMs, try to internalise some of that value. Yet the limitation is practical: most real flow is lumpy and urgent. A system that internalises too much can become brittle or gameable. The reconciliation is scenario-based: for slow, large, predictable flows, structured execution reduces tolls; for fast, small, noisy flows, the open arbitrage loop keeps the road clear. Your job is not to reform the road. It is to choose the lane that matches your cargo.

The fee you pay also funds *liquidation readiness* in lending markets indirectly. When a sharp move hits, arbitrageurs and liquidators compete in the same mempool. If LP fees are attractive, searchers keep idle capital near the venue, ready to act. Markets clear. If fees are anaemic relative to risk, the same wallets may route elsewhere, and your trade faces thinner immediate depth. Again the motif holds: the tollgate hires the crew that keeps the bridge open in a storm. Underpay the crew, and you cross at your peril.

We can make this operational without lapsing into prescription. Translate abstractions into decisions. If a pool's *quoted fee* is low but its *realised slippage* (measured over your size) is high, your effective toll is high. If an aggregator routes you through four pools to save two basis points *before gas*, ask whether a single deep pool saves more *after* gas and failure risk. If a pair sits at a higher fee tier than peers, ask whether its realised volatility justifies it; if not, expect LP migration and price your expectations accordingly. Measure. Compare. Commit.

The motif returns one last time. Tollgates reveal who bears what risk. Stablecoin pairs can afford slim tolls because inventory risk is low; volatile pairs charge more because they must cushion shock. Thin pools charge most of all because they are puddles pretending to be lakes. Arbitrage stitches the surface smooth again, but only if the stitchers are paid and the water still connects to a wider sea of price.

The unresolved tension for any participant is simple to pose and hard to live by: when you press "Swap," do you know which tollgates you are paying—LP fee, slippage, arbitrage gas—and why? Or are you outsourcing that knowledge to an interface that collapses them into a single, soothing number? The market will collect either way. The choice is whether you read the bill before you sign.

Routing and Aggregators

On 23 March 2022, in Ho Chi Minh City, Sky Mavis disclosed that the Ronin bridge supporting its Axie Infinity network had been compromised. Attackers forged cross-chain withdrawals totalling roughly US$600 million. The code on each chain executed as instructed; the route between them was the wound. Many victims had never touched the bridge directly. They had clicked "best route" on a familiar interface, watched their trade split across venues and chains, and saved a handful of basis points. The paradox was brutal: a "better price" on the screen had travelled through a path that was not better at all. It was cheaper until it wasn't. Five words capture the lesson: the route is the risk.

Routers, aggregators, and bridges exist to hide complexity. They promise a single decision—swap A for B—while stitching together a dozen decisions behind the glass. Show: a trader enters a 200,000 USDC → ETH order on an aggregator. Name: *pathfinding*. Explain: the engine computes a route that splits flow across pools, sometimes across chains, aiming to minimise *quoted* cost: fee plus slippage at that moment. Implication: optimisation moves value but also moves *trust*. Each additional hop is a new counterparty, a new contract, a new failure mode. The line between efficiency and exposure is crossed silently, one "Yes" at a time.

Begin with the simplest component, the **router**. Show: Uniswap's Universal Router (late 2022) sequences steps—wrap ETH, swap through multiple pools, route to a recipient—in one atomic transaction. Name: *router contract*. Explain: a router does not hold value; it orchestrates calls to pools and returns the result or reverts entirely. Implication: within a chain, a well-audited router reduces operational risk by compressing steps; the main exposure becomes approval scope and contract upgrades. The behavioural metric is concrete: how many distinct contracts will hold allowance after this swap? If the answer is "the router only," risk is bounded; if the answer includes third-party helpers, it sprawls.

Now zoom out to **aggregators**. Show: 1inch, Matcha (0x), and ParaSwap compete to shave basis points by splitting order flow across AMMs and private RFQ quotes. Name: *best execution*. Explain: aggregators consider gas, pool depth, and expected price impact; they may fragment a single order into five partial fills across three pools. Implication: fragmentation invites microstructure risk. Each partial fill is subject to mempool dynamics, sandwiching, orphans, and non-deterministic gas spikes. A quoted 6 bps improvement can disappear in the scramble for blockspace. The visible behaviour that decides the outcome is mundane but measurable: the *fill ratio at quoted price*. If the aggregator reliably delivers ≥ 95 per cent of the notional at or better than quote, its added complexity is earning its keep; if slippage and retries routinely eat the edge, simplicity wins.

Two named examples anchor these mechanics. First, **0x's RFQ** system, used by Matcha since 2020, sources firm quotes from market-makers that settle on-chain without exposing the entire order to the public mempool. That design reduces price impact for size and blunts sandwich attacks; the market-maker commits inventory risk for the quoted window. Second, **UniswapX** (announced mid-2023, rolling out thereafter) externalised routing to third-party "fillers" who compete to deliver the user's requested swap at the best net outcome, settling with the protocol. Both sought the same prize: better execution with fewer public hops. The implication is precise: routes that *compress* public exposure often outperform in volatile windows, even if they look marginally worse on a static quote.

Bridges raise the stakes. Show: a user accepts an aggregator's cross-chain path from ETH (mainnet) to USDC (Arbitrum) because it is "2–3 bps better" than staying on mainnet. Name: *bridging leg*. Explain: the path introduces at least three new uncertainties: custody (who controls the bridge's escrow), *finality* (how many blocks before the target chain credits funds irreversibly), and *oracle/liveness* risk (how the bridge proves an event occurred). Implication: the few basis points saved are dwarfed by a low-frequency, high-severity tail: a halt, a hack, or a proof delay that forces repricing. The expected value of a tiny edge collapses when multiplied by a non-zero probability of catastrophic loss. This is not rhetoric; it is arithmetic.

History provides two further case studies with dates and consequences. **Wormhole** (2 February 2022) suffered an exploit that drained ~US$320 million in wrapped assets after a signature verification failure; patched funds were later backstopped, but the event revealed how a single validator module could compromise a cross-chain illusion of continuity. **Nomad** (1 August 2022) was drained for ~US$190 million after a contract initialisation error allowed anyone to copy a valid message and cash it; thousands of addresses joined the free-for-all. In both cases, users who arrived via aggregators may never have realised a bridge leg existed. The route had felt seamless; the tolltower they relied upon had been unstaffed.

A credible counter-example tempers blanket scepticism. **Hop** and **Across**, both live since 2021, use designs that reduce trust in a single multisig: optimistic verification with bonded relayers (Hop), or a combination of incentives and canonical bridges (Across) that minimise capital at risk on the fast path. These models improve *time to credit* while bounding trust assumptions. Yet the limitation remains: an extra domain of failure exists. Reconciling this means shifting posture, not rejecting progress. Use fast bridges for low-value, high-urgency transfers when the incremental utility dominates the incremental risk; use canonical routes or direct custody for size. The behaviour is a policy: match the route to the stake.

The motif that threads this discussion is the **map**. A route on your screen is a map that hides terrain: oracles, signers, mempools, relays, RPC providers. When the map offers a shortcut, ask what hill it is skirting. Every abstraction—trust, efficiency, risk—must map to a choice. Trust becomes: which addresses can seize or stall funds on this leg? Efficiency becomes: how many gas-heavy calls and approvals does this route require? Risk becomes: how many independent confirmations until I can net positions without bridge or aggregator assumptions? These questions touch physical acts (counting calls, reading addresses, measuring blocks to finality) and produce metrics: approvals per route, contracts touched, confirmations waited. They turn "better" into something you can audit.

Return to **arbitrage and routing** within a chain. Aggregators that chase the last basis point often split orders across pools with different fee tiers and tick depths. Show: a 500,000 USDC order is split into four legs; two fill immediately, one reverts due to price movement, one suffers from a pending oracle update and executes at a worse tick. Name: *path brittleness*. Explain: multi-leg, multi-pool plans assume state does not shift mid-block; in practice, state shifts constantly. Implication: the combinatorics of failure scale faster than the advertised savings. A single deep pool with a slightly higher quoted cost can produce a lower *realised* cost due to fewer moving parts. The metric here is *effective bps paid* including gas and adverse selection, averaged across repeated trades of similar size and timing. Professionals track that number. Retail can approximate it by back-checking five recent fills against quotes.

Aggregation also interacts with **MEV**. A fragmented order invites more surface for searchers to insert, reorder, or siphon value. Sandwich attacks thrive when a visible trade moves through predictable pools in small fragments; each fragment becomes a snack. Routes that execute as batched, private, or RFQ-style fills reduce that exposure. Matcha's "Protected" quotes, CowSwap's batch auctions, and UniswapX's filler competition all express the same design instinct: reduce visible leakage by compressing time and path. In quiet markets, the difference is marginal. In stressed markets, it is material.

Routers are not innocent either. Approvals to router contracts linger. A malicious or compromised router upgrade can weaponise long-lived allowances. This is not hypothetical. In April 2023, **SushiSwap's** RouteProcessor2 contained a bug that allowed an attacker to divert tokens from users who had granted approvals months earlier. The fix required revoking approvals—a simple act, too often overlooked. The implication is blunt: the safest route is the one that *minimises the set of entities you must trust tomorrow.* A path that reduces approvals and contains them to a single, battle-tested router deserves a premium.

Cross-chain **price improvement** clouds judgement because it presents two incomparable units: a small, certain saving now and a large, uncertain loss later. To reason sanely, convert both to expected terms. If a bridge reduces quoted cost by 4 bps on a £200,000 swap (saving £80) but introduces a one-in-10,000 chance of a freeze that risks a 3 per cent adverse move while funds are locked (expected loss £600), the rational choice is to avoid the bridge. The numbers here are illustrative; your task is to seek the real ones. How often has this bridge halted? How are signers distributed? What is the historical *time-to-final* under load? "Better" is a claim. Test it.

Two more concrete scenes round out the map. In November 2021, on Arbitrum, routing a mid-sized WETH/USDC trade through a single deep 0.05 per cent pool often beat a multi-pool split by 3–5 bps after gas because L2 blockspace was cheap and the deep pool was thick; the aggregator's cleverness had nothing to improve. In September 2022, during Ethereum's Merge week, mainnet priority fees spiked intermittently; aggregators that relied on tightly timed multi-leg routes saw revert rates rise and retries compound gas costs. Traders who forced a single-hop path paid a slightly worse sticker but a lower total. The map had changed. The smartest route was the simplest road that day.

A counterpoint sharpened by practice: *sometimes* the composite route is superior. When stablecoins de-peg locally on one venue and not others, or when tick ranges gap temporarily after a shock, an aggregator that can jump between invariants—Curve's stable-swap here, Uniswap v3's concentrated depth there—earns its fee. The trick is not to worship simplicity blindly. It is to *price* complexity. If fragmentation improves your realised bps with stable delivery and tolerable allowances, take it. If it improves your *quote* but worsens your *outcome*, cancel it. The market does not grade intentions.

We cannot ignore the **infrastructure underneath the map**: RPC providers, indexers, and front ends. An aggregator call that depends on a specific RPC's mempool view can route you into a stale state. A bridge status page fed by a single indexer can show "complete" while the on-chain proof lags. The reliable behaviour here is redundancy: verify critical steps through a second lens—a different RPC, a block explorer, or the wallet's on-device display of exactly which contract you are approving. It adds seconds. It removes surprises.

What, then, is the practical stance for a time-conscious professional? Treat "best price" as a hypothesis. Demand a proof. Read the path. Count the hops. Identify every contract that will hold permission. Ask whether a bridge leg is *worth* the basis points given your tolerance for delay. Keep a mental threshold—say, do not take a cross-chain leg to save less than X bps for more than Y minutes of added settlement risk—and adjust it with market conditions. These are scenarios, not prescriptions. They turn posture into policy.

The motif returns one last time: the map. Interfaces will keep redrawing it, promising brighter roads and shorter drives. Some will be genuine improvements, born of better engineering and saner incentives. Others will be cul-de-sacs with pretty signage. The unresolved test awaits at every "Confirm" prompt that offers you a sliver of improvement for a slice of complexity: are you being paid enough to take *this* road *today*, or is the straight path the wiser purchase?

Red Flags in the Wild

On 1 November 2021, the token *SQUID*, inspired—without licence—by Netflix's *Squid Game*, rocketed on Binance Smart Chain and then collapsed to near zero within minutes as deployers drained liquidity. Exchanges of record were untouched; wallets worked as designed. The losses came from a familiar package of tricks: a fake brand, tilted token parameters (trading restricted and sell tax extreme), and a pool engineered for exit. The interface looked exactly right. The contract did not.

Spoof assets and slanted mechanics flourish because users often read logos, not ledgers. A polished website, an active Telegram, and a "live chart" are theatre that masks simple checks: *which* contract was approved, *who* can mint, *what* the transfer rules are, and *where* the liquidity sits. The pattern is not subtle. Fraud targets attention first. Code follows.

Begin with the simplest red flag: **lookalike tokens**. Show: you type "UNI" into a dex aggregator and see several options with the same name and icon. Name: ticker collision. Explain: ERC-20 tickers are not unique identifiers; any deployer can mint a "UNI." The only thing that matters is the contract address. Implication: execution against the wrong address is not a small mistake; it is unrecoverable. The visible behaviour that counters this risk is prosaic but decisive: retrieve the contract address from a canonical source (the project's documentation, a signed announcement, or a verified registry entry) and match it in your wallet. If you cannot source the address, the trade is not a trade; it is a guess.

Caselet one: September 2020, hours after Uniswap's UNI token launch on Ethereum, dozens of impostor "UNI" contracts appeared on DEX front ends, some with transfer restrictions that prevented selling. Traders who took the wrong address discovered the oldest trap in the book: the **honeypot**. Show: buys succeed; sells revert with a crafted error. Name: sell-blocked tokens. Explain: the token's transfer function rejects transfers to pools or addresses not on a whitelist, effectively trapping buyers. Implication: the market price displayed on the chart is fictional because outflow is impossible. The practical tell is mechanical: test a small sell into the same pool before committing size; inspect bytecode or a vetted scanner for "cannot sell" flags; reject tokens whose verified source is missing or obfuscated.

Caselet two: March 2021, PancakeSwap and Cream Finance warned users after their DNS records were hijacked; counterfeit sites prompted visitors to "reconnect" and pushed approvals to attacker addresses. The protocols were fine. The shopfronts lied. Name: DNS hijack. Explain: an attacker altered registrar records so a familiar URL served hostile JavaScript; the fake UI requested unlimited approvals, then drained wallets. Implication: red flags live not only in contracts but in *routes* to contracts. The defensive habit—*verify before connect*—turns into physical acts: type bookmarked domains, confirm spender addresses on a trusted hardware screen, and compare them with published addresses before signing.

Tilted parameters are the second family of traps. Show: a token sets a **transfer tax** of 10–20 per cent on every move, or increases tax to 100 per cent when sent to an AMM pool. Name: fee-on-transfer / anti-dump tax. Explain: fee-on-transfer tokens rewrite assumptions that routers and UX rely on; some tax only sells, others tax all moves. Implication: slippage must be set high to execute, and a project can raise taxes by governance or hidden switches. You pay in basis points you did not price. The concrete check is to read the token's verified source (or a known audit) for functions like setTaxFeePercent, setSwapAndLiquifyEnabled, or address-based blacklists; then decide whether the policy matches your tolerance. A small transfer tax in a reflection token may be a feature; a configurable confiscation at pool addresses is a weapon.

Third, **mint and pause authority**. Show: a token's ABI exposes mint, pause, blacklist, or setOwner calls owned by an externally controlled account. Name: privileged controls. Explain: many legitimate tokens (for example, USDT) include admin functions for compliance; others retain them solely to rug. Implication: privilege is not evil, but it is power you must price. The behaviour is binary: if an EOA can mint unlimited supply or freeze you, size accordingly or abstain. If ownership is a multi-sig timelocked and disclosed, the risk is bounded. If ownership is an unlabelled EOA, it is not.

Fourth, **liquidity deceit**. Show: a pool displays "locked liquidity" on a badge in the front end. Name: cosmetic lock. Explain: some locks encumber LP tokens in a time-lock contract; others "lock" a trivial fraction while the majority of LP tokens remain free to be pulled. Implication: the withdrawal surface may be larger than the marketing suggests. Inspect actual LP token holder distribution on a block explorer and read the timelock contract. If the largest

LP holder is the deployer or an unlabelled address, the exit risk remains high regardless of badges.

Two more caselets sharpen instinct. July 2020, *YAM Finance* launched with a governance token whose rebasing bug minted excess tokens and broke governance; the flaw was public within hours, funds were later recovered through coordinated migration. This was not malice but haste. The red flag was not a logo; it was unaudited arithmetic. Conversely, August 2022, *Curve Finance*'s DNS compromise redirected approvals to an attacker; the contracts were safe, yet users who trusted the URL without verification lost funds. These paired stories separate intent from impact. Both hurt; one indicts code quality, the other indicts path trust. In both, the *tell* was available: missing audits and rushed parameters; approvals requested by a website instead of a contract address you already knew.

UI tricks are the soft power of deception. Show: a front end pre-populates slippage with "12% recommended," colour-coded green; a timer counts down to a "necessary migration"; a modal blocks your wallet screen with a faux error urging you to "reconnect." Name: coercive UX. Explain: design nudges push you to widen execution windows or sign approvals under duress. Implication: the interface is not neutral; it can tilt parameters against you. The counters are tactile habits: edit slippage yourself; reject arbitrary deadlines; read the exact calldata on a trusted device screen; and if a site ever asks for a seed phrase, close the tab—real dApps never need it.

A credible counter-example tempers hair-trigger suspicion. Some legitimate protocols *must* request sensitive approvals or high slippage *for a reason*. Example: during an initial bootstrap of a thin liquidity pool, a governance UI may propose a large, time-locked approval to a well-known timelock contract so that a single transaction can orchestrate several steps. Or, when redeeming vesting tokens with fee-on-transfer semantics, a higher slippage tolerance may be the only way to pass a programmed tax. The reconciliation is method, not mood: verify the spender contract, confirm it matches published addresses, check whether approvals are time-bound or value-bound, and ensure any unusual parameter maps cleanly to a documented mechanism. If all checks pass, a "strange" request can be legitimate. If they do not, it is not your job to be brave.

Some red flags are statistical rather than dramatic. Show: a token with 95 per cent of supply held by the top three wallets, all created within the same hour as the deployer. Name: concentrated holders. Explain: a thin float plus synchronised wallets equals price fragility; one sell can crater the pool. Implication: the chart's serenity is illusory. The metric is simple: top-holder percentage and contract age from a block explorer. If concentration is extreme and the timelocks missing, treat the tranquil price as a set piece.

Others are temporal. Show: a contract deployed twelve hours ago with "audited" stamped on the website. Name: false provenance. Explain: audits leave on-chain traces—published reports, commit hashes, and version numbers.

Implication: an "audit" with no link or a recycled PDF is a tell. A genuine audit reads like a lab report: scope, methods, findings, severities, and fixes. A real protocol names the firm and the date; a fake one names a mood.

Routers can hide red flags downstream. Show: an aggregator routes your trade through an obscure pool to save two basis points; the pool uses a token with a hidden sell tax, and your transaction fails unless you raise slippage far beyond the norm. Name: path asymmetry. Explain: a "better price" at the quote level becomes a worse execution after taxes, retries, and approvals to unfamiliar spenders. Implication: complexity multiplies red flags. A simple route through a single deep pool you recognise is often the saner purchase. You are not trying to win a screenshot; you are trying to control outcome.

One more caselet underlines the cost of ignoring approvals, the most common prelude to loss. April 2023, SushiSwap's RouteProcessor2 bug allowed theft from anyone who had ever granted an approval to that contract and still held the approved token. Users who had kept approvals tidy—revoking unused spenders periodically—escaped unscathed. Others did not. The "red flag" was retrospective, yet practical: long-lived, unlimited approvals. The cure was maintenance, not myth.

A recurring motif holds these stories together: **the seam**. Every deception exploits a seam between what the user assumes and what the system enforces—between icon and address, between website and contract, between quoted price and execution path, between stated policy and code. Spot the seam, and you reduce the odds of avoidable loss. Miss it, and the market will not forgive you.

We should acknowledge limits. Even careful participants can be caught by a perfect clone served via a poisoned DNS record, or by a novel exploit in a vetted contract. Vigilance is not victory; it is a risk discount. This is a book about literacy, not invulnerability.

Turn abstractions into habits tied to measurement. Trust becomes "do I hold the canonical address I can independently source?" Efficiency becomes "what is my effective bps paid after gas and slippage across five recent fills?" Risk becomes "how many unlimited approvals do I carry, to which contracts, and when did I last revoke?" These are numbers, not vibes. Keep the counts small. Prefer addresses you know.

The market will continue to manufacture convincing fakes, asymmetric parameters, and persuasive interfaces because that is where inattentive money lives. Your defence is not paranoia; it is pattern recognition trained on cases. Which brings us to the test that should hum in the back of your mind the next time a polished token page or a gleaming swap screen invites you to click: what, precisely, is the seam here—and have you checked that it is stitched?

Chapter 4
Lending Markets: Aave and Collateral Logic

In May 2021, as Ethereum gas prices spiked and markets convulsed, a quiet cascade began inside Aave's smart contracts. Liquidators moved in—hundreds of them—buying discounted collateral from over-leveraged borrowers who had fallen below safety thresholds. No panic ensued on the protocol's end. No human froze withdrawals, no administrator halted the system. The code kept clearing positions, restoring solvency block by block. In a week when exchanges glitched and centralised desks scrambled for liquidity, Aave's lending pools functioned with mechanical composure. It was a moment that made an idea tangible: *decentralised credit without human mercy, yet with systemic grace.*

Lending is civilisation's oldest financial act—older than coinage, older than markets—yet DeFi's reinvention of it forces a reappraisal. What happens when collateral, not character, secures a loan; when liquidation is algorithmic rather than negotiated; when interest rates move not by central decree but by utilisation curves? The paradox is magnetic. Decentralised lending protocols promise the freedom to *borrow against yourself,* but they also bind participants to an unforgiving arithmetic: ratios, buffers, and thresholds that define survival. A loan no longer depends on belief in the borrower's future, but on the real-time valuation of their digital past.

The chapter begins here, in this tension between autonomy and automation. Aave, Compound, and similar platforms have made lending programmable. Yet beneath their polished dashboards lies a world of numbers that behave like laws of physics. Over-collateralisation—placing more value in escrow than you borrow—is not a quirk of conservatism but a mathematical necessity. If markets move faster than governance, collateral must always lead. On Aave, that relationship is measured by the *Loan-to-Value* (LTV) ratio and the *health factor*. When your health factor approaches one, liquidation looms. The metaphor of "health" is apt: it's a measure of systemic immunity. Borrow too close to the edge, and you invite the market to euthanise your position.

What makes this discipline powerful is also what makes it perilous. Borrowing against one's own assets feels elegant—a way to unlock value without selling. You retain exposure to your token while drawing liquidity against it, often in stablecoins. Yet that apparent sophistication conceals fragility. When markets rise, leverage feels like strategy. When they fall, it becomes confession. The self you borrowed against begins to vanish. Over-collateralisation, the price of permissionless credit, is both the moat and the trap. Understanding it means seeing lending not as income, but as insurance—insurance against your own impatience.

Aave's architecture turns this logic into code. Each asset has a collateral factor that defines its permissible leverage. Highly stable assets such as USDC can support higher borrowing ratios; volatile ones like ETH or LINK must stay restrained. Behind the screens, interest rates are not set by committee but emerge from a live utilisation curve. When borrowing demand rises, rates climb to attract lenders and discourage further debt. When demand falls, rates soften to stimulate new loans. Stability here is not fixed—it is dynamic equilibrium. Even the so-called "stable" rate is merely a smoothed variable, not a promise. A professional borrower knows this: cost can triple overnight if utilisation spikes. The protocol's fairness lies in its transparency, not its forgiveness.

This fluid pricing turns lending markets into living organisms. During May 2022's deleveraging storm following Terra's collapse, Aave's utilisation soared, rates whipsawed, and liquidations surged. Yet no defaults accumulated. Positions cleared themselves in a sequence that felt brutal but rational. Liquidation, often maligned as punishment, revealed its deeper role: it is *mechanical mercy*. By allowing collateral to be sold when safety margins breach, the protocol prevents contagion. It is the code's equivalent of a heart valve—relieving pressure before the system ruptures. Understanding this reframes liquidation from personal failure to systemic hygiene. It is not panic that liquidates; it is math that resets equilibrium.

To grasp the culture of collateral in DeFi, one must appreciate the human instinct it replaces. In traditional finance, credit rests on reputation, relationship, and regulation. In decentralised markets, credit is geometry: the relationship between collateral, debt, and price volatility. A borrower is not judged; they are modelled. The model's output is immediate: an LTV percentage, a liquidation threshold, a buffer. Those numbers determine whether the position lives another block. It is a financial environment stripped of narrative, governed by vectors. To thrive in it, users must develop new rituals: monitoring dashboards, setting alerts, automating repayments, and maintaining emotional distance. The system rewards vigilance and punishes inattention.

This chapter decodes that vigilance. It translates the abstractions of collateral logic into intuition—what it feels like to manage a position on the edge of a volatile market. Readers will learn why over-collateralisation is not waste but prudence, how to read a health factor as an early warning, and why the most resilient borrowers treat buffers as sacred, not optional. We will examine interest-rate models—how Aave's kinked curves create feedback loops between utilisation and cost, and why the "stable" rate is not a sanctuary but a policy instrument. We will study liquidations through their mechanics rather than their drama: the discount that rewards liquidators, the penalty that disciplines risk-takers, and the triggers that ensure fairness without intervention. Each of these mechanisms reveals a philosophical stance: that security in DeFi is not guaranteed by external enforcement but by internal consistency.

Through this lens, DeFi lending becomes a school of self-discipline. Borrowing against oneself is the ultimate test of judgement: it tempts the rational mind to flirt with irrational thresholds. The line between leverage and learning is razor-thin. Yet for those who understand the mechanics, decentralised credit can be a remarkable instrument. It enables liquidity without intermediaries, arbitrage without permission, and productive risk without central custody. A well-managed loan position is not speculation; it is strategy. The difference lies in awareness—of volatility, utilisation, and liquidation probability—and in the willingness to act before the market acts for you.

Lending protocols like Aave have already outlived the scepticism that once dismissed them as experiments. They have processed billions in loans, survived market shocks, and proven that credit can exist without trust in people—only in contracts. But they also highlight an uncomfortable truth: automation does not abolish responsibility; it transfers it. Every wallet address is its own credit officer, every borrower their own regulator. The reward for literacy is access; the penalty for ignorance is liquidation.

The motif that threads this chapter is *balance*. Between ambition and caution, freedom and discipline, opportunity and fragility. DeFi lending is neither utopia nor catastrophe; it is a mirror that reflects how humans manage risk when intermediaries vanish. Those who master its logic can turn volatility into a tool. Those who ignore it will find that the market's mercy ends precisely where mathematics begins.

The pages that follow unpack that mathematics—not as equations, but as intuition. You will see why lending pools breathe, why collateral thresholds matter, and why liquidation, when understood, feels less like defeat and more like a lesson in structural grace. The goal is not to romanticise risk but to render it legible. For in DeFi, comprehension *is* protection.

And so the question that lingers as we enter the lending markets is deceptively simple: when the only thing standing between you and liquidation is your own ratio, how much safety do you choose to buy—and how often will you check that it still exists?

Over-Collateralisation Explained

On 19 May 2021, as Bitcoin tumbled nearly 30 per cent within a few hours, hundreds of borrowers on Aave and Compound watched their dashboards turn crimson. Health factors that had been comfortably above 1.5 the day before plunged below 1.0. Automated liquidators stepped in. Collateral—Ether, UNI, LINK—was sold off at a discount to repay loans. For some, positions were wiped clean in minutes. Yet the protocols themselves did not falter; not a single lender lost funds. That day was brutal, but it was also a proof of design: *the system did what it was built to do*. The paradox was clear—every liquidation was a failure for an individual and a success for the collective.

Over-collateralisation is the invisible scaffolding of decentralised credit. It reverses centuries of financial logic by making the borrower the guarantor, not the bank. On Aave, to borrow £10,000 in stablecoins, one must typically post £15,000–£20,000 of collateral. This inefficiency by traditional standards is the price of permissionless trust. There is no underwriter, no recourse, and no court. Instead, the protocol maintains balance through ratios—loan-to-value (LTV) limits, liquidation thresholds, and a single metric called the *health factor*. These numbers decide who may borrow, how much, and for how long before code intervenes. They transform credit into geometry.

Show: imagine an address deposits 10 ETH valued at £25,000 and borrows £12,000 in USDC. Name: *Loan-to-Value ratio*. Explain: the borrower's LTV is 48 per cent. If the maximum permitted for ETH is 70 per cent, the loan begins in comfort. As price falls, collateral value declines and LTV rises. When it crosses the *liquidation threshold*—often 80 per cent of the collateral value—the protocol allows liquidators to repay the debt on behalf of the borrower, taking a fee in the process. Implication: the moment of liquidation is not a betrayal; it is a safety valve. It prevents the borrower's default from becoming the lender's loss.

The *health factor* abstracts all this into one number: a dynamic quotient of safety. A health factor of 2.0 means the collateral could lose half its value before liquidation; 1.0 means the cliff is underfoot. The metric is brutally egalitarian. It ignores intention, history, or reputation. The only thing that matters is collateral volatility against debt exposure. When that ratio tightens, liquidators compete to restore equilibrium, often earning a few per cent bonus. Their speed, not sentiment, maintains solvency. On 19 May 2021, over 8,000 such events were recorded in a 24-hour period (Nansen Analytics, 2021). Every one of them protected the system by sacrificing a position.

Why over-collateralise at all? Because volatility in crypto assets is both structural and non-linear. Traditional lenders rely on probabilistic models and legal enforcement. Aave and its peers rely on mathematics and liquidity. If ETH can lose 40 per cent in a day—as history shows—it must be collateralised accordingly. The logic is brutal but elegant: security arises not from prediction but from *preparation*. The market does not forgive under-collateralisation; it arbitrages it.

Show: the MakerDAO collapse of 12 March 2020—"Black Thursday"—when Ethereum gas fees spiked and oracles lagged by minutes. Name: *oracle latency*. Explain: ETH's price crashed faster than liquidation bots could react. Some auctions cleared at near-zero bids, wiping collateral holders while leaving undercollateralised debt. Implication: this episode reshaped collateral design across protocols. Aave introduced wider buffers, faster oracles, and multi-tier liquidation incentives to prevent recurrence. Over-collateralisation ceased to be a choice; it became an axiom.

This principle is often misunderstood by new entrants drawn to the phrase *borrow against yourself*. The phrase sounds empowering—turning dormant capital into productive liquidity. Yet it conceals a psychological trap.

When the collateral asset appreciates, borrowing feels frictionless. A trader holding ETH may borrow stablecoins to stake, farm, or reinvest, believing appreciation will outrun the cost. But when markets reverse, the same mechanism amplifies pain. Selling collateral voluntarily becomes impossible once its price momentum vanishes. Instead, liquidation arrives automatically, indifferent to your plans. What was once liquidity becomes leverage in disguise.

A practical example clarifies the chain reaction. Suppose ETH trades at £2,500 and a user deposits 20 ETH (£50,000) to borrow £25,000 in DAI. If ETH falls 30 per cent to £1,750, the collateral is worth £35,000; the LTV is now 71 per cent—approaching Aave's threshold. A further 10 per cent dip triggers liquidation. A bot repays £25,000 of debt, seizes £27,000 worth of ETH, and leaves the user with £8,000. No fraud occurred. The borrower merely ran out of buffer. The visible behaviour that distinguishes seasoned users from novices is ritual, not brilliance: setting buffer zones, diversifying collateral, using alerts, and repaying early when ratios tighten. These habits are less glamorous than yield farming, but they are what keep autonomy survivable.

One might ask whether over-collateralisation is wasteful. It locks more capital than it releases, creating apparent inefficiency. A counterpoint emerges from *liquidity layering*. Institutions use Aave precisely because it offers predictable safety. By over-collateralising stable positions—say, posting USDC to borrow DAI at low spread—they achieve synthetic liquidity without credit risk. Here, inefficiency becomes stability's subsidy. The protocol functions like a central bank stripped of politics: it demands prudence as a precondition for participation.

A credible limitation exists: over-collateralisation restricts inclusion. If borrowing requires owning excess capital, the model cannot reach those without it. Protocols like Euler (launched 2021) and Gearbox (2022) experiment with *credit delegation*, where one party's over-collateral backs another's under-collateralised borrowing through smart contracts. Yet these systems still rely on reputation—or more precisely, on programmable trust within bounded networks. The trade-off remains unresolved: true decentralisation resists subjective credit scoring, but scaling credit without it remains unsolved.

Over-collateralisation, then, is less a policy than a philosophy. It asserts that solvency must be provable at all times, not contingent on belief. Traditional banks operate on fractional reserves and delayed settlement. Aave operates on atomic verification: every loan, every block, every oracle tick. This inversion is why decentralised lending survived multiple market crises that crippled centralised lenders like Celsius and BlockFi in mid-2022. When human discretion faced panic, smart contracts enforced arithmetic. No emotion, no bailout—just automated balance.

Yet this rigour has emotional cost. Managing a live loan position is behavioural finance in miniature. The screen tempts complacency during rallies and punishes inattention during corrections. The *health factor* becomes a mirror of discipline. Seasoned participants treat it like a heart-rate monitor—healthy ranges preserved, alerts configured, interventions swift. Some use bots to auto-repay or deposit collateral when ratios narrow; others simply avoid thresholds by wider margins. In both cases, security is not a setting; it is a practice.

The motif that runs through these mechanisms is *distance*. The further one stays from the liquidation line, the calmer the experience. Distance is buffer; buffer is freedom. It is the invisible margin that separates autonomy from anxiety. Quantitatively, professionals target health factors above 1.5 or 2.0, translating into 25–50 per cent headroom. Qualitatively, it represents the discipline to sacrifice efficiency for endurance. Every percent of unused borrowing power is an act of humility before volatility.

Two further examples deepen this intuition. First, during the sharp ETH drawdown of June 2022 following Celsius's insolvency, addresses with health factors above 1.7 maintained positions unscathed. Those at 1.2 faced forced liquidations within hours as cascading price drops triggered oracle updates. Second, the same year, MakerDAO's vaults backed by USDC collateral remained untouched; the price-stable asset decoupled them from volatility entirely. The implication is measurable: correlation of collateral with market stress defines survival probability. Borrowing against stability buys certainty;

borrowing against volatility buys excitement—and sometimes extinction.

A counterpoint deserves mention: over-collateralisation can create systemic rigidity. When collateral prices fall, users rush to repay or add funds simultaneously, draining liquidity and accelerating declines. This *liquidation spiral* resembles traditional margin cascades. Protocols mitigate it through rate incentives—raising borrow rates as utilisation increases, throttling new leverage until equilibrium returns. The reconciliation is pragmatic: no system can abolish reflexivity, but transparency allows its participants to prepare rather than react.

Ultimately, over-collateralisation embodies DeFi's central promise and its central warning. It demonstrates that financial safety can be expressed as code, not personality. But it also exposes that code's indifference to intent. Borrowers are not punished for being wrong; they are liquidated for being late. To navigate that reality, one must convert abstract metrics into embodied routine: set alerts, maintain buffers, rehearse reactions. These are not luxuries; they are survival skills for autonomy.

The unresolved tension remains philosophical: if self-custody makes each user their own bank, over-collateralisation makes them their own regulator. How much freedom can individuals handle before they outsource prudence again? At what point does the friction of safety invite a return to centralisation? Those questions, like health factors, never rest. They fluctuate with every tick of the market, reminding us that in decentralised lending, *discipline is the only durable collateral.*

Interest Rates That Move

On 12 May 2022, as Terra's stablecoin unravelled and liquidity fled to safety, Aave's stablecoin markets on Ethereum lurched towards full utilisation. Borrowers watched variable APRs climb within a single trading session while "stable" rates—assumed by many to be placid—repriced upwards as utilisation smashed through their thresholds. The rate doubled in hours. In London, a market-maker who had borrowed USDC the week before at a comfortable single-digit APR faced a cost curve that felt less like a line and more like a staircase. Nothing had broken. The protocol was doing exactly what it advertises: adjusting the price of credit to the scarcity of credit. To the uninitiated, it felt punitive. To the architect, it looked like a thermostat.

Show → name → explain → implication. Show: when borrow demand surges and deposit growth lags, a lending pool creeps towards 100 per cent utilisation. Name: the *utilisation curve*. Explain: in Aave and Compound, interest rates are a function of utilisation with a "kink"—a pre-set optimal point (U*) where the slope increases. Below U*, rates rise gently; above U*, they climb sharply to disincentivise further borrowing and attract supply. Implication: your cost of capital is not merely a market mood; it is a programmable response to crowding. If you borrow at 30 per cent utilisation, you are buying a different risk than if you borrow at 85 per cent.

Two concrete, checkable models anchor the landscape. First, **Compound's Jump Rate Model** (2019, widely deployed on Ethereum) introduced a piecewise-linear borrow function with a steeper slope past the kink, ensuring that utilisation rarely sits at destabilising extremes for long. Second, **Aave v2's interest rate strategy** (live since late 2020) defined both variable and "stable" borrow rate curves with parameters per asset, including an optimal utilisation and two slopes (below and above the kink). Each model uses price to ration access. Neither promises comfort. The mathematics explain May 2022's spike: when fear drives everyone to the same side of the boat, the boat forces some to move.

The motif that threads this subchapter is the **thermostat**. Rates are not opinions; they are regulation-by-geometry. The thermostat does not predict the weather; it responds to it. That responsiveness is what makes decentralised credit resilient and what makes it emotionally expensive for inattentive borrowers.

Let us pin down terms. *Variable* means the rate floats with utilisation, recalculated every block and accruing continuously. *Stable* in Aave's lexicon is not fixed; it is a rate that targets stability by averaging conditions and resisting short-term noise, but it may reprice when the pool is stressed or when governance adjusts parameters. Show: a borrower selects a "stable" rate on Aave's USDC market in a quiet week. Name: *stable borrow rate*. Explain: the rate is set higher than the current variable rate to compensate LPs for bearing rate risk; if utilisation surges beyond U*, the protocol allows the stable rate to reprice within bounds, or even forces migration to variable if safety is at risk. Implication: "stable" buys you friction, not immunity. It slows the thermostat; it does not remove it.

Rates are not abstract. They map to behaviours and decisions. Consider a professional desk borrowing 5 million USDC to fund a basis trade. At 40 per cent utilisation, the variable borrow is seductively cheap. At 80 per cent, cheap becomes contingent. The desk can measure three numbers before committing: current utilisation, distance to U*, and the supply queue. If supply growth has stalled and large liquidations loom (visible in on-chain dashboards), the probability of crossing the kink rises. Each percentage point beyond U* is not a statistic; it is a potential phone call to treasury by nightfall. The discipline is simple. Borrow against room.

Two named examples, places and dates, illustrate both continuity and contrast. First, **Black Thursday (12 March 2020, Ethereum)**: Compound's borrow rates for stablecoins spiked as utilisation surged when collateral values crashed and borrowers scrambled for liquidity, then fell back as liquidations and deposits restored balance. The model did not foresee the crash; it merely priced it. Second, **the DeFi liquidity crunch around Terra (May 2022, global)**: Aave's stablecoin markets saw "stable" rates ratchet upwards and, in some assets, force rebalancing as utilisation pinned at the upper slope. In both cases, the curve worked as designed:

scarce credit became expensive, and the expense pulled the system back from the edge.

A credible counter-example tempers the picture. **MakerDAO's DAI Stability Fee** (2019) did not float with per-block utilisation but with governance: MKR holders voted to raise or lower the fee to modulate DAI supply and peg pressure. That policy tool responded on the order of days or weeks, not blocks. Its slower cadence proved effective in calmer cycles and frustrating in fast ones. Reconciling this with Aave/Compound's curves yields a simple truth: there is no single correct thermostat; there are thermostats for different rooms. Maker's fee targets a macro balance between supply and demand for DAI; Aave and Compound target micro balance in each pool.

Once you accept rates as thermostats, three implications fall into place. First, *cheap today* is not a promise. It is a snapshot of utilisation. Second, *stable* is a premium for smoothed volatility; it still admits jumps when the room overheats. Third, *path* matters as much as price. A borrower who enters a market at 65 per cent utilisation with widening deposit inflows is paying for a different future than one who enters at 88 per cent with outflows.

Now, show how the thermostat shapes risk. When utilisation approaches 100 per cent, lenders cannot withdraw, and borrowers cannot add debt; the pool must attract supply or liquidate risk to reduce utilisation. Name: *liquidity crunch*. Explain: the steep post-kink slope drives borrow rates high enough to motivate capital on the sidelines and to make levered positions uneconomic, prompting deleveraging. Implication: if you run high LTVs with variable borrow near the kink, your risk is twofold: liquidation risk from price moves and funding risk from rate spikes. The second often triggers the first.

Volatility propagates through *re-price events*. Aave's "stable" rates may be rebalanced under defined conditions: sustained high utilisation, or a material change in the reserve's average rate. Show: in December 2021, during a sudden risk-off turn, borrowers on smaller collateral markets saw stable rates tick up as utilisation hit ceilings. Name: *rebalancing event*. Explain: the contract checks conditions and adjusts to protect liquidity providers and system solvency. Implication: "stable until it isn't" is not a gotcha; it is the advertised rule. Treat it as such.

The thermostat metaphor extends to parameter governance. Aave and Compound periodically adjust *reserve factors* (share of interest routed to protocol reserves), *U* (optimal utilisation), and *slopes*. These are governance decisions with measurable effects. Raising the reserve factor reduces lender APY at a given borrow APR, potentially requiring a higher borrow rate to attract the same supply; shifting U* changes where the slope steepens. Professionals watch governance forums because these tweaks alter funding costs without any change in market conditions. Policy is a rate driver. It sits beside utilisation.

All abstractions must cash out into behaviours. Trust becomes "do I understand who can change this curve, when, and how?" Efficiency becomes "what is my all-in cost over the intended holding period under plausible utilisation paths?" Risk becomes "how far can the rate move before my strategy fails?" Each reduces to numbers: rate sensitivity in bps per 1 per cent utilisation move beyond U*; expected time near or above U* under stress; and gap risk between *health factor* and liquidation threshold given higher interest accrual.

A short memory of 2021–2022 helps. During quiet stretches in late 2021, borrowing stablecoins on Layer 2 Aave markets at low single-digit APRs felt routine; cheap blockspace and brisk supply kept utilisation anchored below U*. In Q2 2022, the same assets swung to double digits on mainnet as capital withdrew and liquidations crowded the pipe. The point is not the numbers but the cadence. Rates breathe. They do not hum.

"Stable" rates deserve a closer look because language misleads. Why pay a premium? Because you are insuring against short-term spikes. But insurance has exclusions. Aave's documentation flags that, in extreme conditions, stable borrows can be rebalanced to protect liquidity. The borrower can also switch between stable and variable at a fee when conditions change. Show: a fund enters with stable borrow at 5 per cent, variable at 3 per cent, choosing stable to lock budgeting. Utilisation grinds higher; stable reprices to 8, variable to 10. Name: *optionality*. Explain: the fund can switch to variable to save now, but variable might keep climbing; or remain in stable if it expects reversion.

Implication: rate choice is not moral; it is tactical. The right answer changes as the thermostat moves.

Two further scenes sharpen instinct. November 2020, shortly after **Compound Treasury** was announced in New York as a CeFi wrapper around DeFi yields for institutions, the promise was stable, predictable yield to corporate treasuries while Compound's underlying pools moved with utilisation. This separation of user experience from protocol reality works—until it doesn't—when wrappers face redemption pressure and must pass through volatility. September 2022, during the **Merge** week, mainnet priority fees spiked unpredictably; arbitrage and liquidation timing grew noisier, and utilisation footsteps lagged or raced. Borrow APR curves, especially above U*, exaggerated these micro-imbalances. Those who had modelled sensitivity slept; those who hadn't improvised.

A credible limitation of the thermostat model is that it can create crowd dynamics. When rates spike, everyone wants to repay or refinance. Gas surges. Queues form. Some are locked into "stable" at a poor level after repricing and hesitate to switch due to fees. The reconciliation is behavioural: preparation beats reaction. A borrower with pre-funded repay options, automation for partial deleveraging, and alerts tied to utilisation—not just price—turns a spike into a planned cost rather than a crisis. A borrower without those tools learns a more expensive lesson. The thermostat rewards those who watch the dial.

If this sounds clinical, it is deliberately so. Decentralised credit replaces human discretion with scheduled, visible rules. But that does not make the experience sterile. It makes it legible. The discipline is to turn legibility into habit: measure your exposure to U*, not just your LTV; monitor reserve updates; treat rate curves as living constraints rather than footnotes; and rehearse actions at pre-set thresholds. These are not product tips. They are operating procedures for autonomy.

One might ask whether floating rates are "fair" relative to fixed mortgages or bank loans. The comparison misleads. Banks price credit with balance sheets, capital rules, and cross-subsidies. Aave and Compound price credit with liquidity on tap and no recourse. Fairness here is the absence of surprises: the curve always told you what it would do. If you ignored it, it did not ignore you.

Bring the motif back to the surface. The thermostat sits on the wall, quiet until heat rises. You can ignore it on mild days. You should not architect your house as if mild days are the norm. For borrowers, the house is your position. The thermostat will click. The only unknowns are when and how loud.

We end with a forward test that distinguishes professionalism from bravado. Before you borrow, write down three answers: at what utilisation will your cost become uneconomic; how quickly could the market move from here to there; and what specific transaction will you execute when it does? If the answers are vague, the rate is not your only variable. The variable is you.

Liquidation: The Mechanical Mercy

On 12 March 2020, as Covid panic hit global markets, Ethereum's price fell so fast that MakerDAO's auctions could not keep pace. Gas fees spiked, oracles lagged, and some vaults—over-collateralised minutes earlier—were liquidated at effectively zero bids. The event, later dubbed "Black Thursday", scarred a generation of DeFi users and forced a redesign of Maker's liquidation engine. No malfeasance was required. Arithmetic and latency did the damage. The system survived by sacrificing positions. Mercy for the whole required severity for some.

Liquidation is the protocol's safety valve. It is unemotional by design. When collateral value falls relative to debt and crosses a trigger, third-party keepers repay part of that debt and seize collateral at a discount. The valve opens. Pressure drops. Solvency returns. Show → name → explain → implication. Show: an address on Aave deposits ETH and borrows USDC. Name: *liquidation threshold* and *health factor*. Explain: if the health factor falls to one, the position becomes eligible for liquidation; a liquidator repays a portion of the USDC and receives ETH collateral plus a bonus. Implication: losses crystallise privately so that lenders are protected publicly. Planning beats panic because the rules are legible.

Think of the trigger as a line on the floor. Cross it, and the choreography begins. Aave's mechanism is partial by default: only a slice of the position—up to the *close factor*—is liquidated in each transaction, limiting market impact and giving the borrower a chance to stabilise. Compound employs a similar cap. Maker, by contrast, runs auctions that sell collateral to the highest bidder until the vault is made whole (today with redesigned "clipper" auctions to avoid 2020's pathologies). Different techniques, one ethic: convert volatile, uncertain loss into bounded, transparent loss, fast.

Two named, checkable episodes show both the promise and the limits. First, **19 May 2021, global markets**: ETH and BTC plunged. Aave and Compound processed waves of liquidations smoothly; lenders remained whole, and the protocols never paused. The machines did not flinch. Liquidators competed for bonuses; bad debt did not accrue. Second, **May 2022, Terra's collapse**: stablecoins de-pegged, volatility spiked, and utilisation surged across lending pools. Liquidations again cleared risk, but stress revealed a behavioural weakness: many borrowers had mispriced "stable" borrow costs and ran positions too near the line. In both cases, liquidation worked as a system-level mercy. It kept the pipes open. It punished proximity to the edge.

A credible counter-example refines the lesson. **Black Thursday (12 March 2020, Ethereum)** is the canonical failure mode: latency. Oracles updated too slowly; gas starved bots; auctions cleared at absurd prices. Some vaults took near-total loss while the protocol accumulated shortfall it later socialised. The reconciliation is not to disparage liquidation, but to recognise its dependencies: timely prices, affordable blockspace, and healthy competition among keepers. A valve still needs pressure gauges and a clear pipe.

Liquidation is often misread as moral censure. It is not. It is mechanical. Consider the variables that push a position across the line: asset volatility, interest accrual, oracle cadence, and liquidation parameters. Each maps to a behaviour. Volatility demands buffers; accrual argues for shorter borrowing horizons; oracle cadence warns against assets with thin feeds; parameters tell you how steep the penalty will be. Borrowers who survive shocks act on these facts early. They do not negotiate with a ratio.

Show: a borrower has a health factor of 1.25 on Aave with ETH collateral. Name: *buffer*. Explain: a 20–25 per cent price drop or a funding spike could erase that quickly, especially if correlated assets fall together. Implication: a serious operator maintains a floor—say, >1.5—because they have lived through twelve-sigma days that arrive unannounced. That extra margin is not wasted capital; it is the rent you pay to sleep.

The *penalty* is the valve's incentive. On Aave, the liquidation bonus varies by asset—often a few per cent paid in collateral to the liquidator. Too low, and no one will show up when gas is high and markets are wild; too high, and the system overpays during stress, deepening losses for borrowers.

Governance calibrates these numbers per market with two aims: attract reliable keepers and reduce pro-cyclicality. The metric that matters is observed keeper competition at peak stress: how many distinct addresses successfully liquidate within a five-minute window when prices gap? If that number is small, the valve may stick when most needed.

Liquidation's *scope* shapes its gentleness. Aave's partial liquidations lower leverage incrementally, giving time to act. Compound's close factor historically sat around 50 per cent (configurable), preventing full wipe-outs in one shot. Maker's auctions sell until debt is covered, then return surplus to the vault owner. These design choices are ethics translated into code: constrain harm, reward responders, preserve what can be preserved. None of this moralises. It simply works.

Let us follow the engine step by step. Show: the oracle posts a new price; a health factor flips from 1.02 to 0.98. Name: *eligibility*. Explain: bots monitor mempools and on-chain state; they submit transactions to repay debt and claim collateral. These transactions compete on priority fees; in hot moments, they are bundled through private relays to avoid being front-run. Implication: if gas cost exceeds expected bonus, liquidations stall. Protocols counter by raising bonuses or smoothing oracle updates. Every knob exists to keep the valve responsive under load.

Where does planning displace panic? In *pre-commitment*. Borrowers who survive treat liquidation like fire code. They put extinguishers in the hallway. In practice, that means funding a small reserve in the borrow currency; setting on-chain alerts tied to health factor and utilisation, not just price; pre-authorising repay transactions from a safe wallet; and rehearsing partial deleveraging when the ratio hits a personal trigger above the protocol's. The ritual matters more than the rhetoric. You either have a path to add collateral or repay debt when volatility spikes—or you have a plan to post on social media after the fact.

A recurring motif helps: the **valve**. You neither fear nor worship a valve; you respect it. You learn where it is, what pressure opens it, and what flows when it does. Every feature around liquidation exists to make that valve open cleanly: conservative LTVs, timely oracles, rational bonuses, partial close factors, back-off logic for cascading events. Where users go wrong is standing with their ear pressed to the pipe, insisting they will hear the hiss before it blows. You will not. Markets move first.

Two further caselets ground intuition. **June 2022, post-Celsius stress**: large on-chain borrowers—publicly tracked—approached liquidation as crypto-collateral fell. Liquidator competition was intense; positions were trimmed repeatedly without protocol failure. The public spectacle masked a simple truth: wide buffers would have made the drama invisible. **November 2022, FTX collapse**: on-chain lending markets absorbed shocks with elevated rates and brisk liquidations; centralised venues froze or failed. Mechanised mercy outperformed managerial discretion. Yet a limitation surfaced: where collateral was thinly traded, slippage during liquidations widened, increasing effective penalties beyond parameterised bonuses. Calibration cannot erase market depth.

The human mind rebels at enforced selling. It feels unjust when the algorithm acts without you. But liquidation frees the system from the borrower's timeline. That is the point. You cannot have permissionless lending that waits politely for payday. In this light, liquidation is not catastrophe. It is hygiene. It clears the pipe so everyone else can drink.

This does not sanctify every design. Parameters can tilt too hard. Overly generous bonuses create perverse incentives to "hunt" marginal positions. Over-sensitive oracles can flap eligibility and waste gas. Conversely, stingy bonuses or slow oracles risk under-liquidation, accumulating bad debt that governance later socialises. The art is empirical. Teams study stress windows—how many positions crossed eligibility, how quickly they cleared, how much slippage occurred, how often oracles updated—and retune. Users should read those post-mortems because they describe the real valve, not the brochure.

Language shapes posture. Calling liquidation a "penalty" invites shame. Better to call it a *price*. You paid to borrow. You pay to be rescued from insolvency one block too late. The price is transparent: a percentage of collateral above the debt, plus slippage. That price funds the responders who keep the market solvent when you could not. This framing clarifies decisions. If the expected cost of being wrong is intolerable, you need more distance from the line or a different collateral.

One limitation deserves candour: even with perfect parameters, black-swan latency can still wound good actors. A chain halt, an L2 sequencer outage, or a DNS-level front-end failure can slow your reaction. That is why resilient borrowers separate interface from protocol—bookmarking contract addresses, knowing how to repay directly, keeping a hardware wallet ready—and why they favour assets with redundant oracle feeds. None of this eliminates risk. It relocates it to places you can measure.

Bring the valve back into view. A properly designed liquidation system preserves lenders, resets borrowers, and stabilises pools. It is not a threat; it is a promise. The promise is that risk will be socialised as little as possible and individualised as much as necessary. That promise held in May 2021 and November 2022 across multiple protocols. It failed—partially—on Black Thursday and prompted better engineering. That is what mature systems do. They learn where the valve sticks and file it smooth.

Translate abstractions into two numbers you can live by. First, your *distance* to eligibility, expressed as the percentage move in collateral price—or combined collateral basket—that would push your health factor to one, holding rates constant. Second, your *time to act*, expressed as how long it would take you to add collateral or repay in a stress scenario, including wallet retrieval, RPC reliability, and expected gas. If your time exceeds your distance under plausible volatility, you are borrowing hope. Hope is not collateral.

Liquidation will never feel kind. It should not. But it can be just, in the engineer's sense: predictable, bounded, and quick. That is the mercy. The unresolved test is personal and present tense. If the next twenty-minute candle is ugly and the valve opens, did you choose your distance—and your drill—so the system's mercy includes you? Or are you waiting to negotiate with code?

Use Cases That Actually Make Sense

On 5 January 2022 in London, Aave announced **Aave Arc**, a permissioned pool for KYC'd institutions, with Fireblocks as the initial whitelister. It was a modest press moment with a clear implication: decentralised lending was no longer only for pseudonymous traders. It could be a treasury tool. The design didn't change—over-collateralised borrowing, utilisation-driven rates, mechanised liquidation. The audience did. And that shift, from pure retail speculation to operational finance, points to where lending protocols earn their keep: not in chasing the highest yield, but in funding predictable needs with transparent risk.

DeFi lending makes sense when it behaves like a *scaffold* rather than a trampoline. The scaffold supports something you already do—pay suppliers, extend runway, finance inventory, hedge exposure—without demanding narrative or trust in a salesperson. Show → name → explain → implication. Show: a software company with volatile crypto reserves wants six months of pound-denominated runway without selling core holdings. Name: *treasury runway financing*. Explain: the firm posts liquid collateral (ETH or stETH) to Aave, borrows a modest amount of stablecoins (USDC/DAI) at a conservative LTV, swaps to GBP, and sets calendar reminders tied to the health factor and rate curves. Implication: the company insulates operations from market timing while preserving upside—provided it treats buffers as sacred and rehearses deleveraging. The scaffold holds because discipline holds.

Treasury use is not theoretical. The launch of Aave Arc gave compliance-sensitive desks a venue where custody, KYC, and audit trails could coexist with on-chain transparency. For a finance director, the virtues are prosaic but rare: live collateral ratios, machine-readable liabilities, and no counterparty substitutions hidden in footnotes. The risk is also plain: if the collateral falls and you ignore alerts, liquidation is mechanical. Here the motif of the scaffold returns. A scaffold does not leap; it stabilises. You measure the load, you check the bolts, you avoid theatrics.

Consider a second fit-for-purpose pattern: **basis financing** for market-neutral desks. Show: a market-maker borrows USDC on Aave and shorts an equivalent notional of ETH perpetuals on a derivatives venue such as dYdX or Deribit, capturing funding differentials and exchange rebates. Name: *delta-neutral carry*. Explain: the borrowed capital funds inventory; the hedge suppresses directional risk; the spread pays the bill—until utilisation tightens and borrow

APR spikes, or funding flips. Implication: the trade makes sense only if the desk monitors two thermometers—Aave's utilisation-rate curve and the perp's funding—and codifies exit rules. The visible behaviours that separate professionals from tourists are banal and decisive: size positions to survive a jump to the post-kink borrow slope, pre-approve repay transactions, and use alerts on both venues. The carry exists. It is earned, not granted.

A third sensible use: **staker liquidity**. Show: an ETH-staker holds liquid staking tokens (for example, Lido's stETH, introduced December 2020) yet needs fiat for tax or payroll. Name: *cash-against-yielding collateral*. Explain: the staker borrows stablecoins against stETH on Aave, continuing to earn the staking yield while funding short-term needs. Implication: align maturities; keep LTV low to withstand price basis moves between stETH and ETH; treat the liquidation threshold as a hazard line, not a suggestion. This is a textbook scaffold: it respects the asset's cash flow and uses credit as a bridge, not a bet.

Fourth, **DAO treasury smoothing**. Show: a grant-giving DAO with a volatile token treasury wants predictable quarterly disbursements in stablecoins without immediate token sales that could depress price. Name: *runway smoothing via over-collateralised loans*. Explain: a portion of the treasury is posted as collateral; stablecoins are drawn each quarter at preset caps; if token volatility increases, the DAO automatically tops up collateral from a reserve bucket or reduces grant size. Implication: governance translates policy into parameters—minimum health factor, maximum borrow per epoch, emergency unwind rules—so that execution is dull. Dull is the point. Public money should move like a metronome.

Two named, dated examples ground these patterns. First, **Aave Arc (London, January 2022)**: its permissioned pool enabled corporate treasuries and funds—those with fiduciary and regulatory constraints—to operate with DeFi's transparency without violating internal controls. The concrete outcome was not spectacular yields but access: CFOs could test working-capital lines on chain. Second, **MakerDAO's Peg Stability Module (Ethereum, December 2020)**: though not a lending market per se, the PSM institutionalised low-friction stablecoin swaps that many treasuries used for liquidity management around DAI, often in tandem with Aave/Compound borrowing. The implication across both cases is sober: when primitives are simple and parameters explicit, organisations can compose them into risk policies without drama.

Now the counter-example. **Recursive leverage loops**—depositing a stablecoin, borrowing the same stablecoin, redepositing, and repeating to inflate headline APY—look clever and feel safe, until they are not. The **Euler Finance** exploit in March 2023 (London-based team; Ethereum mainnet) did not fail because recursion is inherently evil; it failed because a code path allowed attackers to strip the scaffolding. Users who had looped exposure discovered that leverage magnifies contract risk just as surely as it magnifies price risk. Reconcile the lesson this way: where your return depends on rehypothecating the *same* exposure, you are building extra floors on the scaffold without strengthening the foundations. Use credit to bridge dissimilar risks (inventory ↔ cash flow), not to echo the same one.

Behind each use case sits a decision rule you can measure. *Trust* becomes "do I know which contracts can move my collateral and debt, and under what governance?" *Efficiency* becomes "what is my realised all-in bps after borrow APR, slippage, and volatility buffers over the period I intend to hold?" *Risk* becomes "what move in collateral price, or what shift in utilisation past the kink, would force liquidation or blow the spread, and how fast could that happen?" These translate to behaviours: maintain health factors >1.5 for operations; cap borrow at a percentage of expected cash inflows; set alerts on utilisation as well as price; rehearse the exact sequence that repays or adds collateral.

There are also **geographies** where lending makes sense because payment rails do not. Show: a design studio in Lagos invoices a client in London and faces variable settlement delays and FX haircuts. Name: *short-term invoice bridging*. Explain: the studio posts crypto collateral, borrows stablecoins for two weeks to pay staff, and settles the loan when the pound arrives. Implication: the scaffold supports working capital without predatory rates—*if* the studio is honest about buffers and sets a liquidation line far from noise. The same geometry helps a freelancer in Buenos Aires smooth income without holding ballooning local currency, though regulatory specifics remain jurisdiction-dependent and must be respected. The pattern is not ideology. It is cash-flow engineering.

Where does **credit delegation** belong? Protocols such as Aave introduced delegated credit primitives (2020–2021) whereby an over-collateralised address allocates borrowing power to a counterparty under contractual constraints. This can fund known partners—suppliers, service firms—without pulling assets into a bank. The limitation is obvious: reputation re-enters through the side door. Smart contracts can cap exposure and automate penalties, but they cannot will honesty into existence. The scaffold gains a new joint; it also gains a new failure mode. Used inside bounded relationships—with legal agreements and arbitration—it works. Sprayed at strangers, it is wishful thinking.

Inventory finance for on-chain businesses is another credible use. NFT marketplaces, miners (historically), or validator operators often have volatile treasuries and periodic fiat costs. Borrowing stablecoins against a basket of correlated assets to match predictable outgoings—electricity, hosting, salaries—can be rational if the LTV is low and the maturity tight. The detail that makes or breaks the case is *correlation*. A miner posting only the coin they mine as collateral courts a double shock (price down; revenue down). A validator posting stables or liquid staking derivatives for a short window better respects the physics.

You do not hang a scaffold from the same beam you are testing.

One might ask whether **SME lending via under-collateralised protocols**—for example, Goldfinch (San Francisco, launched 2021)—belongs here. It can, with caution. The sensible slice is the one that treats DeFi as a funding rail and keeps the underwriting off-chain with firms who know how to read balance sheets and recover loans. The on-chain part—incentives, transparency, disbursement—adds value. The credit decision remains human. That does not insult decentralisation; it clarifies where it ends. The scaffold holds because a wall, not a slogan, bears the load.

Two more caselets sharpen instinct. **November 2021, Arbitrum**: borrowing USDC on Aave's L2 at low single-digit APR to fund marketing spend for a token launch looked rational because blockspace was cheap, liquidity was deep, and utilisation sat well below the kink. Teams that monitored rates and kept health factors wide saw stable costs. **September 2022, Ethereum mainnet (Merge week)**: priority fees spiked sporadically; liquidations and arbitrage timing jittered; utilisation kissed upper slopes. The same borrow that looked benign a month earlier turned brittle. The difference was not philosophy. It was parameters and preparedness.

A scaffold is also a choice *not* to build. Where use cases fail the test is where borrowing becomes a substitute for decisiveness—refusing to sell an asset you should sell, or looping exposures to simulate yield. You will recognise these because they need a story to justify themselves. Sensible cases do not. They point to a cash flow and a calendar.

Translate the chapter's abstractions into three operating questions before you open a credit line. What is the *purpose* of the borrow, and can you name the cash inflow that services it without further borrowing? Where is the *scaffold* strongest—asset choice, LTV, rate curve, oracle quality—and where will you add redundancy? How will you *exit*—the exact transaction, not a hope—if volatility or utilisation moves against you? If the answers are crisp, you have a use. If they are mist, you have a temptation.

We end where we began: with institutions stepping onto the stage. Aave Arc's London announcement was not a coronation. It was a signal. Lending protocols earn relevance when they disappear into operations—quiet scaffolds under ordinary work. They will fail loudly wherever they promise trampolines. The unresolved, practical question sits with every treasurer, desk head, and builder who has access to a borrow button and a balance of collateral: will you use the scaffold to support load you can measure, or to attempt a jump you cannot land?

Chapter 5
Staking, Yield, and Where Returns Come From

In November 2021, as crypto markets roared to their peak, a banner on a lending platform promised *"20 per cent fixed APY—risk-free."* Within six months, the platform—Terra's Anchor Protocol—had imploded, erasing billions in deposits and rewriting the public understanding of "yield" in decentralised finance. Those who had asked *who pays me, and in what risk?* saw what others did not: the return had no revenue beneath it. It was not yield. It was subsidy disguised as certainty. The wreckage clarified a question that should never again be optional: where does the yield actually come from?

The question is older than crypto. Every interest payment since Mesopotamian grain loans has had a payer. In traditional finance, that payer is visible—borrowers, fees, trade spreads, taxes. In decentralised systems, the line blurs: code replaces intermediaries, governance mints tokens, and protocols distribute "rewards" that may or may not connect to productive activity. Yield, unexamined, becomes theology. What this chapter restores is the anatomy of return—the mechanisms, not the slogans—and the humility to trace who funds what, through how many layers, and at what hidden leverage.

Staking, the anchor of most base yields in decentralised finance, begins cleanly enough: validators secure a network, earn newly minted tokens and transaction fees, and distribute those earnings proportionally to delegators. It is the blockchain equivalent of earning rent for maintaining a property. Yet the moment that yield is tokenised, re-wrapped, and pledged again—through "liquid staking", "restaking", or "vault strategies"—the clarity fogs. Each derivative adds convenience and composability, but also a new link in the chain of claims. When everything yields, few stop to notice that many yields are the same coin, promised twice.

To grasp staking's promise, one must first see its restraint. A validator's reward is grounded in measurable work: uptime, correctness, and stake weight. The network's inflation rate defines the total pool of rewards, and slashing defines the cost of failure. This is *base yield*: protocol revenue that corresponds to the service of consensus. The moment a staking token is re-deposited into another protocol that issues a new token or pays incentives in kind, that yield becomes *manufactured*. It may persist for months. It may look indistinguishable on a dashboard. But the economic difference is fundamental: one is earned; the other is paid to you by a future participant. The surface number conceals the question of sustainability.

The motif that threads through this chapter is *lineage*. Every yield has a family tree. Trace it far enough, and you discover whether it ends in fees, inflation, or circular promises. During 2023, the rise of "restaking" protocols like EigenLayer (Seattle, mainnet launched June 2023) revealed how short those genealogies could be. Users deposited staked ETH, pledged it again to secure additional services, and earned extra rewards. The mechanism looked elegant. But from a systems view, it stacked obligations: if any underlying layer failed or suffered slashing, the same collateral bore multiple claims. Leverage, in a new vocabulary, had returned. The discipline was no longer to find the highest yield, but to map the chain of dependencies until one saw daylight.

Yield, in this sense, is narrative discipline. Every protocol that promises return without external revenue is telling a story. Some stories are fine: "we are bootstrapping participation." Others are deception. The line between subsidy and Ponzi is not moral—it is mathematical. The former expects to end; the latter cannot afford to. The intelligent participant learns to follow cash flow as a hydrologist follows water: source, flow, evaporation, and floodplain. Protocol rewards, staking income, arbitrage capture, liquidity provision, and governance emissions all belong in that map, each carrying its own risk density.

That discipline extends to liquidity provision, where *impermanent loss* remains the quiet predator of the unwary. The phrase itself—so sterile, so theoretical—conceals the human experience of watching a balanced position decay as prices diverge. Yet impermanent loss is not a bug; it is the cost of providing liquidity in volatile markets. It is the rent paid to maintain symmetry. The key is understanding that loss is "impermanent" only until you withdraw: once you do, the loss becomes realised. A narrative walkthrough can make this intuitive, showing how price moves shift your token mix and how the arithmetic rewards those who hold volatility steady. Once internalised, impermanent loss ceases to be mysterious—it becomes a risk premium you can measure.

From that clarity grows the practice of *position sizing*. The great unspoken rule of decentralised finance is that every strategy, no matter how automated, is human in its failure mode. Hardware breaks, contracts update, oracles lag, wallets misclick. Survivors allocate by exposure, not excitement. They keep critical funds in cold custody, allocate a smaller share to productive staking, a smaller still to active strategies, and an even smaller to experimental yields. This chapter translates that principle into numbers—not prescriptions, but ratios that keep autonomy survivable. In this world, speed is not the advantage; *staying solvent* is.

Yield is not the enemy of prudence. It is its test. To recognise where returns come from is to reclaim financial adulthood in a system that too often celebrates permanent adolescence—the next token, the next multiplier, the next epoch. Base yield reminds us that honest return requires work done or risk borne. Restaking shows how easily leverage hides beneath convenience. Liquidity provision exposes the arithmetic of loss that pretends to be income. And sizing decisions translate philosophy into posture.

The deeper message of this chapter is temporal. Yields tempt with immediacy: annualised returns, daily rewards, real-time dashboards. But the underlying systems are slow—validators accumulate trust over months; protocols amortise risk across cycles; healthy positions survive winters. When the mania fades, what remains is *time discipline*: an awareness of what kind of risk pays you, how often it pays, and whether you could still sleep if it stopped.

We will treat yield not as spectacle but as evidence—proof that value was created somewhere, by someone, for someone else. Where that proof is missing, the return is counterfeit. The craft lies in learning to tell the difference before the market reminds you. The scaffold of this chapter stands on that distinction: base versus manufactured yield, visible versus stacked risk, the arithmetic of impermanent loss, and the design of portfolios that assume error before profit.

At its heart, staking is about trust turned mechanical. Yield is trust measured in numbers. And restaking is trust recycled, sometimes too often. The unresolved question, one that will echo through every case and diagram that follows, is simple and disquieting: if yield is the language of DeFi, can you still tell when the speaker is lying—or have we all started to believe our own fluency?

Base Yield vs. Manufactured Yield

On 7 May 2022, as Terra's UST stablecoin began its death spiral, Anchor Protocol's once-boasted "20 per cent fixed APY" became meaningless. Within 72 hours, over **$14 billion** in deposits vanished from its smart contracts (data:

DeFiLlama, May 2022). What Anchor had labelled "yield" was not income from any productive activity. It was a subsidy—funded by newly minted governance tokens and marketing budgets—paid to attract deposits that, in turn, were used to sustain the price of the same asset generating the rewards. The loop was perfect in its circularity and fatal in its logic. It answered no question about *who pays* and *in what risk*.

That question—so simple it feels naïve—is the core diagnostic of yield. When a protocol distributes tokens or interest, one must trace the cash flow back to a payer and a service rendered. If none exists, the yield is manufactured, not earned. The distinction is not moral. It is thermodynamic. Base yield arises where value is created outside the loop: block rewards, transaction fees, borrower interest, arbitrage profits, or any real economic activity that pays someone for a task. Manufactured yield, by contrast, is internal heat: emissions and incentives used to mimic productivity until the external energy arrives—or the system burns through itself.

Show → name → explain → implication. Show: Ethereum's transition to proof-of-stake (The Merge, 15 September 2022) created a predictable stream of validator rewards—paid in ETH, derived from transaction fees and network issuance. Name: *base yield*. Explain: each validator performs measurable work (proposing and attesting to blocks) and earns a pro-rata share of these revenues, roughly 4–5 per cent annualised in mid-2023, as reported by

Beaconcha.in. Implication: the yield corresponds to a real service—security. The network pays for trustlessness. If staking stopped, the chain would halt. That linkage makes the reward credible, finite, and analysable.

Contrast this with **Anchor (Terraform Labs, 2021–2022)** or **OlympusDAO (launched March 2021, Athens pseudonymic origin)**, whose "APYs" reached four digits. Those returns were priced not by risk but by imagination. Olympus minted OHM to pay OHM holders, sustaining itself through reflexive belief that others would buy tomorrow. Anchor subsidised UST deposits with LUNA emissions that inflated away the base. Neither extracted revenue from an external payer; both inflated internal promises. The numbers dazzled, until the loop closed.

A credible counter-example complicates the picture. **Curve Finance**, launched January 2020 in Switzerland, distributed CRV governance tokens to liquidity providers alongside trading fees. The token incentive was inflationary, yet the pool fees were genuine—collected from actual trades of stablecoins and used to reward LPs. Manufactured and base yield coexisted. The former bootstrapped liquidity; the latter sustained it. The reconciliation lies in recognising *temporal layering*: emission as ignition, revenue as fuel. When protocols fail to switch sources, they stall.

Base yield answers the "who pays" question in clear language. In staking, the payer is the network; in lending, it is the borrower; in AMMs, it is the trader. Manufactured yield dodges the question or disguises it behind tokenomics. The observable behaviour is different. Base yield contracts when use falls; manufactured yield often rises when participation slows, as teams amplify incentives to attract new entrants. A healthy protocol breathes with usage metrics—total transactions, fees collected, borrow volume—while an unhealthy one inflates its own lungs.

The motif of *oxygen* clarifies the difference. Base yield is the oxygen a system produces by genuine metabolism—blockspace sold, credit priced, liquidity used. Manufactured yield is the oxygen pumped from a tank to keep a dying patient pink. Both can sustain life temporarily, but only one can last without constant intervention.

Take **Ethereum's staking returns** versus **liquid staking derivatives** (LSDs). The former earns base yield: consensus rewards and fees. The latter—say, stETH from Lido (launched December 2020)—earns the same base yield, then layers liquidity incentives on top, such as Curve pool rewards or additional governance emissions. For months, stETH-holders received compounded incentives from several directions. Yet the aggregate yield was a blend: part base, part manufactured. When market conditions changed and token emissions declined, only the base remained. Those who mistook temporary boosts for structural income learned that oxygen tanks empty fast.

The counterpoint is that manufactured yield is not always dishonest. It can serve as *bootstrapping capital*. Compound's COMP distributions (launched June 2020, San Francisco) created a market for governance tokens while stimulating borrowing and lending volumes. The incentive was explicit, temporary, and linked to measurable activity. It functioned like a start-up's marketing rebate. The issue arises when protocols forget the expiration date and call the rebate "income."

Show another contrast. **Aave's lending markets** generate base yield because borrowers pay interest in real time. The interest rate responds to utilisation—when liquidity is scarce, rates rise. The APY a depositor earns is traceable: it comes from another participant's decision to borrow. By contrast, yield farms that reward deposits without any borrowers rely purely on emissions. There is no economic counterparty, only a conveyor belt of tokens. When that belt stops, the yield vanishes without a trace of unpaid debt, because there was never a payer.

The philosophical question is not "is it sustainable?" but "is it reciprocal?" Every credible yield sits on a completed loop of risk and payment. Validators risk slashing to secure the chain; lenders risk default to earn interest; LPs risk impermanent loss to collect fees. Each trade is a wager against uncertainty, and the yield compensates that wager. Manufactured yield decouples risk and reward, replacing uncertainty with token inflation. It produces *price movement*, not *service*.

Metrics make the difference visible. Base yields correlate with exogenous variables—network usage, gas fees, transaction count, borrow utilisation, volume. Manufactured yields correlate with endogenous ones—

token price, emission schedule, treasury runway. If the return doubles because the token price doubles, not because usage grew, it is not yield; it is reflexivity.

Yet reflexivity can be functional if understood. During 2021's growth phase, token emissions accelerated adoption. Protocols needed initial liquidity to reach fee equilibrium. In that context, emissions acted as venture financing paid in kind. But as 2022 proved, those subsidies must taper. The failure to taper is what turns a bootstrap into a noose.

The motif of oxygen returns: base yield breathes freely; manufactured yield gasps without subsidy. Recognising which you are inhaling is the discipline of survival. The technical lens—cash-flow tracing—becomes a moral one only when users forget to look.

The question *"who pays me, and in what risk?"* should be as habitual as checking the weather. It demands an explicit answer before capital is deployed. If a yield is paid by borrowers, the risk is default. If by traders, the risk is volatility. If by protocol emissions, the risk is dilution. If by market narrative, the risk is belief. Each can be priced, but none can be ignored.

A subtle limitation tempers this neat division: some base yields depend indirectly on token inflation. Ethereum's validator rewards, though grounded in fees, also draw from new ETH issuance. The network effectively taxes holders through inflation to pay security providers. The risk is systemic rather than circular, yet the mechanism resembles a state paying soldiers with seigniorage. The reconciliation lies in transparency. Everyone knows the rate of inflation and its purpose. Manufactured yield hides it. Base yield declares it.

When investors compare yields across DeFi and traditional markets, they often forget time and compounding. A "10 per cent" return paid in volatile governance tokens is not the same as 10 per cent in fiat stablecoins; the risk units differ. The base/manufactured distinction reframes the conversation from *how much* to *from where*. Asking who pays forces a recalibration of appetite.

Two more instructive examples close the circle. **Yearn Finance (launched July 2020)** aggregates yields from underlying protocols, most of which originate in genuine borrower or trading activity. Its automation makes base yield more accessible. **Wonderland (launched September 2021, Avalanche)** did the opposite: it issued its own token, TIME, to pay astronomical "rebase" yields sourced entirely from dilution. The former compounded external yield; the latter self-consumed. Both used the same vocabulary. Only one could answer the oxygen test.

Base yield can be boring. It often is. Four to six per cent annualised on staked ETH, or low-teens lending rates during volatile cycles, feel pedestrian beside the fireworks of 1000 per cent APY. Yet boredom is a feature. It signals that returns have a payer, and that payer has limits. Manufactured yield promises constant motion; base yield endures because it pauses with the system's breath.

Every advance in DeFi—liquid staking, restaking, credit delegation—returns to the same diagnostic. Trace the yield. Follow it through contracts, bridges, wrappers, and treasuries until you reach a human or protocol that performs work or assumes risk. Stop when you find air. If you loop back to your starting point, you have found the circle.

The unresolved test is this: as staking derivatives proliferate and governance incentives blur the boundary between reward and subsidy, can you still identify the base yield beneath the marketing layer? If not, the question answers itself. You are not being paid for risk. You are being paid to forget it.

Restaking and Rehypothecation

In June 2023, in Seattle, EigenLayer opened deposits for a new idea with an old name: *restaking*. Holders of staked ETH, already pledged to secure Ethereum, could pledge it again to secure additional services—new oracles, data layers, or middleware. One key bears many claims. In weeks, deposits hit caps and waiting lists formed. The reward was simple to advertise: more yield on the same collateral. The risk was harder to see: if a downstream service failed, a slashing event could propagate backwards into the base stake. The promise was stacked. So was the peril.

Restaking is explicit rehypothecation. It reprises a familiar pattern from prime brokerage and shadow banking, now rendered on-chain. Show → name → explain → implication. Show: you hold stETH (Lido's liquid staking token, launched December 2020) that earns base ETH staking rewards. Name: *restaking*. Explain: you pledge that stETH (or re-staked ETH via a wrapper) to a protocol such as EigenLayer, which in turn delegates it to operators securing Actively Validated Services (AVSs). If an AVS detects malicious behaviour or a contract-defined fault, it can request slashing of the underlying stake. Implication: a single asset now bears several performance promises. You earned a second stream of tokens; you accepted a second route to loss.

Rehypothecation has always traded opacity for convenience. In 2022, Celsius Network's bankruptcy in New York revealed customer assets repeatedly re-pledged across counterparties; when markets turned in June, collateral chains jammed, withdrawals froze, and balance sheets broke. The reuse of the same collateral through multiple layers meant that the failure of one actor imperilled many. DeFi is more transparent than that, but transparency does not equal simplicity. A token can be wrapped, staked, re-staked, lent, and LP'd before it reaches a dashboard; each stop adds a promise and a path for seizure. The map matters.

To see why stacked pledges alter risk, follow the path of a single ether. First pledge: to Ethereum's validator set. The network pays base yield—issuance and fees—in exchange for honest participation. Second pledge: to an AVS that piggybacks the same validator's identity. The AVS pays an additional reward—its own token, fees from users, or emissions funded by investors. Third pledge: the resulting receipt token is supplied to a lending market at a discount, where it backs borrow. A downturn hits. The AVS misbehaves, or is attacked, and requests slashing for a cohort of operators. Your base stake is docked. Simultaneously, the AVS token falls, reducing the value of your recent rewards; the lending market marks collateral down and moves towards liquidation. Three layers, one move, multiple claims. Nothing fraudulent happened. Geometry did.

The language that clarifies this is *correlated slashing*. If the same validator set secures many AVSs, a fault in any one can trigger slashing across a common base. Correlation increases with operator overlap and with AVS designs that rely on similar assumptions (the same data availability, the same committees). The metric to watch is the *overlap ratio*: the percentage of your staked position that sits with operators simultaneously responsible for more than one AVS you support. A low overlap ratio means faults are more idiosyncratic; a high ratio means they are systemic. Most dashboards do not show this number. You must infer it: list your operators, list your AVSs, count the intersections.

A paired concept is *maturity mismatch*. Base staking has exit queues and withdrawal delays; AVS slashing can be faster. Lending markets have liquidation thresholds triggered by oracle updates in minutes, not days. If a slashing event reduces your stake on day one but the withdrawal queue to reconstitute collateral extends to day five, your lending position may breach health factors before you can adjust. Here the metric is *time-to-access* versus *time-to-loss*: how long to move collateral compared with how quickly a slashing-induced price change can force liquidations. If the latter is shorter, you are running hot.

History supplies two cautionary, checkable episodes that, while not "restaking" in the strict sense, map the same physics. In June 2022, the *stETH–ETH basis* widened under stress as large centralised borrowers—Celsius among them—sold stETH for liquidity. stETH never ceased earning base rewards, yet the derivative deviated materially from ETH; users who had pledged stETH in lending markets learned that *derivative risk* compounds *funding risk.* Prices corrected later, but the lesson endured: even a high-quality wrapper can trade at a discount when collateral chains are crowded. In March 2023, the Euler Finance exploit revealed how quickly composability can become correlation, as attackers used flash loans and logic bugs to drain collateral; positions that depended on the uninterrupted exchangeability of receipts found that assumption falsified for hours. Both episodes remind us that stacked promises bind timing as well as value.

A credible counter-example tempers fatalism. Redeploying collateral *can* be sensible when each layer's risk is orthogonal and capped. Consider MakerDAO's admission of stETH as collateral (post–December 2020) with conservative debt ceilings and liquidation ratios. The protocol acknowledged basis risk (stETH depegging from ETH) and sized exposure accordingly. Similarly, EigenLayer has explored operator isolation and AVS-specific slashing scopes—attempts to confine the blast radius of faults. These do not erase risk; they localise it. The reconciliation is pragmatic: the danger is not reuse per se; it is reuse without *bounded correlation* and *bounded size*.

The discipline that makes stacked pledges survivable is *path tracing*. Ask—methodically—four questions before adding a layer. Who can seize or slash this asset at each contract hop? Under what conditions, signed by whom? What is the withdrawal or exit timeline at each hop? Where are oracles or governance decisions able to introduce non-market risk? Convert each answer into a behaviour. If two layers share a seizure authority (for example, a multisig of overlapping operators), treat them as one risk. If an exit is slower than a likely liquidation, lower LTVs or skip leverage. If an oracle updates slowly relative to price, avoid strategies that depend on precise marking.

We can make these abstractions measurable. Define a simple *rehypothecation ratio*: the number of distinct claims that can reduce your principal per unit of collateral. Base stake alone has one. stETH in a lending market (collateral subject to stETH–ETH basis and liquidation) has at least two. stETH, re-staked to secure an AVS with independent slashing rules, then supplied to a lending market, now has three or more. The number is imperfect but instructive. A higher ratio does not forbid action; it raises the bar for buffers and reduces acceptable position size.

A second metric is *coverage adequacy*: some restaking frameworks advertise "slashing insurance" or operator bonds that compensate delegators in the event of faults. Measure the notional of these funds relative to re-staked TVL and to the plausible loss from correlated slashing. If coverage is two per cent of exposure and a bad event could cost five per cent, you are self-insuring the gap. Note who pays claims and how quickly. Insurance that requires governance votes during crisis is theatre.

Rehypothecation also invites *liquidity mirages*. A token may trade with tight spreads and deep depth under calm conditions because market-makers recycle it quickly through wrappers and AMMs. In stress, those same market-makers de-risk simultaneously, and the path that made liquidity look deep becomes a maze of one-way doors. Watch *inventory turnover*—how long it takes for a unit of the receipt token to return to base redemption under normal flow—and imagine it doubling. That is your stress baseline.

Two named, dated examples of apparently safe reuse sharpen instinct. First, *Curve's stETH–ETH* pool across 2022 often provided narrow slippage due to concentrated liquidity and incentives; when large sellers hit, the pool imbalanced and price moved to clear inventory that could not instantly redeem. Second, *Aave's* inclusion of LSTs such as stETH allowed conservative borrowers to access stablecoins while continuing to earn base yield; those who maintained wide health factors rode out the 2022 basis moves; those who ran near liquidation discovered that basis and rate spikes compound. In both cases, reuse worked when discipline did. It failed where sizing failed.

The motif that threads this subchapter is the *claims map*. Every wrapper is a road. Every pledge is a tollbooth. The art is not to avoid roads; it is to know which roads converge. Draw it. From your wallet outward, list the contracts that can move or mark your asset: staking contract, wrapper, restaking manager, AVS registry, lending market, router. For each, note the authority (on-chain threshold? multisig?), the oracle, and the exit timeline. The picture is unglamorous. It is also the difference between a clever yield stack and a correlated margin call.

None of this argues for purism. Restaking may secure valuable public goods—a new oracle network, a data availability layer, a shared sequencer—more cheaply by reusing existing trust. In aggregate, that efficiency could be a public benefit. The risk materialises if governance underprices slashing, or if the same operators dominate multiple AVSs, turning one clever architecture into a single point of human failure wearing many masks. The fix is structural: caps per AVS, diversity of operators, transparent slashing charters, fast disclosure of incidents, and cross-protocol drills. Drills matter. They force the question: when an AVS requests slashing, who vouches the evidence, and how fast do claims settle?

There is also a political dimension. Restaking reallocates security budget from a base chain to secondary services. If those services pay high rewards, they bid validators' attention away from base duties; if they pay too little, they import risk without resilience. The balance will be fought in governance: how much base risk to accept for how much peripheral utility. That argument is healthy. It makes value explicit.

A final, sober complication: sometimes layers are added invisibly by intermediaries. A custodial "staking product" may restake without the depositor's informed consent; a yield aggregator may route receipt tokens into strategies with nested leverage. Documentation lags. Dashboards simplify. Your defence is dull: read the contracts your tokens approve; monitor allowances; prefer primitives with clear slashing policies over composites with vibrant marketing. Show me the charter. Name the slasher. Explain the evidence. Implication: if clarity is scarce, risk is dear.

We return to the five-word sentence that framed the opening: one key bears many claims. That phrase is either an opportunity or a warning depending on whether each claim is understood, bounded, and paid for with appropriate return. The unresolved test is practical and immediate. Before you accept an extra percentage point for reusing your collateral, can you draw the claims map from your wallet to the base chain and mark every entity with seizure or pricing power over your position? If your pencil stalls at layer two, the yield you see is not the only number that will move.

Impermanent Loss Without the Headache

On 19 June 2022, Bancor suspended its much-promoted impermanent loss protection after sustained market stress, a decision announced by the Tel Aviv–based team with immediate effect. Liquidity providers who believed they were insulated discovered the protection itself depended on a reservoir of protocol fees and emissions that had thinned. The pools continued to function; the promise did not. It was a clarifying scene: impermanent loss (IL) had never left. It had merely been socialised and, for a season, hidden. The market brought it back into view. That day, a thousand dashboard numbers gained context. So did the phrase *provide liquidity*.

Impermanent loss is not a monster under the bed. It is the arithmetic of keeping a balance between two assets while prices move. Uniswap popularised it; v2 made it simple; v3 made it sharp. The rule is mechanical: an automated market maker (AMM) holds reserves in a mathematically defined ratio. When one asset re-prices, the pool sells what is rising and buys what is falling to keep the ratio intact. That is the job. The loss arises when, at withdrawal, the value of your pool position is less than what you would have had by simply holding both assets separately. In calm markets with ample fees, the difference can be small or positive after income. In directional markets, the difference can be painful. The pool behaved correctly. Your outcome reflects what the pool *is*.

A narrative walkthrough turns this from abstraction into muscle memory. Show: you deposit equal values of ETH and USDC into a constant-product pool at £2,000 per ETH. Name: the *book-keeper's balance*. Explain: the pool is a scale; it must keep the product of reserves constant. If ETH rallies to £2,400, arbitrageurs step in, selling ETH to the pool until its price matches the market. Your share of the pool now contains less ETH and more USDC than when you entered. You have earned fees on the trades that rebalanced the pool, but you hold fewer of the appreciating asset than a passive holder. Implication: your performance equals *fee income minus divergence loss*. The fees are visible. The loss is not theft; it is the cost of being the other side for the entire time the market moved.

Turn the dial in the other direction. If ETH falls to £1,600, the pool buys ETH as it drops; you end up with more ETH and less USDC than you began with. You have accumulated the volatile asset while it declined. Again, you collected fees throughout. Again, your PnL relative to holding depends on the magnitude of the move versus the fees earned. There is no moral in this. There is only geometry. The pool enforces mean reversion in inventory; your outcome depends on whether the market rewarded that exposure during the period you provided it.

Two concrete, named examples show where this geometry helps and where it hurts. First: **Curve's 3pool**

(DAI/USDC/USDT, launched January 2020 on Ethereum) employs a *stable-swap* invariant that flattens the price curve around parity. Because the three assets are designed to trade at $1, the pool absorbs large amounts with minimal price impact. Liquidity providers earn fees from heavy flow while exposure to divergence is tiny. IL exists, but it is measured in basis points and usually dominated by fee income. The pool suits treasuries and market-makers because the shape of the curve matches the assets' behaviour. The scale is built for balance.

Second: **Uniswap v3's ETH/USDC pools** (May 2021 onward) introduced *concentrated liquidity*. LPs choose price ranges; capital only works inside those bands. When prices live inside your range, fees are rich and IL modest. When prices trend outside, your position goes "out of range": you hold one asset only and earn no fees until you rebalance. In 2022, research from Uniswap Labs reported that a large subset of passive LPs underperformed simple holding due to range mismanagement and volatility that pushed positions out of range for extended periods. The mechanism wasn't broken; the practice was. Concentration increases fee density and increases the need to tend the garden.

A credible counter-example tempers fatalism. During periods of high, two-sided activity—launch weeks, macro volatility spikes, or busy options expiries—the fees in major pairs have, at times, exceeded divergence loss even for moderate range widths. Professional LPs who model flow and reset ranges proactively have harvested net positive

PnL. Reconcile the cases like this: IL is a *drag term* you must budget for. Fees are a *credit* you can nurture with placement and maintenance. The system neither guarantees nor forbids profit. It rewards alignment between your range and the market's breathing.

To make this intuitive, treat the pool as a tide pool, not a vault. Water flows in and out with price. You cannot freeze it. You can, however, place your stones where the tide most often lingers. In practice that means choosing ranges around recent realised volatility rather than around hopes; measuring fee-to-range utilisation over rolling windows; resetting when price spends too long near an edge; and accepting that sometimes the tide will sprint. These are behaviours, not beliefs. They reduce surprises.

Pair every abstraction with a visible decision. *Trust* becomes the choice to deploy only against assets whose behaviour you understand—stablecoins in a stable-swap; major pairs in wide bands. *Efficiency* becomes your observed fee APR per unit of "time in range". *Risk* becomes the maximum adverse move you can tolerate before a position goes one-sided, translated into a range width in percentage terms. Write the numbers down. If your tolerance is a 15 per cent move and recent realised volatility is 10 per cent per week, a narrow band around the mid is a wager, not a provision of service.

Sizing follows from this arithmetic. The market pays you to warehouse inventory risk. It does not pay you to be brave. One method that emerges from practice, not dogma, is to tier exposure by how much maintenance a position demands. Capital that cannot be watched frequently belongs in *wide* ranges or in correlated-asset pools where the invariant limits IL (Curve stables; ETH/stETH). Capital that can be tended daily can sit in *moderate* ranges in deep pairs with robust fee flow (WETH/USDC), with pre-written rules for resets. Capital allocated to *active* experimentation—the granular tick-farming strategies some funds run—should be sized as research: explicitly small, explicitly temporary, explicitly measured.

Use two more named contexts to ground the instincts. In **May 2021 (Uniswap v3 launch)**, many LPs deployed tick-tight ranges to capture fees in ETH/USDC. Fee income was initially striking, then choppy; as price trended, ranges went idle and resets consumed gas. Those who widened bands to volatility-aware corridors accepted lower peak APRs yet sustained accrual longer. In **June 2022 (stETH/ETH dislocation)**, Curve LPs in the stETH/ETH pool learned that "correlated" is not "pegged": as redemptions clogged and sellers sought liquidity, basis widened, and IL appeared where it had seemed negligible. In both cases, the pool worked precisely. The surprise lay in assumptions about the assets, not the invariant.

It helps to name the arithmetic cleanly. For constant-product pools, IL as a function of price change Δ can be expressed in closed form; you needn't memorise it, only its shape: convex, growing with divergence. Fees accumulate roughly linearly with flow through your range. That slope depends on both *volume* and *how much of that volume trades where you are present*. This explains why the same notional in a shallow altcoin pair can lose more, faster, than in a deep major. The tide is choppier; the scale is smaller; a single step sloshes everything.

UI framing can mislead. Front ends often display "pool APR" as if it were portable to any LP. It is not. It is a *historical pool-wide average*. Your range will capture a subset of that flow. The more concentrated and intelligently placed the range, the closer you get. The more you miss the action, the more that headline becomes fiction for you. The right response is not cynicism. It is calibration: back-check your last week's fees against the displayed APR and your time-in-range to see whether your placement aligns with the pool's centre of action.

The Bancor pause belongs here again, as a caution about socialising IL. Insurance models can make sense—mutualising idiosyncratic shocks with transparent rules, caps, and premia. But they cannot repeal convexity. When a market moves far and fast, the cost of being the counterparty arrives for *someone*. If it is not the LP, it is the insurer; if not the insurer, it is the token holders; if not them, it is the user through slippage. A sensible LP assumes the bill will come and asks only *when, how large,* and *for what service in return.*

Motif, once more: the scale. AMMs sell a service—continuous, permissionless liquidity. You rent the scale. Your rent is IL. Your income is fees. The craft is to choose a scale whose fulcrum matches market reality and to charge appropriately with range and size. Dogma—"never LP" or "always LP"—fails because it ignores the market's mood and your own logistics. Some readers will, rightly, prefer to hold assets outright and avoid inventory service. Others will treat LP as a business, with rota, rules, and budgets. Both are respectable. Only unpriced conviction is not.

Three practical diagnostics keep this human. First, *fee-to-drag ratio*: over your intended holding period, do fees at your planned range exceed the expected IL for plausible price paths? This can be estimated with realised volatility and back-tests of pool flow. Second, *reset cost burden*: are the gas costs and operational frictions of maintaining your range small enough that they don't consume the edge? If not, widen the band or reconsider the venue (Layer 2 often helps). Third, *sleep test*: will a 20 per cent move overnight leave you one-sided and unhappy? If yes, your range is a screenplay, not a strategy.

A final counter-intuition matters. Sometimes the right LP decision is to go *out of range* by design. A stablecoin/volatile pair can be used to stage exits or entries over time: deposit at a band above spot to sell into strength via fees, or below spot to accumulate. You are not seeking net fee profit; you are seeking execution with rebate. It is a patient limit order wearing an LP's clothes. This is not the business of market-making. It is a treasury tactic with clear intent and capped risk.

The unresolved test remains deliberately simple. Before providing liquidity, can you write—on one line—what market behaviour you are being paid for, what price path would make you underperform a holder, and what size and range make that trade-off acceptable? If the sentence is crisp, the pool is a tool. If the sentence wobbles, the pool will teach you. The scale is there, humming, indifferent. The question is whether you are prepared to pay its rent for the time it keeps your balance.

Position Sizing for Humans

On 12 June 2022, in New Jersey, Celsius froze withdrawals. Overnight, a platform marketed as safe became a block of trapped balances. Five months later, on 8 November 2022 in Nassau, FTX halted its own. Traders who had concentrated working capital on a single exchange discovered that "access" is a position in itself. Some had cold wallets ready and operating float sized for a bad week. Others had everything hot and everything halted. Two dates, two places, one lesson. Survival beats speed, every time.

Position sizing begins where headlines end: with the mundane arithmetic of *how much can you afford to lose in one place, in one way, on one day*. It sounds defeatist. It is pragmatic. You do not win DeFi by outrunning risk; you win by isolating it. The motif that will anchor this subchapter is the *firebreak*. Foresters do not hope a blaze will spare them. They cut lines in advance to deny it fuel. In finance, those lines are custody tiers, strategy buckets, and limits you obey when the screen glows red.

Show → name → explain → implication. Show: a desk keeps 70 per cent of long-term holdings in hardware wallets with multi-signature recovery, 25 per cent in yield-bearing but redeemable positions, and 5 per cent in hot wallets for trading. Name: *tiered custody sizing*. Explain: each tier has a purpose and a cap; caps reflect both exposure and *time-to-liquidity*. Cold is for permanence; warm is for income with exits measured in hours or days; hot is for execution, backed by replenishment rules. Implication: one failure mode—an exchange pause, a bridge incident, a UI compromise—can hurt, but cannot cripple. The firebreaks are real. They cost some efficiency. They buy endurance.

The second line is *single-point-of-failure budgeting*. Show: you compute a number—the maximum percentage of total net worth you will allow any single contract, venue, or signer set to imperil. Name: *SPoF cap*. Explain: it converts anxiety into a metric. If your SPoF cap is 10 per cent, you refuse to route a trade, a farm, or a delegated-stake arrangement that breaches it, no matter how glossy the APR. Implication: you pre-commit to an appetite. You do not renegotiate with panic. You dissolve FOMO with arithmetic.

The third is *drawdown design*. Show: a fund models a 30 per cent market drawdown plus a concurrent liquidity shock (withdrawal queues, gas spikes, oracle lags) and asks how the portfolio behaves. Name: *stress envelope*. Explain: it is not a prediction; it is a rehearsal. You size loan buffers, LP ranges, and staked token allocations so that forced actions are rare. Implication: when the envelope is tested, you reduce position sizes, not standards. A plan replaces improvisation.

Two named, checkable episodes give these abstractions teeth. Celsius's pause (June 2022) trapped users whose operating capital and treasury reserves lived on one platform. Those who had sized hot exposure to a week's needs and the rest to self-custody rode out the halt at the cost of inconvenience, not insolvency. FTX's freeze (November 2022) punished concentration even more. Teams that had *measured* venue risk—allocating per exchange caps, enforcing daily sweep rules, and rehearsing cold-to-hot replenishment—saw interruption, not extinction. In both cases, position sizing *by tier* turned reputation shocks into workflow snarls.

A credible counter-example refines the story. Over-fragmentation carries its own hazard. The Parity multi-sig freeze in November 2017 trapped hundreds of thousands of ether due to a contract bug. Some teams had prudently moved sizeable treasuries into that then-standard multi-sig to reduce operational risk; in so doing, they concentrated smart-contract risk. The reconciliation is practical rather than doctrinaire: diversify *across failure modes*, not merely across logos. A two-of-three multi-sig guarded by the same library as everyone else is a crowd, not a hedge. Firebreaks that share timber burn together.

Translate ideals into behaviours and numbers. *Trust* becomes "how many distinct keys—human or code—must fail to lose more than X per cent?" *Efficiency* becomes "what

APR am I truly giving up by keeping Y per cent cold, and is the foregone return worth the variance reduction?" *Risk* becomes "what is my maximum daily loss if two assumptions fail at once—say, a 20 per cent price gap plus a bridge halt?" You can measure each. You can decide before dawn.

Position sizing across *strategies* uses the same firebreak logic. Staking sits near the core: base yield, protocol-level risk, predictable cash flow. Liquidity provision lives a ring farther out: fee income with inventory risk that rises with volatility and falls with range width. Leverage belongs further still: cheap when utilisation is calm, lethal when borrow curves kink. Experimental strategies—restaking layers, new vaults, freshly launched perps—sit at the perimeter. The allocation rule is not a moral hierarchy. It is a bet on *what hurts first*. When markets stress, perimeters fail before cores. You size the perimeter so that its failure is a bruise, not a fracture.

A second pair of examples adds texture. MakerDAO's Peg Stability Module (December 2020, Ethereum) gave treasuries a predictable, low-friction way to balance stablecoin exposure; protocols that sized their liquidity operations around it rather than around thinly traded stables found their "cash" behaved like cash. By contrast, the June 2022 stETH–ETH basis widening punished desks that had sized borrowing and LP positions as if a wrapper could not diverge. Those with modest LTVs and perimeter sizing for basis risk saw drawdowns they could narrate and manage. Those who built cores on the assumption of perfect liquidity met the margin clerk. The implication is blunt. The closer to the centre a position sits, the more boring it should be.

Sizing also means *time budgeting*. Do not only count capital. Count minutes. A position that needs hands-on range resets does not belong in a bucket you can touch weekly. A loan that can reprice 300 basis points above the utilisation kink does not belong in a treasury that closes on Fridays. Assign each strategy a *maintenance cadence* and size it to your calendar, not your ambition. If you cannot maintain it, you do not own it. It owns you.

Humans need heuristics. The point is not to ossify them into dogma but to make them explicit. One workable pattern for an individual or a small treasury reads like this in behaviour, not percentages: keep long-duration reserves in cold wallets with social recovery tested quarterly; stage a smaller "income" slice into base-yield primitives with same-day exits; keep an even smaller "active" slice for LP and basis trades that you can tend; and cordon a tiny "R&D" slice for new code paths where you assume zero recovery in a stress event. The words *tested, same-day, tend,* and *assume* do the sizing. They embed time, liquidity, and humility into risk.

A complementary sizing lens is *scenario fidelity*. Name a plausible bad week for each bucket. For cold, the scenario is key loss or compromised signers; you mitigate with shards, passphrases, and rehearsed recovery. For base yield, the scenario is protocol governance changing parameters or exits slowing; you mitigate with caps per protocol and a second route to unwind. For LP, the scenario is a 20–30 per cent price move plus fee drought; you mitigate with wider bands and smaller notional. For leverage, the scenario is a rate spike above the kink plus a price gap; you mitigate with pre-funded repay and stricter LTV. You do not need to predict. You only need to prepare.

Human fallibility is the constant. We misclick. We defer. We rationalise. That is why sizing rules work when they *bind behaviour*. Create *hard stops* that trigger when metrics breach lines you set in calm. Health factor hits 1.5? Reduce borrow by N per cent. Liquidity utilisation crosses U*? Switch rate mode or repay. Exchange balance exceeds the weekly float cap? Sweep. You do not debate the rule at midnight. You execute it. Firebreaks burn ugly only if they are cut late.

There is also the question of *governance concentration*. A venue that relies on a single multisig with five known signers is a different risk than one governed by a timelocked DAO with fail-safes. Size accordingly. If a decision by a handful can freeze assets, assign that venue to the perimeter even if its brand lives at the centre of the discourse. Conversely, if a protocol exposes on-chain parameters, audits, and live risk dashboards, you can move it inward—cautiously—because transparency lowers model error. You are not trusting more. You are measuring better.

A counterpoint deserves space: too much caution is also a position. In September 2022 during the Merge week, some desks withdrew entirely from mainnet lending, fearing chain instability, and thereby missed attractive, *short-lived* borrow dislocations visible to those who had sized a small "opportunistic" bucket with strict stop rules. The return was not moral superiority; it was readiness. The lesson is not to hunt drama. It is to keep a tiny, fenced patch of capital trained for brief, asymmetric moments—sized to zero regret if it idles, sized to zero ruin if it trips.

The role of *measurement* cannot be overstated. Keep three numbers live and visible. First, *SPoF exposure*: the percentage of assets controlled by the top single contract, venue, or signer set. Second, *liquidity runway*: days of obligations payable from assets that redeem within 24 hours. Third, *perimeter loss capacity*: the absolute amount you can lose in experimental strategies without touching core plans for six months. Update weekly. Numbers nudge behaviour more reliably than slogans.

Institutions face an extra dimension: accountability. A CFO must defend sizing to boards and auditors. The elegance of DeFi is that you can *evidence* prudence: addresses, caps, timelocks, on-chain histories. Convert heuristics into policy artefacts—whitelists for spenders, caps per protocol encoded in contracts, automated sweeps. If you mean it, codify it. A rule that lives in a slide deck is not a rule. It is an intention waiting to fail.

Return to the motif. Firebreaks are cut against *directional* risk and against *structural* risk. Directional is price and rate movement. Structural is custody, code, and governance.

Sizing across both dimensions denies risk the chance to combine. Celsius and FTX were structural fires. Parity's bug was structural. The stETH–ETH dislocation was directional. A portfolio sized only for one will meet the other at the worst time.

All of which leads to a quiet philosophy. You are not choosing position sizes to maximise the next quarter's chart. You are choosing which promises you can keep to yourself in a bad hour. "I will never have more than X per cent in a single signer set." "I will be able to meet Y months of obligations from assets that liquidate within a day." "I will never borrow above a health factor of Z without an automated repay." These sentences look dull in print. They sound beautiful when markets lurch and you are bored by your own resilience.

The unresolved test is personal and immediate. Before you deploy the next pound, can you answer—without opening an app—how much a single failure could cost you by morning, how long it would take to regain control of your funds, and which rule will fire first if stress arrives at dinner? If any answer feels fuzzy, the size is wrong. Cut the firebreak now, while the forest is quiet.

Chapter 6
Security Threats and Defences

At 3:17 a.m. on 14 April 2023, a developer in Seoul watched helplessly as $25 million drained from a DeFi protocol he had helped build. The code had been audited twice; the exploit took nine seconds. Within minutes, blockchain analysts traced the path through a contract interaction that none of the auditors had marked as critical. It was not a backdoor; it was a misplaced assumption. The exploit was later labelled a "logic inconsistency"—a phrase that hides the human story beneath: tired eyes, a missed edge case, a smart attacker. In a system where code holds money directly, security is not a checklist. It is a living relationship with doubt.

DeFi's defining promise—open, permissionless value transfer—carries its shadow: open, permissionless attack surface. The same transparency that lets anyone verify flows lets adversaries map them. The same composability that fuels innovation compounds vulnerability. When protocols talk to each other, they also inherit each other's weaknesses. A bug in one contract becomes a contagion in another. And while we speak of "hacks", most collapses begin not with code but with people—an engineer who clicked a poisoned link, an investor tricked by a forged domain, a community member persuaded by a fake moderator's direct message. The bridge most often breached is not technical; it is human.

Security, in DeFi, is the study of how trust decays and how discipline restores it. Audits, bug bounties, and formal methods are the industry's visible armour—but they are not guarantees. They are probabilistic mirrors of diligence. An audit proves that someone looked carefully, not that everything was safe. Formal verification catches what is expressed, not what is assumed. When the Ronin Bridge exploit in March 2022 cost $625 million, the root cause was not novel cryptography but an insufficient quorum: five of nine validator keys controlled by a single entity. The line between "mathematical security" and "organisational shortcut" proved shorter than anyone wanted to admit.

To professionalise scepticism is to reverse the reflex of trust. A smart contract, however elegant, should first be treated as an adversary. What does it *want* from you? What permissions does it request? Who can change it? The explorer becomes your microscope: its "Contract Created" timestamp, its list of holders, the pattern of transactions after launch—all signals that speak before marketing does. A contract deployed a week ago with three holders and a sudden jump in total value is not an opportunity; it is a test of your patience. The skill is not paranoia; it is perception.

Social engineering remains the quiet killer. When MetaMask began warning users of "fake support" in 2022, it was responding not to a single event but to an epidemic of impersonation. Scammers learned that urgency outpaces logic: "You have a pending security issue—click here." They mirror tone, icon, even typo patterns of legitimate staff. The best defence is behavioural: *slow the click*. Pause, verify sender addresses character by character, confirm through known public channels. This reflex cannot be automated; it must be trained. Every seasoned operator has a scar from one almost-click.

The paradox is that as systems become more decentralised, the human attack surface widens. Private key compromise, seed-phrase leaks, and wallet-draining approvals all bypass cryptography entirely. It is humbling to realise that the weakest link in a trustless network is still trust misplaced. The distinction between technical and social threat collapses: the exploit starts in the inbox and ends on-chain. To navigate that frontier, you must think like both engineer and anthropologist—aware of code's precision and human fallibility's persistence.

Audits are no longer enough. The mature stance treats them as weather reports: informative, not binding. A clean report means "checked under these conditions". The next release, integration, or dependency can shift the terrain. The rigorous practitioner supplements external audits with internal rehearsals—what if scenarios, chaos drills, white-hat simulations. When ChainSecurity discovered a potential exploit in MakerDAO's multi-collateral DAI contract hours before activation in November 2019, it was these feedback loops that bought time. Maker paused, fixed, redeployed. The difference between vigilance and luck is practice.

This chapter will follow the logic of defence through four concentric circles. The innermost is code: bugs, exploits, audits, and the emerging promise of formal methods that attempt mathematical proof of safety. Around it lies the human layer: phishing, impostors, and the behavioural hygiene that separates caution from paralysis. Beyond that, visibility: learning to read on-chain evidence—contract ages, liquidity flows, ownership concentrations—so that independent judgment can replace marketing narratives. The outermost circle is response: how to compress chaos into steps when something goes wrong. The plan—revoke, quarantine, rotate, report—is not glamorous. It is survival written as procedure.

The through-line is humility. Security in decentralised finance is not a product to purchase or a status to claim; it is a discipline of continuous doubt. Each exploit retells the same fable: hubris before loss, then clarity after. The professional learns to reverse that order—to doubt first, lose less, and teach the reflex. Audits can be bought. Prudence cannot. And the real innovation in DeFi's security future may not be better code, but better culture—the quiet pride of a user who pauses, reads, and clicks slowly while others rush.

When this chapter ends, the reader should not feel invincible. They should feel *equipped*: alert to what they can control, aware of what they cannot, and confident that good habits beat good luck. The test is personal: if your next mistake cost nothing but time, would your defences hold? The honest answer is where security begins.

Bugs, Exploits, and Audits

At 11:04 UTC on 30 March 2022, the Ronin Bridge—used to transfer funds between Ethereum and the blockchain game *Axie Infinity*—was drained of approximately $625 million in ETH and USDC. The breach went unnoticed for nearly six days. The attackers had compromised five of nine validator keys, allowing them to approve withdrawals at will. Audits had been conducted. None had flagged this as a critical weakness. The code was sound; the assumptions were not. The lesson was brutal and simple: in decentralised systems, security fails not only at the edge of code but at the edge of imagination.

Every exploit begins as a sentence in code that behaved exactly as written—but not as intended. Software, in the cryptographic age, is no longer a map for machines; it is a contract with money. A misplaced arithmetic operation, an unchecked return value, or an off-by-one error can turn logic into loss. In April 2022, the Beanstalk protocol, a credit-based stablecoin system on Ethereum, suffered a $182 million theft when an attacker used a *governance flash loan* to gain voting control long enough to pass a malicious proposal. The smart contract did not malfunction; it executed flawlessly. What failed was the human model of what "safe" meant. Bugs are rarely villains. They are ghosts of assumptions.

To professionalise scepticism, one must begin where engineers often end: the audit. The term evokes assurance, yet in practice, it is probabilistic scrutiny. An audit is not a guarantee; it is a second pair of eyes, bound by scope, time, and human limits. When auditors sign reports, they sign a *snapshot in time*—a promise that, as of that commit hash and that repository, no known vulnerabilities of a given type were found. It is not a forward shield. The moment new code is deployed, or a dependency updates, that comfort decays. In March 2020, MakerDAO faced cascading liquidations during a price oracle delay; its code had been audited and stress-tested, yet no one had modelled gas spikes of that intensity. The code stood firm. The environment did not.

A useful motif here is the *mirror*. An audit reflects what is visible, not what is true in every light. Show: a team deploys a yield protocol and commissions two audit firms—Trail of Bits and Quantstamp—to review it. Name: dual auditing as a confidence tactic. Explain: each firm reads the same code through its own lens, applying static analysis tools, fuzzing techniques, and manual review. Both produce reports. The community celebrates. Then an integration two weeks later introduces an untested function via an external call. The mirror, fixed to last month's light, shows nothing new. Implication: security is a process, not a certificate.

Bugs follow patterns. Reentrancy, overflow, uninitialised storage, misused delegate calls, and unchecked access controls are not exotic; they are recurring grammar errors in the language of solidity. The DAO hack of June 2016—when $60 million in ether was siphoned from an Ethereum-based venture fund—exploited a reentrancy flaw that allowed recursive withdrawals before balances updated. Six years later, similar vulnerabilities resurfaced in smaller protocols, despite formal lessons learned. The repetition is not technological but behavioural: developers trust abstractions they did not build, auditors skim familiar code paths, users anchor to audits as absolution. The cycle continues until a new failure restarts attention.

Formal methods offer a different lens. Unlike human audits, they seek mathematical proof that code satisfies specified properties under all possible conditions. Tools such as Certora's Prover or Coq formal verification frameworks attempt to exhaustively validate that "if this, then never that" holds true across every execution path. In 2021, Compound Finance used Certora's system to formally verify its core lending logic—proving, in essence, that collateral could never be withdrawn beyond permitted bounds. When a separate upgrade bug later distributed excess COMP tokens worth tens of millions, the verified logic was not at fault; the *deployment script* was. The proof's boundary had been precise, and therefore brittle. Formal methods reduce risk, but only for the world they describe.

Contrast this with an approach that blends automation and community audit: *open review*. Yearn Finance, a yield aggregator launched in 2020 by Andre Cronje, relied not on a single audit firm but on persistent community scrutiny. Every contract was open, every deployment public. Bugs were found, debated, patched, redeployed—often in hours. The system was messy, yet adaptive. The credible counter-example here is not chaos but scale: open review thrives in small, engaged ecosystems. In complex multi-contract architectures, few possess the bandwidth or incentive to audit continuously. The reconciliation lies in layering: formal verification for core invariants, independent audits for broad hygiene, and community visibility for operational drift.

Audits fail most often where curiosity stops. Many reports include phrases like "low-severity issue" or "out of scope". These are invitations for attackers. A low-severity misconfiguration can become high-severity when combined with another overlooked function. An "out-of-scope" dependency can inherit a vulnerability from a different protocol. The Poly Network hack in August 2021, which drained $610 million before funds were returned, exploited a cross-chain message verification flaw that none of the component audits covered because each team assumed the other's code was secure. The bridge between scopes was the bridge that broke.

The professional learns to treat reports as *maps of assumptions*. Each "resolved" or "acknowledged" note hides an untested future state. A well-read auditor's report should be annotated like a pilot's checklist: where are the limits, what parameters changed since, who holds upgrade authority, and how are new dependencies reviewed? In this frame, scepticism becomes respect. You respect the work by not worshipping it.

Scepticism also extends to *tooling*. Automated scanners such as Slither and MythX identify thousands of potential issues per codebase. They are indispensable for scale, yet they breed complacency. False positives can dull intuition; false negatives can breed false confidence. The discipline is to use machines for pattern detection, not for judgement. The question "why does this not trigger an alert?" is more valuable than "what did it flag?". The professional learns to listen to silence as much as to signal.

In a maturing industry, the economics of security are shifting. Audit firms now command six-figure fees and multi-month queues. Some protocols spend more on audits than on development. This is progress of a kind, but it risks creating an *audit monoculture*—where safety is outsourced, and reputational badges replace architectural thinking. The corrective is to integrate security upstream: threat modelling before design, invariant definition before line one of code. Audits then validate preparation, not patch improvisation.

History reminds us that security cultures evolve only after losses. The aerospace industry adopted redundant systems after crashes; the financial sector codified segregation of duties after frauds; open-source software learned version control through failure. DeFi is still absorbing its own blood price. Each exploit adds to a canon of case studies that, properly read, teach not despair but discipline. The great irony is that decentralisation magnifies individual responsibility. There is no central authority to compensate victims. Therefore, prudence is no longer optional. It is fiduciary.

The motif of the *mirror* returns. Every audit is a mirror held to the current state of code. The reflection can be polished, detailed, even beautiful—but it remains static. The adversary, by contrast, moves. They test the edges of light, looking for where the reflection stops. The professional response is not to polish harder but to keep the mirror moving—to audit continuously, to verify updates, to question dependencies.

Where does this leave the practitioner? With a paradox worth holding: trust audits enough to act, distrust them enough to watch. Use them as instruments of learning, not insurance. Ask not only "has this been audited?" but "by whom, when, for what, and against which assumptions?" Then act as if no one has. The tension will never resolve completely. It is not meant to. That tension—the refusal to relax into certainty—is the heartbeat of real security.

Social Engineering is the Real Bridge

On 20 February 2022, OpenSea, the largest NFT marketplace, suffered what at first looked like a contract exploit. Panic spread across Twitter and Discord: wallets drained, prized digital artworks vanished, and whispers of a new "zero-day" flaw rippled through the community. Yet when the dust settled, the codebase was fine. The attackers had not breached a smart contract—they had breached people. They posed as OpenSea support staff, sending direct messages to users who were already nervous about a scheduled contract migration. The victims clicked a link, signed what they thought were safe approval transactions, and authorised their own theft. A hundred NFTs changed hands. The bridge the hackers crossed was not digital but psychological.

DeFi's most potent vulnerability is not code complexity but human confidence. Where a protocol's logic demands precision, human conversation invites ambiguity. A contract cannot be flattered, frightened, or rushed; a person can. Social engineering thrives not by defeating cryptography but by mimicking credibility. It weaponises empathy, authority, and routine. In decentralised finance, where users hold direct custody of assets and rely on interfaces that blend social and technical trust, this intersection is perilous. The same chat window that delivers community updates can deliver ruin.

Show → Name → Explain → Implication. Show: a Telegram group buzzing with token launch anticipation, where "admin" messages look identical whether authentic or fake. Name: *channel mirroring*. Explain: attackers clone official community groups, lure users with time-sensitive announcements, and post counterfeit links that lead to signature requests. Implication: the battlefield is perception. The victim's interface looks normal; the danger lies in the invisible signature payload. A moment's haste converts curiosity into loss.

The *illusion of familiarity* is the oldest trick in the digital con. In April 2021, a scam targeting MetaMask users spread across Twitter DMs, using profile photos of legitimate support staff and language lifted directly from the wallet's FAQ. The scammers offered "quick help" for pending transactions and linked to a site that harvested seed phrases. Tens of thousands of dollars disappeared in minutes. The victims were not naïve; they were overloaded. The attackers did not need malware when mimicry sufficed.

Social engineering adapts faster than technical defence. After the collapse of FTX in November 2022, panic opened fresh attack surfaces. Scammers circulated "claim refund" forms through Discord, exploiting both urgency and grief. The victims were not careless—they were emotional. The tactic worked because it framed theft as restitution. This inversion—posing as rescue rather than risk—is a recurring pattern. As blockchain interactions become more normalised, the emotional triggers remain ancient: fear of loss, desire for help, trust in symbols of authority.

Contrast these digital con artists with an earlier analogue. In 2013, a spear-phishing campaign against employees of the Associated Press tricked them into sharing login credentials. Moments later, the AP's hacked Twitter account falsely reported explosions at the White House, briefly erasing $136 billion in market value before recovery. The parallels with DeFi are eerie: one compromised credential, one believable message, cascading systemic consequence.

Whether it's a journalist or a yield farmer, the vector is the same—trust repurposed.

Counter-example sharpens understanding. Some argue that decentralised systems, by virtue of transparency, should be resistant to social engineering. After all, every transaction is visible, every signature verifiable. Yet visibility is not the same as comprehension. Most users cannot read bytecode or parse approval traces in real time. Attackers know this and disguise malicious requests as benign operations. The visual language of wallets—green ticks, verified icons, confirm buttons—creates a rhythm of consent. The reconciliation is clear: transparency without literacy is camouflage, not clarity.

The motif of the *click* threads through all these stories. One click to connect a wallet. One click to sign a message. One click too fast. Each interface compresses complex cryptographic authority into gestures measured in milliseconds. The attacker's goal is to accelerate that gesture. Slow-click reflexes—pausing to check domain names, contract addresses, and social channels—are the human equivalent of two-factor authentication. They buy time for reason to catch up with trust.

Formal security frameworks treat human error as a residual variable; in DeFi, it is central. Most major protocols now include "phishing disclaimers" on their interfaces, but these act as warning labels, not shields. Some developers, like those behind Uniswap Labs, have begun blacklisting known scam URLs directly within front-ends, effectively embedding reputational filters into code. Yet this approach raises its own paradox: decentralisation's ethos is openness, but safety often requires curation. The balance between freedom and protection remains unsettled.

Case studies show that *context* determines vulnerability. During the 2020–21 bull run, fake airdrops proliferated. Attackers exploited FOMO by dropping counterfeit tokens into legitimate wallets, each with a website promising instant conversion. The only way to "claim" was to connect and approve—authorising a drain. The victims were not tricked by design, but by narrative. They assumed success must involve recognition, and recognition must arrive through the channels they already used. It was a social story disguised as a financial one.

Professional scepticism reframes this dynamic. Security experts now treat *social surface area* as quantifiable exposure. The more channels a protocol maintains—Twitter, Discord, Telegram, Reddit—the more opportunities exist for impersonation. Each platform multiplies trust dependencies. During 2021, Compound Finance limited direct support interactions after impostors flooded their Discord, replacing human moderation with automated ticketing and signed support responses. The result: slower responses, fewer compromises. Efficiency decreased. Integrity improved.

The credible counterweight is accessibility. Excessive scepticism can alienate newcomers and erode participation. A system so fortified that no one dares interact ceases to be decentralised in practice. The reconciliation lies not in universal caution but in *rehearsed caution*. Train reflexes, not fear. Encourage communities to stage mock scams—controlled phishing drills that demonstrate, without harm, how persuasion feels. This mirrors cybersecurity training in traditional sectors, adapted for on-chain life. Culture becomes defence.

Human stories make the lesson visceral. In 2022, a developer known as "0xN" shared that he had lost access to funds after a fake Metamask update prompted him to enter his seed phrase. The site looked identical to the real one, right down to the support icon. His postmortem was not bitter—it was pedagogical. "I wasn't tired or greedy," he wrote. "I was just fast." That line has since become a shorthand in DeFi circles for the cost of speed. Every signature has velocity; wisdom lives in friction.

Speed is the enemy's ally. Platforms now experiment with built-in *cooling periods* for high-risk approvals—brief delays before large transfers or new contract permissions take effect. Argent wallet introduced such timelocks in 2021, allowing users to cancel suspicious actions before execution. This design borrows from behavioural economics: replace "trust" with *time to verify*. The slower the bridge, the safer the crossing.

The motif returns: the click. Technology promises instant confirmation; security demands deliberate hesitation. To cultivate that habit is not to retreat from innovation but to preserve it. A decentralised system survives only if its users remain decentralised thinkers—questioning, verifying, resisting pressure.

The unresolved tension lies here. Can a community built on openness also cultivate scepticism without cynicism? Can speed coexist with safety when the same interface demands both? The next social-engineering wave will not announce itself with malicious code, but with empathy perfectly timed. When that message arrives—friendly, plausible, urgent—pause. The bridge is you.

On-Chain Signals That Matter

At 12:24 UTC on 17 April 2022, Ethereum block 14602789 recorded an odd choreography: a nine-figure flash loan, a governance vote, and a drain of collateral from Beanstalk's contracts—all within minutes, all perfectly visible on Etherscan. The post-mortems would take days; the on-chain story took seconds. Anyone who opened the transaction page could trace the money's route from lender to proposal to theft, step by step, long before social feeds agreed on a narrative. Read the chain before tweets. The lesson was not that explorers solve every puzzle, but that they offer primary evidence when noise surges.

Explorers are X-rays. They do not predict; they reveal. With a few habits—the right tabs, the right heuristics—you can turn wallet pop-ups and marketing threads into verifiable claims: how old a contract is, who can upgrade it, how concentrated the holder base is, where liquidity sits, and whether a "partnership" shows up as flows rather than adjectives. This is not forensic theatre. It is day-one safety. If autonomy is the burden of DeFi, independent visibility is your leverage over uncertainty.

Show → name → explain → implication. Show: you land on a token's page and see "Contract Created: 3 days ago." Name: *contract age*. Explain: most catastrophic failures happen in young code; three days is not proof of harm, but it is a signal to shrink size or wait. Implication: *time* is a risk discount you can measure. Mature contracts—USDC (deployed 2018), Aave's core money markets (v2 live since late 2020)—have endured more block-time and more eyes. Age does not sanctify, but it filters.

Next, the *verified source code* badge. When a contract publishes its source and the explorer attests that the bytecode matches, you can read functions, modifiers, and roles. This enables a second signal: *who can do what?* Click "Read/Write as Proxy" if the contract indicates a proxy pattern; then follow "Admin" to the implementation address and governance timelock. If an "owner" can pause transfers or mint at will, the risk is not abstract; it is a permission sitting behind a private key or multisig. Implication: *role power equals counterparty risk*. You do not need to fear it. You do need to size it.

Holders matter. Not as slogans, as distributions. Open the "Holders" tab for a token and look at concentration: top 10 wallets, percentage in each, and labels—"Uniswap V2 Pair", "Treasury", "Deployer". Name: *holder concentration*. Explain: if one or two EOAs hold the lion's share outside liquidity pools and treasuries, price is a hostage to a decision. If most supply sits in contracts labelled "staking" or "masterchef", check those contracts' admins. Implication: marketing says "community". The ledger says "who can crash this". Believe the ledger.

Liquidity lives in pools. Click through to the token's main AMM pair and inspect LP token holders. Name: *liquidity custody*. Explain: if the pair's LP tokens sit in an unlabeled deployer wallet, liquidity can be pulled without warning. If they sit in a time-locked contract or a reputable locker, exit risk falls. If the pool is split across thin, obscure venues, slippage will punish you when you most need to sell. Implication: your personal liquidity is only as strong as the weakest pool you rely on. Size positions to the exit, not the entrance.

Flows tell stories words won't. The "Transactions" and "Internal Txns" tabs reveal whether a project that trumpets partnerships has actually moved funds to, or integrated with, the named counterparty. Name: *flow verification*. Explain: a "strategic collaboration" with a lending market should show deposits, borrows, or reserve factor changes; a "custody integration" should show movements between labelled cold wallets. Implication: if announcements leave no footprints, treat them as theatre until the chain disagrees. Evidence beats copy.

Two named, checkable examples illustrate how these signals separate narrative from reality. First, **Curve's 3pool** (DAI/USDC/USDT; launched January 2020 on Ethereum).

Its contracts are verified; admin parameters are governed by a DAO with visible timelocks; liquidity is deep and custody distributed across LP holders and gauges with public addresses. An explorer view shows multi-year age, predictable parameter changes, and constant, high-volume flows. Each of these is an X-ray sign of structural resilience. Second, **the stETH–ETH pool on Curve during June 2022**. A glance at the pool's "Reserves" and trade history showed a rapidly widening imbalance—more stETH than ETH—as large actors sought exits. No rumour was needed. The on-chain ratio told you liquidity would slip before press did. Both cases show why explorers are not optional. They compress confusion into state.

A credible counter-example tempers overconfidence. **USDC depegged briefly in March 2023** after the failure of Silicon Valley Bank exposed Circle's banking links. On-chain, USDC looked old, verified, and widely held—strong signals. Yet the peg moved because off-chain trust moved. The explorer could not show banking risk; it could show how quickly traders rotated to other stables, and where liquidity thinned first. Reconciling this teaches humility: on-chain signals are necessary, not sufficient. They illuminate what *is*, not what *must be*.

Part of professionalising scepticism is learning to read *approvals*. Before you sign a transaction, copy the contract address and paste it into an explorer. Click "Token Approvals" (or use a reputable approvals dashboard) and review allowances you have already granted to that address. Name: *approval surface*. Explain: most large personal losses start with unlimited approvals to malicious or compromised contracts. The explorer shows the live state: an approval you forgot, an allowance set to max. Implication: revoke is not drama. It is hygiene.

Explorer breadcrumbs also reveal *dev and deployer behaviour*. Inspect the deployer address: did it fund itself from a fresh, exchange-funded wallet moments before launch (common in fly-by-night deployments), or from long-standing multisigs linked to known teams? Does the deployer still hold admin keys, or has control migrated to a timelock or DAO? In October 2020, when Uniswap airdropped UNI and launched governance, the deployer and governance contract addresses were public, balances readable, and timelocks visible. The signals did not guarantee success; they established provenance. Conversely, tokens that rotate deployers or hide admins behind privacy tools increase your *model error*. Implication: unknown is not evil; unknown at size is reckless.

Bridges deserve extra caution. On explorers, bridge contracts often show huge balances and frequent internal transactions. Name: *bridge blast radius*. Explain: a bug in message verification or a compromised validator set can drain funds across chains, as the **Ronin** incident (March 2022) and **Wormhole** (February 2022) demonstrated. On-chain, you can check whether a bridge uses a multisig with labelled signers, whether there is a timelock on upgrades, and whether recent transactions include emergency admin calls. Implication: composability magnifies both convenience and catastrophe. If you must cross, cross where the signage is legible.

Not all signals are in the code. *Gas* is a tell. Spikes around a token's trades may reflect MEV bots arbitraging thin liquidity; constant failed transactions near a contract can indicate users struggling with slippage or traps. *Event logs* are a second tell: large "Mint" or "Burn" events outside documented schedules, or unusual "Transfer" events to new, unlabeled contracts, should trigger caution. And *function names* matter: if a token includes setTax, blacklist, or swapAndLiquify in a speculative microcap, you are not guessing at risk. You are reading it. Implication: words inside code outweigh words on websites.

Make abstraction operational with a tabletop drill. You hear of a new yield vault. What do you ask the chain? Contract age and verification? Yes. Admin powers and upgradeability? Yes. Holder concentration? Yes. Liquidity custody and LP token holders? Yes. Flow evidence of the touted strategy (deposits into Aave, trades on a DEX, bribes claimed)? Yes. Off-chain claims like audits? Check the report hash and see whether the exact bytecode was audited. Now trace the next hop: where do users exit in stress? If the answer is "the same thin pool everyone else uses", you have a self-answering question on size.

Two further examples show explorers as instruments for *independent timing*. In **May 2021**, at Uniswap v3 launch, fee growth in major pairs could be seen by watching per-pool fee accumulators and LP positions by tick range. LPs who looked first adjusted ranges with data; those who waited for threads trailed. In **November 2022** after FTX's halt, stablecoin flows into and out of centralised exchange wallets labelled on Etherscan and Nansen showed confidence deterioration hours before public statements did. The chain did not say "insolvent". It said "leaving". That was enough.

A limit must be stated plainly: explorers can create false certainty. A verified contract tells you what functions exist, not that they are safe. A DAO timelock shows parameter changes, not whether delegates understand them. Labels can be wrong or lag reality. The correct response is not cynicism; it is *triangulation.* Cross-read addresses across multiple explorers; follow links to implementation contracts; check time stamps against governance forums; correlate on-chain flows with known announcement times. If the story lines up, risk falls. If it diverges, reduce exposure or demand better evidence.

Turn the X-ray back on yourself. Your own wallet page shows a biography of risk: old approvals you forgot to revoke, airdropped scam tokens sitting like landmines, and a cluster of interactions with contracts you barely remember. Clean it. Revoke with intention. Tag addresses you trust. Create a watchlist of contracts whose parameter changes should ping you (Aave interest rate strategies; Maker vault collateral updates; Curve pool weights). Independent visibility is not only for others. It is for you.

The motif returns: the X-ray. It does not judge; it shows structure. A professional learns to look through skin and marketing to the bone—age, permissions, holders, flows. From that anatomy, posture follows: size smaller in youth; diversify when holders are narrow; exit faster when liquidity is thin; demand governance clarity when admin reach is long. The reward is not omniscience. It is fewer surprises.

One last scene to hold. In August 2021, during the Poly Network breach, the attacker began returning funds days later, leaving messages in transaction data fields. The explorer made a theatre of it, but the substance was still the ledger: where the money was, who could move it, and under what code. Opinion shifted hourly. State did not. That is the promise of on-chain literacy.

The unresolved test is simple and personal. Before you act on the next "opportunity", can you, within five minutes on an explorer, answer four questions: how old is the contract; who can change it; how concentrated are holders; and where will your exit trade clear under stress? If not, are you comfortable outsourcing those answers to someone whose incentives you cannot see? The chain is not a prophecy. It is a mirror. Learn to look.

Personal Incident Response

At 08:00 on 20 September 2022, in London, Wintermute disclosed a major DeFi theft triggered by a vulnerability in a vanity-address tool. Within hours, the firm had fenced compromised hot wallets, restored market-making on selected venues, and began negotiating with the attacker from the address that drained funds. What stood out was not the loss; it was the tempo. The response unspooled like muscle memory: isolate, rotate, communicate. No slogans. Just steps. That same month, after a DNS hijack on Curve Finance's front end misdirected users to malicious approvals, those who had rehearsed revocation routines detached their wallets calmly while others learned, live, what an "allowance" meant. Breathe. Follow the plan now.

"Incident response" sounds corporate until you need it in your own wallet at midnight. In decentralised finance, there is no helpdesk that can reverse time. Your only advantage is preparation that compresses chaos into minutes and preserves capital by forcing sequence. The motif throughout is the *checklist*. Aeroplanes rely on them because stress erases working memory. So does a live drain. Four verbs guide everything: revoke, quarantine, rotate, report. Each is a behaviour you can practise; each turns abstraction into action.

Show → name → explain → implication. Show: you notice an approval pop-up you do not expect, or an unfamiliar contract appears in your signer history. Name: *trigger recognition*. Explain: incidents rarely announce themselves with sirens; they arrive as small mismatches—an ask for "unlimited" where you expected a number, a domain homograph, a token you never bought landing in your wallet. Implication: the first skill is not technical; it is attentional. Train yourself to stop when something feels off. Friction is a feature.

Revoke is the first verb because most losses begin with permission, not a trade. On Ethereum and EVM chains, token approvals grant contracts the right to transfer your assets within limits you set. When those limits are "infinite"—the default in too many interfaces—you have created an open tab the attacker can run up. The behaviour is plain: maintain a shortlist of reputable approval viewers bookmarked; when suspicion rises, check allowances for the last contracts you touched and set them to zero. This is not a talisman. It is plumbing. The metric that matters is *time-to-revoke*: the minutes it takes from noticing trouble to executing a revocation. You can measure it. Practise until it is under five.

BadgerDAO's front-end compromise in December 2021 taught this lesson with cruel clarity. Users interacted with a familiar site that silently injected approvals to a malicious contract. Those who throttled their allowances routinely—or who had practised revocation—suffered less. Those who treated approvals as harmless suffered more. The implication is hard-edged: caution around approvals is not paranoia; it is hygiene. If your workflow normalises "max" allowances to anonymous contracts, an incident is not a question of *if*. It is a calendar entry.

Quarantine is the second verb and the most neglected. Once you suspect compromise, your instinct is to move *everything* everywhere. That impulse can compound damage: you sign more transactions on a poisoned machine, you expose clean wallets to tainted allowances, you migrate across bridges during volatility and pay dearly for slippage. Quarantine means *cordon and contain*. Stop interacting with the suspected interface. Disconnect wallet sessions. Power down the compromised device and switch to a known-clean one. If funds must move, move only what is necessary to a pre-prepared, *sterile* address whose seed and signing path have never touched the suspect environment. The visible behaviour here is the existence of that sterile address before trouble. If you do not have it, you improvise under stress. That is when errors multiply.

Quarantine also applies to *venues*. If the incident relates to a specific dApp or bridge, do not "test" with small amounts through the same route to see if it was you or them; that converts a suspected failure mode into a confirmed one. In August 2022, when the Nomad bridge was exploited and open copying of the attacker's transactions began, some users attempted partial withdrawals through the same contracts. They lost what they tried to save. Quarantine would have meant stillness: wait, gather facts, use an alternative route when trusted parties publish a safe path.

Rotate is where autonomy becomes work. If you detect compromise of a seed phrase, passphrase, or hardware device, *new keys* are not optional. They are the only restore. Rotation has layers: change passwords on any custodial accounts linked to the compromised device; regenerate fresh seed phrases on hardware wallets you initialise on a clean machine; migrate critical assets to these new addresses; revoke residual allowances from the old accounts *after* assets have moved, not before, to avoid signing extra messages on a poisoned signer. A credible limitation lives here: rotation is slower than revocation. During 12–13 March 2020 ("Black Thursday"), gas prices spiked so sharply that many users could not push transactions for hours. The reconciliation comes from rehearsal: pre-fund a small gas reserve in a secondary wallet so that rotation is not throttled by the very panic that demands it.

Rotation also means *changing communication channels*. Social engineers often pair technical compromise with impersonation. If your Discord, Telegram, or email account ties to your Web3 identity, assume those contacts are at risk. Announce from a verified secondary channel that you are rotating; do not reply to inbound offers of help. During the OpenSea phishing wave of February 2022, scammers cloned staff profiles and reached out to victims mid-incident offering "assistance"; victims who rotated keys but kept talking to the wrong people re-exposed themselves. The practice is dull: silence first, then broadcast *once* from a place your counterparts can verify.

Report is the last verb because clarity follows containment. Reporting serves three functions: it alerts others, it creates forensic artefacts for later claims, and it helps you think. Good reports are specific: contract addresses, transaction hashes, block times, domains. Avoid adjectives; provide links. Teams cannot help if they must decode your emotions first. In November 2019, when ChainSecurity warned MakerDAO of a pre-launch vulnerability, the quality of the report—the invariants at risk, the exact code path—bought decision time. Your version will be humbler but can follow the same ethos: facts first, theories later.

Two named, checkable cases show these steps turning panic into protocol. Wintermute's September 2022 disclosure coupled admission with a timeline, addresses, and a path forward; counterparties could filter signals from noise because they had data. Curve's September 2022 DNS incident produced a clear directive from the core team—"do not use the site; use contracts directly"—and a list of known-bad domains. Users who had practised direct contract interaction via explorers, or who followed dev-signed advisories, were able to revoke and rotate without chasing rumours. In both scenes, the decisive factor was neither code nor cleverness; it was prepared behaviour.

A credible counter-example tempers neatness. Not every revoke–quarantine–rotate sequence produces salvation. Some attacks are too fast. In March 2023, when a widely used wallet connector dependency was compromised for a brief window, thousands signed malicious approvals within minutes. Gas surged; mempools clogged; revocations competed badly. Users who had rehearsed still lost funds. The reconciliation is sober: preparedness reduces harm; it does not eliminate it. The lesson is not despair but *redundancy*. Multiple hardware wallets, multiple RPC endpoints, multiple routes for announcements—these reduce the chance that a single jam turns injury into amputation.

Turn abstractions into metrics you can manage. *Exposure surface*: count active approvals across your top five addresses each month; keep it low. *Time-to-safe*: measure how long it takes you to (a) detect and (b) revoke and (c) move to sterile storage on a clean device; compress with practice. *Key freshness*: record the date each seed was generated; rotate any that share history with suspect software or public computers. *Comms integrity*: list where you will post in a crisis—Twitter, a signed message from your address, a DAO forum—and test that your peers recognise those signals.

Practise, then automate what you can. Schedule quarterly "chaos drills" on a Saturday morning: simulate a front-end compromise; attempt revocation from a burner laptop; move a trivial amount to a sterile address; post a mock incident note with hashes and block times. Time yourselves. You are not training for a certificate; you are inoculating reflexes. In institutional settings, codify this as runbooks: who holds the hardware spares; who has sign-off to pause operations; which multisig threshold can act without quorum during a live drain; how to rotate guardians in a smart-contract wallet without bricking access. Dull? Deliberately. Drama is the enemy.

Move from solo to team by pre-assigning roles. In a DAO treasury, one signer owns detection (monitoring alert feeds and on-chain watchers), another owns containment (pushes revokes, pauses automated strategies), a third owns communication (publishes signed updates). Separation of duties is not bureaucracy; it is latency management. Human throughput declines under stress. Split the work.

Incident response also extends to *post-incident* discipline. After containment, you must close the loop. Catalogue what failed—tooling, posture, judgement. If the trigger was a homograph domain, buy close spellings. If it was a hasty signature, adjust wallet settings to require explicit gas and nonce confirmation. If it was an approval you forgot, create a monthly revoke habit. Public post-mortems matter because they turn private errors into communal memory. When Nomad's team documented their bridge's flaw and retrieval effort (August 2022), they armed others against similar designs. Tragedy becomes textbook.

A word on emotion. You will feel shame. It is misplaced. Attackers are professionals. You are outnumbered. What matters is not whether you were duped but how quickly you transmute embarrassment into procedure. The checklist is medicine for the amygdala: it swaps rumination for sequence. Revoke. Quarantine. Rotate. Report. Then rest. Then review.

Limitations deserve honesty. Revokes can fail if the network is congested. Hardware can brick. A "sterile" address can later be contaminated by habit. Reporting may invite opportunists. Accept these as parameters, not excuses. The countermeasure is *diversity*: a second hardware wallet from a different vendor; a second browser profile that never installs extensions; a second RPC provider in your wallet settings; a second person who can carry the plan if you are asleep.

The motif returns: the checklist. You are not building heroics; you are building a habit of *order under pressure*. The craft is to make the first move so obvious that you can execute it half-asleep, to make the second move so practised that your hands know it, and to make the third move so well-defined that you trust it even when your pulse disagrees. There is dignity in that.

One last scene to keep. During the MakerDAO turbulence in March 2020, a handful of teams saved positions by scripting repayments that fired automatically when collateral ratios hit a pre-set line. They had converted intention into automation. That is the end-state of personal incident response too: a plan so rehearsed that, when the message arrives—friendly, plausible, urgent—you act slower where it matters and faster where it counts. Which brings us to the forward test that matters. If your wallet buzzed now with a signature you did not expect, could you, within five minutes, revoke what needs revoking, move what must move, swap to fresh keys, and tell the people who must know—without asking anyone what to do first? If the answer is not yet, your plan is not a plan. It is a wish. Fix it while the screen is still calm.

Chapter 7
The Regulatory Weather

In December 2020, a few paragraphs buried deep within a U.S. Treasury proposal sent ripples through the decentralised world. The document, published in Washington under Secretary Steven Mnuchin, suggested new recordkeeping rules for self-hosted wallets. No bans, no seizures—just data. Yet within hours, crypto markets reacted as if a storm warning had been issued. Discord servers buzzed with talk of "wallet surveillance," legal think-tanks drafted rebuttals overnight, and a simple bureaucratic consultation became a referendum on sovereignty. For regulators, it was paperwork; for developers, it was prophecy. The question was not whether rules were coming, but what kind of weather they would bring—and who would be left standing when the clouds cleared.

DeFi has always existed at the edge of legal geometry. The code executes in public, but its authors live in private; the functions mirror those of banks, brokers, and exchanges, yet the wrappers dissolve on contact. Lending, swapping, custody, market-making—each has its counterpart in legacy finance, each carries an invisible twin in the law. What makes the discussion volatile is not ignorance but translation. When regulators speak of "custody," they imagine possession through intermediaries; when DeFi practitioners hear the same word, they think of keys. When lawmakers say "disclosure," they mean paperwork;

developers mean open source. Both sides talk of "integrity," but one means ethics, the other means hash verification. The task of this chapter is not to take sides but to make these mismatched languages intelligible to each other.

Regulation, like weather, is cyclical, uneven, and inescapable. It does not arrive everywhere at once. The European Union drafts MiCA (Markets in Crypto-Assets Regulation) to define obligations for stablecoins and service providers; Singapore crafts the Payment Services Act to channel innovation through licensing; the United States debates whether tokens are commodities, securities, or neither. Each jurisdiction measures risk through its own moral barometer—consumer protection in Brussels, financial integrity in Washington, competitiveness in Dubai. For a protocol that lives on-chain, these lines mean little until an exchange delists, a bridge freezes, or a stablecoin becomes untradeable overnight. Jurisdiction may be an offline idea, but its consequences are on-chain.

What makes prudence valuable here is *ambiguity*. The rules are not yet written for the medium DeFi inhabits, yet their shadows already shape it. Most projects cannot wait for legal certainty; they must act under probability, not promise. The professionals who thrive are those who learn to *track* the weather—to follow central bank speeches, Financial Action Task Force updates, and enforcement actions as signals rather than threats. This form of literacy, half legal and half behavioural, is the new due diligence. It is the difference between operating *under* scrutiny and operating *in spite of* it.

The most charged frontier in this landscape is identity. KYC—Know Your Customer—was once a slogan for gatekeepers; in DeFi, it has become a puzzle for engineers. The ideological version of the debate pits privacy against compliance, liberty against order. The operational version is quieter but more consequential: how can a system prove legitimacy without exposing identity? Privacy-preserving compliance patterns—zero-knowledge proofs of personhood, selective disclosure credentials, wallet scoring based on behaviour rather than name—are already in live testing. Projects like Polygon ID, zkKYC by zkSync, and the Financial Action Task Force's 2023 pilot programmes hint at a world where transparency and discretion coexist uneasily but productively. Yet every technical fix carries a social cost. Too much verification, and anonymity dies; too little, and access vanishes. DeFi's ideological debates mask an engineering dilemma: how to encode trust without surrender.

The regulatory theatre often turns on optics. When the Office of Foreign Assets Control (OFAC) sanctioned Tornado Cash in August 2022, the shock was not only about privacy but about precedent. A *smart contract* had been blacklisted—a neutral protocol treated as an entity. GitHub accounts vanished, front-ends went dark, and governance tokens plunged. But the contract itself persisted. No decree could un-write it. The episode revealed the friction between code's permanence and law's conditionality. Sanctions and delistings can change liquidity overnight, but they cannot erase the underlying logic. The professional question, then, is not "Will DeFi survive regulation?" but "How will it adapt to its rhythms?"

History offers perspective. Every wave of financial innovation has met its regulatory reckoning: joint-stock companies in the 17th century, derivatives in the 1980s, peer-to-peer lending in the 2010s. Each began in legal grey zones; each matured through confrontation. Regulation, at its best, does not extinguish new forms—it teaches them to survive sunlight. Yet for participants, the early phases always feel existential. In 2021, Uniswap delisted certain synthetic assets from its interface, not because the contracts were illegal, but because legal *uncertainty* carried reputational risk. The contracts continued to function independently; the front-end folded under pressure. For users who believed "decentralised" meant invincible, this was an education. Function survives; visibility can vanish.

The motif of *weather* runs through these stories deliberately. A storm does not choose sides. It tests structure. DeFi's open architecture makes it unusually exposed—any change in legal temperature can condense instantly into operational frost. Yet storms also clarify: they reveal which bridges are load-bearing and which roofs were built for calm skies. The most enduring projects will be those that design for regulatory volatility—modular governance, composable compliance, liquidity diversification across jurisdictions. The point is not defiance but resilience.

This chapter will trace that terrain in depth: how DeFi's core functions map onto regulated analogues; how jurisdictional variability shapes strategy; how privacy-preserving compliance is evolving; and how design can absorb rule changes with minimal collateral damage. Beneath each topic runs the same question: *what does responsibility look like when rules are unfinished?* For the architect of a protocol, for the investor holding tokens across continents, for the researcher tracing flows that straddle legality and innovation—the challenge is to remain both informed and adaptive, sceptical yet constructive.

The deeper insight is that regulation is not external to DeFi; it is becoming *internalised* within it. Smart contracts now embed compliance logic; DAOs debate sanctions lists; wallets offer built-in risk scoring. The frontier is no longer "code versus law" but "law inside code." As this convergence accelerates, the distinction between regulators and developers blurs: both are writing rulebooks, one in statutes, one in Solidity.

The chapter ends where the forecast begins—with uncertainty. No one can chart the weather precisely, but everyone can read the barometer. The professionals who endure will be those who treat regulation not as a storm to outlast but as a climate to inhabit. The question is not whether decentralised finance will fit the rules, but whether it can evolve fast enough to define them.

Same Functions, New Wrappers

In June 2022, at the headquarters of the U.S. Commodity Futures Trading Commission in Washington, a panel convened to discuss decentralised derivatives. The officials found themselves in an odd mirror: liquidity pools behaving like clearing houses, automated market makers replicating quote-driven exchanges, and governance tokens distributing rights that once belonged to shareholders. The chair, Rostin Behnam, remarked that "the functions are familiar, the forms are not." It was a moment of recognition and discomfort. The financial system had met its reflection in code, stripped of human intermediaries but humming with the same incentives. The issue was no longer novelty, but jurisdiction—who was in charge when nobody held the keys?

The motif of the mirror recurs because DeFi does not invent finance; it refracts it. A decentralised exchange clears trades, a lending protocol allocates capital, a liquidity pool provides market depth, a stablecoin anchors confidence. Each mirrors a regulated analogue: exchanges, banks, market-makers, and currencies. The differences lie not in purpose but in custody, disclosure, and integrity—the pillars on which regulatory oversight rests. DeFi challenges each by replacing institutional accountability with cryptographic transparency. What was once enforced by law is now enforced by logic. Yet mirrors, while accurate, are not reality. They invert.

Show → name → explain → implication. Show: Uniswap executes a trade between two tokens through an automated pool rather than a broker. Name: *decentralised exchange function equivalence*. Explain: the mechanism performs the same role as a regulated exchange—price discovery, matching, settlement—but without human intermediaries or central custody. Implication: functionally identical outcomes arise through divergent risk channels. Market abuse in traditional exchanges centres on insider information; in DeFi, it centres on miner extractable value and sandwich attacks. The label changes; the ethical test remains.

Custody is the first axis of difference. In regulated finance, custodianship is a profession—banks and brokers safeguard client assets under fiduciary duty. In DeFi, custody collapses into possession: whoever controls the private key owns the asset. This disintermediation is both liberation and liability. Mt. Gox's 2014 collapse illustrated the perils of custodial opacity; users lost 650,000 bitcoins when entrusted control turned fraudulent. DeFi emerged partly as a reaction to that event, promising self-custody and verifiable reserves. Yet self-custody also transfers operational risk to individuals who may misclick or lose seed phrases. A protocol like Aave does not "hold" user funds; it locks them in contracts accessible only by code. If that code is flawed, no regulator or trustee can restore what vanishes. The implication is profound: the line between custodian and user blurs into software, and accountability migrates from people to design.

Disclosure is the second axis. Traditional finance demands ex-ante disclosure: prospectuses, audited statements, and periodic filings reviewed by agencies such as the SEC or FCA. DeFi flips this temporal order. Smart contracts publish code first; participants read—or fail to read—its logic. Audits exist, but they are market signals, not regulatory requirements. In August 2021, Compound's upgrade bug distributed $90 million in unintended rewards to users because of a single misconfigured line. The contract was public, the risk visible, yet disclosure without comprehension proved hollow. The contrast underscores the difference between *disclosed* and *understood*. Regulators measure integrity through documentation; DeFi assumes transparency equals fairness. The mirror shows a truth regulators know well: transparency without literacy is theatre.

Integrity, the third axis, binds the system's social contract. Regulated finance maintains integrity through licensure, sanctions, and legal deterrence. DeFi replaces these with incentive alignment and game theory. Slashing mechanisms, governance votes, and immutable ledgers aim to internalise moral hazard. MakerDAO's overcollateralisation rule functions as a self-imposed prudential standard; Curve's time-locked governance prevents sudden parameter manipulation. Yet both rely on voluntary participation rather than statutory enforcement.

In October 2021, the CFTC fined the decentralised prediction platform Polymarket $1.4 million for offering unregistered event contracts. The fine targeted the corporate entity behind the front-end, not the protocol's logic, demonstrating that integrity in law still maps to human actors even when code executes autonomously. The implication is that decentralisation can redistribute responsibility but cannot erase it.

Two named examples clarify the symmetry. First, **Aave**, launched January 2020, operates as a decentralised money market. It pools deposits, prices risk, and issues collateralised loans—functions indistinguishable from a wholesale lender. Yet it does so through algorithmic interest rate curves and liquidation bots rather than credit officers. Second, **Uniswap**, first deployed November 2018, offers spot exchange with continuous liquidity via automated market makers. It performs precisely the role of an exchange but removes listing committees and market-makers as intermediaries. Both replicate financial infrastructure through code. Their strength lies in auditability; their weakness lies in the absence of recourse. If an error occurs, you can prove it happened but not compel correction.

A credible counter-example complicates the narrative. **Terra's collapse in May 2022** was not a failure of disclosure—the code and mechanism were public—nor of custody, since users held self-sovereign tokens. It was a failure of design integrity: an algorithmic promise that could not survive market pressure. Traditional finance has analogues—Long-Term Capital Management's 1998 failure, for instance—but regulation there provided structured resolution. In DeFi, collapse unfolds in real time, with no circuit breakers, no lender of last resort, no legal framework for redress. The reconciliation lies in recognising that functional equivalence does not guarantee systemic equivalence. Same outputs, different fault lines.

Custody debates converge on one recurring legal question: *when does control equal responsibility?* In September 2023, a U.S. court examined whether developers who deploy immutable smart contracts can be considered custodians. The reasoning oscillated between metaphors—writing code as authorship versus operating infrastructure as control. For regulators, "custody" implies ongoing authority; for developers, deployment severs it. This mismatch suggests a future where legal definitions evolve to accommodate non-human actors. Until then, prudence demands that projects operating interfaces or DAOs that earn fees assume fiduciary-like duties even without formal classification. Ethics often precedes law.

Disclosures, too, will evolve under pressure. The European Union's MiCA regulation, passed in April 2023, requires crypto-asset service providers to publish whitepapers akin to prospectuses, outlining risks and governance structures. While aimed at intermediaries, the spirit of MiCA foreshadows expectations that will likely extend to DeFi aggregators. Projects that voluntarily issue audit summaries, code provenance statements, and token distribution breakdowns pre-empt this scrutiny. The difference between proactive and reactive transparency is survival. A lesson from aviation applies: checklists codify lessons before regulators demand them.

Integrity, the hardest pillar to formalise, depends on the social layer. Trust migrates from institutions to communities, but communities fracture. DAOs offer democratic control yet face voter apathy and capture. The June 2022 *Solend* incident, where a DAO attempted to seize a whale's position to prevent liquidation cascades, mirrored the discretionary power centralised exchanges once held. The vote reversed after backlash, proving that decentralisation constrains authority but not temptation. The implication is not that DeFi is less ethical, but that it rehearses old dilemmas in new syntax. Governance remains the mirror where ideology meets consequence.

The motif returns: the mirror. Each reflection of a regulated function in DeFi forces a reckoning about what regulation *really* protects. Custody rules protect against loss; DeFi replaces them with self-reliance. Disclosure rules protect against asymmetry; DeFi replaces them with radical transparency. Integrity rules protect against misconduct; DeFi replaces them with immutable logic and social consensus. Whether these substitutes suffice depends on human comprehension. Code can express fairness but cannot enforce understanding.

Across these axes, the same functions invite divergent virtues. A central bank prizes stability; a protocol prizes neutrality. A regulator demands identification; a network demands permissionlessness. Yet both aspire to the same end: orderly transfer of value. This convergence is why policymakers now speak of "same risk, same rules," even as they struggle to define which risks apply. In that ambiguity lies both threat and opportunity. The profession of compliance is slowly becoming an engineering discipline; the profession of engineering, a branch of ethics.

One must acknowledge a limitation. Equivalence between DeFi and traditional finance holds primarily at the micro level—transactional functions, capital flows, pricing. At the macro level—monetary policy, systemic stability, consumer protection—the parallels break down. DeFi lacks a central authority to coordinate stimulus, guarantee deposits, or resolve disputes. Yet, even that absence is instructive. It reminds us that regulation evolved as a response to failure. The open question is which failures DeFi must endure before its own adaptive regulation crystallises.

A quiet implication threads through this comparison: convergence is inevitable. Regulated entities will adopt DeFi primitives for efficiency; DeFi protocols will integrate compliance features for legitimacy. Fireblocks' institutional custody platforms already bridge regulated custody with smart-contract automation; Chainlink's proof-of-reserve feeds enable on-chain attestations aligned with audit standards. The wrappers may differ, but the logic is coalescing. Over time, the boundary between "decentralised" and "regulated" may prove less like a wall and more like a membrane—porous, adaptive, alive.

The forward test is simple but consequential. When you look into the mirror of DeFi's architecture, do you see a reflection of finance as it was, or a prototype of finance as it might become? The answer depends not on code alone but on whether integrity, transparency, and accountability—those ancient, regulated virtues—can be reborn in autonomous form. The weather ahead will decide which reflection hardens into reality.

Jurisdictional Variability

On 10 August 2022, the U.S. Treasury's Office of Foreign Assets Control sanctioned Tornado Cash, a privacy protocol on Ethereum. Within hours, its website was down, its GitHub repository removed, and its developer, Alexey Pertsev, arrested in Amsterdam. Yet the smart contract itself kept running—unstoppable, unowned, and defiantly neutral. What made this episode historic was not the arrest, but the asymmetry: the same code that was deemed illegal in one jurisdiction continued operating legally in another. DeFi had run headlong into the patchwork of national sovereignty. It was no longer a question of whether decentralised systems could outpace the law, but whether the law could meaningfully define where *any* of this was happening.

Regulation assumes geography; DeFi dissolves it. A protocol can be coded in Berlin, deployed from Singapore, governed by token-holders in Buenos Aires, and used by a trader in Nairobi. The architecture ignores borders, but enforcement does not. Each jurisdiction carries its own definition of "security," "custody," or "transfer," often drafted before blockchain existed. When these definitions collide, the same transaction may be legal in one place, restricted in another, and unclassified in a third. This variability is not chaos—it is the terrain. Professionals who treat it as noise misread the weather; those who map it find advantage.

Show → name → explain → implication. Show: A project lists a token on a decentralised exchange without realising that, in the United States, similar instruments have triggered securities actions. Name: *jurisdictional mismatch.* Explain: because the token is globally accessible, regulators anywhere can assert reach over its distribution if it touches their citizens or infrastructure. Implication: decentralisation does not neutralise geography; it multiplies it. The new competence is not coding but cartography—knowing which legal climates your protocol inhabits.

Consider two named, checkable examples. In April 2023, the European Parliament passed MiCA, the Markets in Crypto-Assets Regulation. It created clear licensing regimes for stablecoin issuers and service providers, establishing a single framework across 27 member states. The intent was certainty: if one met MiCA's standards in Paris, one could operate in Prague. Across the Atlantic, in June 2023, the U.S. Securities and Exchange Commission filed cases against Binance and Coinbase, alleging that several traded tokens constituted unregistered securities. No statute defined this; enforcement by interpretation did. The European approach sought coherence; the American approach, deterrence. Both sought integrity, yet through different instruments. The implication for DeFi builders is structural: identical conduct can invite licence in one jurisdiction and litigation in another.

A credible counter-example tempers this polarity. Switzerland's Financial Market Supervisory Authority (FINMA) has, since 2018, treated blockchain projects under a "technology-neutral" lens—same activity, same risk, same rules. This allowed projects such as Aave and Curve to register foundation entities in Zug without collapsing under regulatory uncertainty. Yet neutrality has limits. When sanctions law entered the conversation, even Swiss exchanges delisted certain privacy tokens. The reconciliation is pragmatic: technology neutrality ends where political consensus begins.

Jurisdictional variability is not static; it evolves by precedent and pressure. The Financial Action Task Force (FATF), a global body headquartered in Paris, publishes "recommendations" that function as moral gravity. Its June 2019 guidance extended anti–money laundering obligations to "virtual asset service providers," a phrase elastic enough to stretch over exchanges, custodians, and arguably, DAO operators. By June 2023, only 29 of FATF's 98 member jurisdictions had fully implemented those standards (FATF, 2023). This gap reveals a subtler truth: global uniformity exists rhetorically, not practically. The map of enforcement resembles weather fronts—dense in the U.S. and EU, sparse in Latin America and Africa, unpredictable in Asia.

The motif of *weather* fits because guidance behaves like climate: local, changing, and consequential. A stablecoin issuer designing for the eurozone must now account for MiCA's "e-money token" classification; one designing for the U.S. faces 50 state money-transmitter regimes. Each choice carries compliance drag. Projects with the discipline to track these fronts—reading central bank speeches, regulator consultations, and policy drafts—build resilience. Those who ignore them wake up under new skies.

The professional virtue here is *prudence under ambiguity*. Prudence is not paralysis; it is the art of acting amid uncertainty. In August 2021, dYdX geo-blocked U.S. users pre-emptively, citing regulatory ambiguity. Critics called it overcautious; the project called it survival. When enforcement finally arrived for similar derivatives protocols, dYdX's self-restraint proved prescient. The visible behaviour of prudence is the decision to *limit* exposure before law compels it. Metrics include the number of jurisdictions served, the frequency of legal audits, and the time from guidance publication to internal policy update. These are not abstractions; they are operational signals of maturity.

Jurisdictional awareness also extends to disclosures and language. The same whitepaper that reads as an open technical description in London may be treated as a prospectus in New York. The same DAO token that grants voting rights in Lisbon may resemble an unregistered share in Toronto. The skill lies in reading legal intent, not just text. For example, the UK's Financial Conduct Authority (FCA) distinguishes "promotions" from "information," a nuance that can determine whether a community announcement breaches law. Projects that monitor regulator consultations—such as the FCA's March 2024 crypto marketing rules—can pre-empt compliance before enforcement crystallises.

To navigate such complexity, some DeFi teams adopt "regulatory arbitrage" as a strategy—incorporating entities in favourable jurisdictions while serving global users. Singapore's Payment Services Act (2019) and the Virtual Asset Regulatory Authority (VARA) regime in Dubai have become popular for this reason. Yet arbitrage is not immunity; it is delay. Binance, initially registered in the Cayman Islands and operating globally, faced coordinated investigations in 2023 despite its decentralised posture. Jurisdictional fog may conceal risk, but it rarely dissolves it. The professional standard must evolve from "Where can I go?" to "Where can I endure?"

Prudence also means resisting false clarity. Policymakers themselves operate under uncertainty, drafting frameworks that often lag technology by years. When the U.S. Treasury sanctioned Tornado Cash, the legal debate turned on whether code could be sanctioned as an entity. No court had yet defined the ontological status of a smart contract. The case became jurisprudence in real time. For developers and institutions alike, the lesson was sobering: legal categories are being invented mid-flight. The virtue, therefore, is not certainty but *adaptation*—designing operational models that can bend without breaking when interpretations shift.

A practical manifestation of this virtue is "jurisdictional diversification." Teams increasingly split governance, treasury, and development functions across multiple legal entities in different countries, reducing the chance that a single regulator can immobilise all operations. MakerDAO's foundation dissolution in 2021 and transition to decentralised governance was not just ideological; it was jurisdictional resilience. The same principle animates multi-signature treasuries distributed across time zones and continents. Geography, once an administrative detail, becomes a risk parameter.

Yet variability also breeds opportunity. Jurisdictions compete. Liechtenstein's Blockchain Act of 2020 explicitly recognises tokenised assets as property. France's Autorité des Marchés Financiers (AMF) offers "PSAN" licences for digital asset service providers willing to meet transparency requirements. Each regulatory innovation invites experimentation. The implication for professionals is strategic: regulation is not merely a constraint; it is a differentiator. Entities that operate cleanly within clear jurisdictions attract institutional capital sooner. Transparency, paradoxically, becomes a moat.

The counterpoint must be addressed. Absolute compliance is impossible for protocols that are borderless by design. Smart contracts cannot verify nationality; they cannot distinguish between a user in Tokyo and one in Tehran. Enforcement, therefore, often targets interfaces, developers, or front-end operators—the human choke points. Some view this as betrayal of decentralisation; others see it as the inevitable compromise between autonomy and accountability. The reconciliation lies in design: separating immutable protocol layers from jurisdiction-sensitive access layers allows systems to function globally while front-ends adapt locally.

This discussion circles back to prudence. The professionals who thrive in DeFi's regulatory weather exhibit a distinct posture: they neither hide from law nor worship it. They track guidance the way sailors track tides—aware of patterns, alert to shifts, and humble before uncertainty. Their competitive edge is not arrogance but literacy: knowing when a draft bill becomes law, when an enforcement pattern hardens into precedent, when a consultation hints at direction. Knowledge becomes navigation.

Jurisdictional variability will not vanish; it will deepen. As blockchains host real-world assets—bonds, carbon credits, and identity credentials—the collision between national sovereignty and global protocols will intensify. Forks may emerge not just for technical reasons but for regulatory divergence: one version compliant with European data laws, another resistant to U.S. sanctions. The map will fragment, but innovation will persist within those fractures.

The motif returns—weather. To thrive under it, one must read clouds, not curse them. The forward test is simple: when the next policy shift arrives, will your organisation react with panic or with process? Prudence under ambiguity is not passivity; it is choreography. The storm is already overhead; the task is to move with its rhythm, not against it.

KYC, Privacy, and Selective Disclosure

On 10 August 2022 in Washington, the U.S. Treasury's Office of Foreign Assets Control sanctioned Tornado Cash; two days later, Dutch authorities arrested developer Alexey Pertsev in Amsterdam. The contracts still executed. The website vanished. GitHub accounts were removed. The paradox was stark: code that ran everywhere met rules enforced somewhere. What, exactly, must one reveal to use money? What, precisely, may a system verify without exposing a person? The aperture narrowed and widened at once. Hold that image. The *aperture*—not a wall—determines what passes from identity into action.

The ideology is familiar: one camp treats anonymity as a right, the other treats verification as a duty. The operations are harder and more interesting. DeFi's practical frontier is not "KYC or not" but *what* is proven, *to whom, for how long,* and *under whose control*. The space between secrecy and surveillance isn't empty; it's a design surface. We can shape it. We should.

Show → name → explain → implication. Show: a lending market wants to admit counterparties that meet anti–money laundering standards without collecting names. Name: *selective disclosure*. Explain: instead of handing over documents, a user presents a cryptographic proof—"I am over 18", "I am not on a sanctions list", "I am a resident of an approved jurisdiction"—derived from attestations held off-chain or on a permissioned ledger, validated on-chain with zero-knowledge proofs. Implication: the protocol enforces policy without warehousing identity. Disclosure becomes a knob, not a binary switch.

Two concrete, checkable examples anchor the conversation. First, **Aave Arc** (December 2021) launched a permissioned pool for institutions, with Fireblocks acting as the initial whitelister in New York and Tel Aviv. The function mirrored traditional onboarding—Know Your Customer checks, recordkeeping, audit trails—while retaining smart-contract settlement. The aperture narrowed: participants proved they were "good actors" to a gatekeeper; beyond that, their trading remained pseudonymous to the public chain. Second, **Polygon ID** reached general availability in March 2023 under Polygon Labs, offering decentralised identifiers and zero-knowledge credentials that let users prove attributes (age, residency, accreditation) without revealing underlying data. Here, the aperture became programmable: credentials could be re-used across dApps; revocation lists could be published; proofs expired on schedule. In both cases, ideology ceded the stage to mechanics. Verification became a product, not a sermon.

A credible counter-example forces humility. **Worldcoin**, launched July 2023, promised proof-of-personhood using biometric "orbs". Kenya suspended operations in August 2023 pending investigation in Nairobi; European data authorities raised GDPR concerns. The aperture was too wide—biometric capture to fight Sybil attacks—and too narrow—opaque governance and uncertain data deletion. The reconciliation is operational: privacy-preserving compliance must satisfy *two* auditors, the cryptographer and the regulator. It must prove the right thing *and* prove that nothing else is retained.

To separate ideology from operations, begin with four verbs that turn abstractions into behaviours: *minimise, partition, attest, expire*. Minimise: collect the least possible data to meet a policy, then commit—publicly—to deletion schedules. Partition: keep attestations with issuers (banks, exchanges, national ID providers) and present only proofs to dApps; never centralise raw identity inside the protocol. Attest: use credential formats (W3C verifiable credentials, BBS+ signatures) that support zero-knowledge predicates, and make issuers accountable for false positives. Expire: time-limit both credentials and proofs, forcing renewal and revocation hygiene. Each verb is visible. Each can be audited. Each tightens the aperture.

Zero-knowledge techniques are not slogans; they are circuits with constraints. Consider a practical pattern: *zk-sanctions screening*. An exchange or regulated VASP issues a credential stating "this wallet is not currently on X list" with a serial that can be revoked. The user later proves set membership *or* exclusion to a smart contract without revealing the list entry or their name. No raw list is uploaded; no addresses are leaked to the public chain. The trade still clears. The risk surface changes: reliance shifts to the issuer's fidelity and the revocation oracle's uptime. You can measure both—service-level agreements, incident logs, and on-chain liveness of revocation registries.

A second pattern: *proof of residency for market access*. Some jurisdictions permit trading certain tokens only to local residents. A credential issuer (say, a bank in Paris) signs a residency statement. The user proves "EU resident" to a DEX front-end, which unlocks features client-side while the contract itself remains neutral. Here the aperture sits in the interface, not the chain. The benefit is agility; the cost is fragmentation—the same contract behaves differently by front-end. Trackable metric: divergence between interface policy and protocol neutrality. If divergence widens, pressure builds for protocol-level enforcement. Know your *policy locus*.

Critics will argue that any gate is censorship by another name. Practitioners learn to ask a duller, harder question: *where should the gate live?* Embed it on-chain and you harden rules but risk ossifying law inside code; keep it off-chain and you preserve neutrality but invite regulatory heat to the interface. The pragmatic answer is layered: encode *capabilities* on-chain (support for revocation registries, hooks for proofs-of-attribute) while allowing communities to choose front-ends that enforce different apertures for different jurisdictions. The chain stays credibly neutral. The boundary adapts.

The political economy of KYC also matters. Verification power is market power. If a single custodian of credentials dominates, you swap state surveillance for corporate choke points. A resilient design spreads issuance across many attesters: banks, exchanges, eID schemes (Estonia's e-Residency, India's Aadhaar—each with distinct risks), even professional bodies. Compete on service levels and liability regimes, not on hoarded data. Add *accountability hooks*: if an issuer's false positive rate exceeds a threshold, proofs from that issuer lose priority or trigger extra checks. This is not romantic. It is governance by metric.

Privacy has costs. Proving a thing without showing it is computationally heavier than showing it; proofs consume gas and engineering time. But cost is a design parameter. Teams can amortise with batching, off-chain proving, and proof aggregation (Halo, PLONK, Groth16 each with different performance envelopes). They can also *price* privacy: offer fee rebates or lower margin requirements to users who present stronger credentials because their risk profile is better understood. This turns ideology into basis points. It is how systems change behaviour at scale.

A separate friction is usability. Wallet UX still renders signatures in ways that baffle even professionals. If selective disclosure requires three extra clicks and ten extra seconds, users will defect to laxer venues. The fix is craft, not creed. Use human-readable prompts that say, plainly, "Proving you are not on List X" with an issuer's name and a link to their policy. Display expiry. Offer one-tap revocation. Show the *aperture* to the user at the moment of consent. If you cannot render it in a sentence, you probably cannot defend it in court.

Regulators are not blind to this frontier. The **FATF** (Paris, 2019 guidance; updates through 2023) extended the "Travel Rule" to virtual asset service providers, asking them to share sender and recipient information. That rule built for bank wires has spawned *privacy-preserving Travel Rule* pilots: encrypted data exchange between VASPs with proofs of possession rather than public broadcasts. Meanwhile, the **EU's MiCA** (April 2023, Brussels/Strasbourg) frames obligations for service providers and significant stablecoin issuers, not for immutable protocols, hinting at a compromise: compel the edges, tolerate the core. The aperture narrows at the periphery and remains open in the centre.

Not every privacy primitive travels well across jurisdictions. What Germany treats as proportionate may breach the UK's marketing rules; what Singapore licences under the Payment Services Act may fall foul of U.S. securities doctrine by association. Professionals must track *policy temperature* like traders track volatility: subscribe to consultations, map enforcement actions, maintain a register of "proofs accepted" per venue. Then adapt. Prudence under ambiguity is a habit, not a mood.

We should address the hardest case: sanctioned addresses and taint analysis. Protocols increasingly consume risk scores from analytics firms that label flows as "high risk" based on heuristics. This is useful for triage; it is dangerous for rights. Heuristics are not law. A privacy-preserving posture sets *appeal paths*: users can present countervailing proofs (source-of-funds attestations, clean-history credentials) to reduce friction without doxxing themselves to the chain. The decision remains at the interface; the record is off-chain; the proof is minimal. The system keeps its dignity.

The aperture motif returns because it rescales the debate. Privacy is not a castle to defend; it is a camera to configure. A well-tuned aperture reveals *enough* for integrity and *no more* for appetite. That configuration is a policy choice expressed as code. We can argue it in public. We can measure it: average credential age; revocation lag; percentage of users satisfying policy with zk proofs versus document uploads; number of attesters whose credentials a dApp accepts (concentration risk). Metrics turn values into operations.

Stories teach reflex. After the **OFAC/Tornado Cash** shock (August 2022), many teams quietly sketched "dual-rail" plans: a neutral protocol rail untouched by jurisdictional toggles and a regulated access rail with selective disclosure. Some added proof-of-human options that used *Semaphore-style* group membership proofs—"one person, one vote"—for governance without deanonymising wallets. Others cut support for privacy tools entirely. Two years on, the most resilient projects are those that kept both rails alive and documented their apertures. They can show a minister an audit trail without showing the internet a passport.

There is an unresolved tension. Selective disclosure depends on attesters whose incentives may drift, and on proofs whose mathematics most users will never understand. Trust migrates but never disappears. The forward test, therefore, is not "Is this pure?" but "Is this *proportionate, revocable,* and *portable*?" Proportionate: prove only what a policy rationally requires. Revocable: turn off credentials fast when facts change. Portable: let users carry proofs across venues to avoid re-exposure. If a system fails any one of these, the aperture is wrong.

The question you must answer—architect, investor, or operator—is disarmingly simple. When your protocol must show something about a user, do you know *exactly* what, to whom, for how long, and with what exit? If you can specify that in a sentence a judge could read aloud and a user could accept with a click, you have separated ideology from operations. If not, the camera is pointing at the wrong thing. Adjust the aperture before someone else does it for you.

Risk of Rule Changes

On 10 August 2022 in Washington, the U.S. Treasury's Office of Foreign Assets Control added Tornado Cash smart contracts to its sanctions list. Within hours, front-ends went dark, GitHub accounts disappeared, and stablecoin issuers froze tainted balances. Yet the contracts kept executing on Ethereum. One rule change flipped—and portfolios moved. A week later, in Amsterdam, a developer was arrested; in London and New York, exchanges revised terms; in DAO forums, emergency proposals multiplied. Nothing in the code had altered. The law had. Rules move markets fast. A switch had been thrown.

Forks, sanctions, and delistings are not distant hypotheticals; they are the switches that can convert assumptions into losses overnight. Forks redraw what "the chain" means; sanctions redraw what "legal tendering" means; delistings redraw what "liquid" means. Each event changes the meaning of the assets you hold without changing the bits you own. That asymmetry is the risk. It is also where design can help. The motif of this subchapter is the *switch*. We will return to it because good architecture ensures that when a switch is thrown, the blast radius is small.

Show → name → explain → implication. Show: on 20 July 2016, following *The DAO* exploit, Ethereum executed a contentious hard fork to reverse the theft. Name: *consensus split*. Explain: a portion of miners and users rejected the fork and continued the original chain, creating Ethereum Classic

(ETC). Implication: the "same" ether did not exist; two histories did. Holders who controlled their own keys received assets on both chains. Those whose assets sat in custodial pools were credited at the custodian's discretion, sometimes after delay. The design choice—self-custody versus pooled custody—determined whether the switch produced optionality or confusion.

Forks are rule changes encoded in state. They may be planned (protocol upgrades) or reactive (crisis responses). Either way, they force a practical question: what exactly do you own? If your claim to value relies on a single canonical chain, a fork turns that claim into a bet on social legitimacy. If your claim relies on redeemability against off-chain assets, a fork tests contracts and issuers rather than consensus. The protective design here is dull but decisive: maintain independent control of keys; track whether the assets you hold are native or wrapped; and know where the "right" chain is determined—in client software defaults, in exchange listings, or in governance votes. The answer decides price.

Sanctions are rule changes at the border between code and law. The Tornado Cash episode made that border visible. Stablecoins such as USDC include freeze functions for compliance. In August 2022, Centre blacklisted addresses linked to those contracts, rendering some balances inert at the contract level. The switch was literal. Funds became unspendable not because holders lost keys, but because an issuer toggled a bit to meet a legal instruction. This is not a moral judgment; it is a risk parameter. The implication is quantifiable: if a strategy uses assets with issuer control, the strategy inherits issuer policy risk. Measure it by reading the code (freeze functions), the policy (blacklist criteria), and the governance (who can add an address, how quickly, under what quorum).

Delistings are rule changes at the venue. On 22 December 2020, after the U.S. Securities and Exchange Commission filed suit against Ripple, multiple American exchanges delisted XRP. Liquidity thinned; price gapped; arbitrage paths closed. Long-only holders saw valuation crumble; market-makers saw inventory trapped; companies using XRP for treasury or remittance flow had to redesign routes in days. A listing is an access promise. A delisting is a door closing. The implication is behavioural: treat exchange access as a variable, not a constant, and size positions so that a single venue's policy cannot strand you.

Two further, checkable examples sharpen intuition. In March 2023, the collapse of Silicon Valley Bank triggered a temporary USDC de-peg as markets digested the location of Circle's reserves. While not driven by a statute, the regulatory environment around bank resolution shaped price within hours. The "safe" stablecoin traded at a discount; DEX pools rebalanced; risk systems that assumed parity had to be re-coded while live. In November 2022, the freeze at FTX cascaded into token relistings and risk-limit changes across other exchanges. Some projects found liquidity erased not by failure of code, but by a shift in gatekeeper confidence. In both episodes, the switch was reputational but functioned like policy: a rule changed elsewhere, and your local reality shifted.

A credible counter-example tempers fatalism. After Ethereum's proof-of-stake Merge in September 2022, a minority of miners and exchanges backed a proof-of-work fork (ETHW). Most users ignored it; prices reflected that indifference. For self-custodied holders, the fork produced an extra token that could be sold without touching the original position. The switch existed, but the design—keys held, assets identifiable, execution pathways clear—turned potential harm into optionality. Reconciliation: not every rule change is a disaster. Resilience is the ability to benefit from disagreements about the rules.

Design choices can minimise collateral damage when switches flip. Consider *asset layering*. A protocol that accepts only a single, centrally issued stablecoin concentrates policy risk. One that accepts a basket—USDC, USDT, DAI—with conservative haircuts spreads it. MakerDAO's collateral framework illustrates this: DAI's peg relies on diversified backing and governance-controlled parameters that can be adjusted with timelocks. The implication is operational: baskets blunt switches. The cost is complexity. That cost is usually worth paying.

Consider *upgrade paths*. Upgradeable proxy contracts enable fast responses to bugs and regulation, but they also create governance attack surfaces and potential compliance choke points. Immutable contracts reduce discretionary risk but cannot adapt quickly to new rules. There is no universal answer. A design that uses proxies with timelocks and clearly published admin keys admits agility while preserving due warning. A design that hard-codes critical invariants and isolates them from upgradeability contains blast radius. The practical measure is the *timelock delta*: the time between a parameter change proposal and execution. Longer deltas improve predictability under rule changes; shorter deltas improve responsiveness to crises. Choose, document, and communicate.

Consider *jurisdictional distribution*. Teams that concentrate infrastructure—front-ends, DNS, API gateways, and multisig signers—in a single country tie uptime to one legal climate. Teams that split these across regions, use content-addressed hosting, and publish verified IPFS hashes reduce the chance that a single administrative order can turn off lights. In August 2022, Curve's DNS was hijacked; users who knew the verified contract addresses or alternate front-ends avoided the trap. In sanctions episodes, teams with multiple canonical front-ends could comply where needed and remain operable elsewhere. Infrastructure is policy in waiting.

Consider *oracle independence*. Delistings and sanctions can distort price feeds. Oracles that aggregate across venues and publish methodologies reduce the chance that one venue's switch becomes everyone's reference. During USDC's March 2023 wobble, projects that drew on multi-venue or time-weighted feeds experienced less whipsaw than those keyed to a single exchange pair. The design principle is quantifiable: define maximum venue weight, publish fallbacks, and simulate venue outages in tests. The metric is a mouthful but matters: *price integrity under venue failure.*

Now return to forks. A practical pattern reduces harm: *claim discipline.* After a split, some tokens accrue value on both chains. If a protocol's contracts rely on the pre-fork chain ID or on canonical addresses that do not exist on the fork, interactions there may be unsafe. Good design prevents accidental execution on unsupported forks by checking chain IDs and pausing gracefully. Good operations publish post-fork instructions: how to access assets on each chain, which versions they will support, and how prices will be treated in oracles. Clarity reduces opportunistic loss.

Sanctions invite a different design response: *capability separation.* Keep the core protocol credibly neutral, but make space at the edge—front-ends, routers—for selective disclosure and regional policy. This reduces the chance that the core will be seen as an entity with obligations, while enabling compliance where law speaks clearly. After Tornado Cash's listing, some protocols embedded deny lists into interfaces; others accepted proofs that funds were not tied to sanctioned flows. The split is not hypocrisy. It is containment.

Delistings suggest a treasury lesson: *liquidity redundancy.* A DAO that keeps working capital in a single exchange, or a token that relies on one pool, accepts an avoidable hazard. Redundant rails—CEX and DEX pairs, multiple bridges, alternative stabilisation routes—ensure that when one switch is thrown, you can still move. The measure is concrete: the number of independent paths to fiat or to a reserve asset that survive if your top venue disappears for a week.

All of this sits atop culture. The fastest way to shrink a blast radius is to admit that switches exist. Teams that publish *rule-change runbooks*—who decides, where to post, what to pause—move from shouting to sequence when events hit. When OFAC acted in August 2022, projects with pre-written comms and on-chain emergency controls looked prepared rather than panicked. Users notice. So do regulators. Scepticism is professionalised by rehearsal.

A further, uncomfortable point: some assets are designed to be switchable. Freeze and clawback functions are not bugs; they are compliance features. If you rely on such assets for core collateral, you inherit that feature. You can model the risk by reading admin roles in contracts, checking signers on multisigs, and tracking prior exercises of those powers. You can also place those assets at the perimeter of your design: useful for interfaces, dangerous in core safety modules. Repeat the earlier motif. Where do you want the switch to live?

A limit must be stated. No design fully neutralises political risk. If a major jurisdiction bans a class of interaction and exchanges obey, spreads widen; liquidity will migrate; models dependant on frictionless movement will suffer. Even on-chain, social consensus can splinter over values, as with the 2016 fork. The point of architecture is not invincibility; it is graceful degradation. Systems that fail in small pieces live to be improved. Systems that fail in one piece become case studies.

There is also opportunity in volatility born of rule changes. When venues delist, pairs become mispriced. When forks occur, assets trade at confused discounts. When sanctions carve the network, liquidity pockets form. Those who map policy and design for optionality can supply needed services at fair margin without courting regulatory heat. Ethics and enterprise can align if you choose what to serve, and to whom, with care. That is a design choice too.

The switch motif returns because it forces plain speech. If a law or policy changed tomorrow, which literal switch in your system would someone need to flip to keep users safe? Can a guardian pause a module? Can an oracle shift to a quarantine mode? Can your treasury move across rails without begging a single gatekeeper? If each answer has a named operator, a documented path, and a public rationale, then a rule change is a stress test, not a death sentence.

The unresolved test is personal and immediate. Pick one asset you rely on and one venue you cannot live without. Now ask: if a fork split that asset's chain next week, or if a sanction made that venue unusable in your country tomorrow, what exactly happens to your position by morning? Where is the switch, who holds it, and what is your second route? If the answers are guesses, you are not managing risk; you are hoping for weather. Design so that when someone else throws the switch, your lights dim but do not go out.

Chapter 8
Real-World Use and Future Directions

In August 2021, the government of El Salvador made Bitcoin legal tender. The announcement was met with cheers, scepticism, and a fair amount of global confusion. Within six months, a more pragmatic story had emerged beneath the headlines: merchants were accepting Bitcoin only when converted instantly into U.S. dollars through the Lightning Network; the state-backed wallet, Chivo, quietly integrated a dollar-denominated stablecoin; and everyday users—market vendors, taxi drivers, small shopkeepers—were measuring their comfort not by ideology but by predictability. The grand experiment, often framed as radical, had distilled to a simple operational truth: what people value most in money is *working money*. Stable, quick, low-friction. The underlying technology mattered less than its ability to keep promises in motion.

That same insight echoes across every serious application of decentralised finance that has survived hype cycles. The speculative fever that once defined the sector is cooling into something subtler and more consequential: functional integration. Across continents, stablecoins settle wages, remittances, and B2B payments faster than correspondent banks. SMEs experiment with on-chain treasuries not because they wish to "go crypto," but because the architecture offers liquidity management tools they cannot easily access elsewhere. Credit, long dependent on identity and collateral, begins to borrow new language from data—

reputation, attestations, verified history—while regulators and developers cautiously sketch bridges between privacy and disclosure. The industry's headline has shifted from "disruption" to "assimilation."

The paradox is worth pausing on. DeFi's earliest evangelists promised a world without banks, yet its most durable achievements increasingly serve banks' customers. The same infrastructure once marketed as an escape route now underpins settlement for fintech firms and cross-border payrolls. This is not capitulation; it is evolution. Technologies mature when their idealists lose monopoly over their narrative. What remains is the *plumbing*—the quiet endurance of stablecoins, automated market makers, and collateralised lending protocols, operating in the background like routers of value. As the speculative gloss fades, their utility becomes visible precisely because it ceases to demand attention.

Payments and remittances illustrate both progress and friction. Stablecoins now settle billions of dollars daily—transparent, auditable, near-instant—but the rails still depend on interfaces subject to compliance choke points. A coffee exporter in Nairobi may receive USDC faster than a SWIFT wire, yet must still pass through local conversion hurdles, tax rules, and the daily liquidity rhythm of mobile-money ecosystems. The gains are real; the frictions, equally so. This chapter explores those balances: where efficiency ends and policy begins; where technology's reach still meets cash drawers and customs desks.

Small-business treasury management, by contrast, reveals how DeFi's design can align with conservatism rather than speculation. The image of DeFi as reckless leverage obscures a quieter trend: SMEs using tokenised treasuries to hold diversified stable assets, earn modest yields through vetted protocols, and automate reporting through on-chain transparency. The innovation here is procedural. Governance becomes process. A digital wallet can enforce quorum votes, spending limits, and audit trails with more precision than many legacy systems. Yet prudence remains the anchor—teams learn to treat automation as delegation, not abdication.

Identity, reputation, and credit form the next frontier—and the next moral hazard. On-chain reputation promises to extend credit without collateral by transforming behaviour into trust. It also threatens to ossify bias if built carelessly. The systems that grade or attest must do so with clarity about what they measure: repayment history, not personality; verified outcomes, not affiliations. Zero-knowledge proofs, decentralised identifiers, and selective disclosure tools offer technical scaffolding for privacy-preserving verification, but cultural alignment will determine their legitimacy. A credit system is not only a database; it is a mirror of what a community values as reliability. DeFi's challenge is to reflect virtue without revealing everything.

And then there are the questions of endurance. Amid the constant reinvention of terminology and tokenomics, a few primitives have demonstrated staying power. Stablecoins, by binding cryptographic certainty to monetary stability, have become the de facto backbone of digital liquidity. Automated market makers (AMMs) continue to redefine price discovery and capital efficiency, their algorithms adjusting not only balances but beliefs about how markets should behave without intermediaries. Collateralised lending remains the most functional bridge between decentralised logic and traditional finance, its governance now tested through multiple market cycles. These are not trends; they are *infrastructure*. The rest—synthetic assets, yield farms, fleeting governance tokens—has faded or will. What survives tends to do something boring well.

Threaded through all of this is a broader reckoning with what decentralisation actually delivers. The early dream of total autonomy now collides with operational realism: users want recourse when errors occur, regulators demand auditability, and enterprises need predictable accounting. The future of DeFi may therefore look less like an alternative universe and more like a substrate—a transparent layer under traditional systems, invisible yet indispensable. That prospect does not dilute the project's significance; it completes it.

To read this chapter is to move from speculation to implementation. We will examine how stablecoins quietly power migrant wages from São Paulo to Manila, how small firms in Warsaw or Lagos treat DeFi tools as extensions of corporate banking, how on-chain identity could redefine creditworthiness for freelancers in Mumbai or students in Nairobi, and which design patterns are likely to persist once the rhetoric cools. Each case underscores a single motif: survival through utility.

The closing movement of this chapter looks forward with humility and precision. Predictions in this field age badly; patterns endure. We will ask not what will *explode* next, but what will *remain*. The signal will come from those who stop announcing revolutions and start reconciling spreadsheets, from protocols that survive rule changes because they serve plain human needs. DeFi's future, paradoxically, may be its normalisation—a return to the quiet satisfaction of systems that simply work. The excitement, then, is not over. It has changed frequency. The next revolution will sound like reliability.

Payments and Remittances

On 10 October 2023, in Quezon City, the Philippines, a nurse named Maria Santos received her monthly remittance from her sister in California. It arrived as USDC on a mobile wallet linked to a local exchange. The transfer took forty-five seconds and cost thirty-seven cents. Her sister, accustomed to paying nearly 7% in remittance fees through Western Union, had saved the equivalent of a week's groceries. Yet when Maria walked to a nearby pawnshop to convert her digital dollars into pesos, she waited forty minutes and paid another 2% to access cash. The rails had changed; the friction had not vanished. The global system of value transfer—built for speed, burdened by borders—had met its newest test case: stablecoins as everyday money.

Stablecoins have become the invisible engines of global remittance networks, often without their users knowing it. Behind an app interface in Nairobi or Caracas sits an Ethereum or Tron contract that reconciles balances more efficiently than the correspondent banking web it shadows. In 2023, Chainalysis estimated that over $500 billion in stablecoins moved through "off-exchange" wallets, much of it in developing markets. Yet this headline number conceals nuance. Stablecoins are no longer experiments; they are *rails*. But rails alone do not guarantee smooth travel. They require roads—liquidity providers, local on-ramps, and clear rules. Each step where the chain meets human life still costs time, trust, or both.

Show → name → explain → implication. Show: when Argentina's inflation surged past 120% in August 2023, merchants began quoting prices in Tether (USDT), not pesos. Name: *informal dollarisation through stablecoins*. Explain: citizens turned to crypto not for speculation but as a hedge against domestic currency collapse, using peer-to-peer markets on Telegram and Binance P2P. The transactions cleared near-instantly, but settlement in cash remained slow and uneven, subject to the same gatekeepers that DeFi was meant to replace. Implication: efficiency in bits does not erase inertia in bricks. A digital dollar still needs a human to redeem it.

The Philippines offers another lens. The country is one of the world's largest remittance corridors, receiving over $36 billion in 2022 (World Bank). OFWs—Overseas Filipino Workers—are effectively an alternative monetary authority. As fintech firms layered stablecoin transfers atop the traditional corridors, fees dropped from an average of 5% to below 2% for users able to stay within digital rails. Yet adoption plateaued. Why? Because regulation of on-ramps remained patchy, bank integrations inconsistent, and retail literacy limited. A single mistyped address could freeze wages for a month. The friction migrated; it did not disappear.

Contrast that with **Brazil**, where regulatory clarity has produced the opposite outcome. The Central Bank of Brazil's *Pix* system, launched in November 2020, now settles millions of instant payments daily. In 2023, stablecoin gateways such as Mercado Bitcoin and Nubank integrated Pix deposits and withdrawals. The pairing allowed users to swap reais for USDC or BRL-pegged tokens seamlessly, embedding crypto liquidity within a compliant domestic system. It is a glimpse of what synthesis looks like: stablecoins as *underlays* rather than alternatives, operating quietly beneath regulated infrastructure. The implication is powerful: once stablecoins become plumbing, their controversy fades.

A credible counter-example tempers the enthusiasm. Nigeria's 2021 crackdown on crypto trading, coupled with repeated naira devaluations, pushed users towards informal exchanges. Tether volumes soared, but price spreads widened to 10–15% on bad days. Market opacity replaced institutional friction. A transaction that clears in seconds means little if its exchange rate moves in minutes. The lesson is practical: disintermediation without transparency simply substitutes one form of uncertainty for another. Real efficiency arises not when intermediaries vanish, but when they become accountable.

The quiet motif here is *friction*. It recurs not as failure, but as feedback. Each remaining bottleneck signals where DeFi meets the material constraints of geography and law. Consider the moment a stablecoin exits a screen: point-of-sale terminals that cannot yet read QR codes; cashiers unsure whether a token is "real money"; compliance teams freezing transfers until they can label the counterparties. Each is a drag coefficient on the otherwise frictionless physics of code. To reduce it, systems must either integrate or outlast. Integration means working with banks, regulators, and payment processors to translate digital certainty into legal assurance. Outlasting means building parallel economies that prove too efficient to ignore. Both paths are visible today.

From a technical standpoint, stablecoins work. USDC's settlement latency is under a minute; transaction costs on efficient chains can fall below a cent. The human layers—interfaces, compliance checks, cash conversion—consume the rest of the cost stack. This division clarifies the opportunity: what remains to optimise is not protocol throughput, but coordination. Projects such as Circle's *Cross-Chain Transfer Protocol* (CCTP), launched April 2023, aim to make stablecoins portable across blockchains without custodial bridges. That solves one side of friction—the technical. The social side lags. Governments remain cautious, banks defensive, and many users still define trust by the ability to reverse a mistake.

We can measure progress by outcomes rather than rhetoric. The **Stellar Development Foundation** partnered with MoneyGram in October 2022 to pilot global USDC cash-out points across 180 countries. It worked: remittances from the U.S. to Kenya cleared in minutes. But the partnership also reintroduced a familiar intermediary—the agent network—now operating atop digital settlement rails. The cost savings were modest, the reliability improved. The rails had evolved, but the human topology remained. Similarly, **Visa's stablecoin settlement trials** (August 2023, Singapore) demonstrated that large corporates could move treasury funds across partners in hours instead of days, but always within a regulated perimeter. The experiment's outcome was neither radical nor negligible; it was incremental. And incrementalism is the hallmark of adoption.

The counterpoint lies in community-led remittance corridors. In Venezuela, peer-to-peer stablecoin networks such as *Reserve* and *Venezuela Remesa* operate beyond banking access, processing household transfers through mobile apps. Here, friction reduction equates to survival.

Yet these systems depend on fragile trust loops—local liquidity providers who convert tokens to cash, often manually. When one node fails, the corridor seizes. This is where theory meets anthropology: the efficiency of an algorithm is constrained by the patience of a person.

The implication for professionals and policymakers is that stablecoin payments are neither miracle nor menace; they are infrastructure under construction. Each jurisdiction builds its version differently. Singapore licenses USDC under the Payment Services Act; Hong Kong drafts rules for fiat-backed tokens; the European Union's MiCA regime, live in 2024, codifies disclosure and reserve requirements. The direction is uniform: integrate the functionality, regulate the custody, preserve the audit trail. The friction that remains is often regulatory latency—the time between innovation and interpretation.

Behind these developments lies a subtle shift in mindset. The goal is not *replacing* money transfer systems but *disaggregating* them. Each function—verification, settlement, custody, compliance—can be modularised and recombined. A stablecoin acts as the settlement module, not the entire stack. This modularity explains why fintech firms now use DeFi without advertising it: they import just enough cryptographic certainty to remove an internal bottleneck, leaving customer experience unchanged. Stablecoins are ceasing to be products and becoming verbs.

A philosophical note deserves mention. Payments are the most mundane and most political of human activities. They determine who can participate in markets and under what conditions. DeFi reframes this by separating the right to transact from the privilege of being recognised by an institution. Yet that freedom carries operational responsibility. A self-custodied wallet is powerful but unforgiving; an unregulated exchange can be efficient until it collapses. Stability, therefore, demands more than peg maintenance—it demands governance, clarity, and a shared definition of fairness.

The motif of friction returns one final time. It is not something to be eliminated, but understood. Friction reminds systems that they exist within societies, not apart from them. It slows recklessness and forces adaptation. The history of payments—whether through the Venetian giro banks of the 14th century or the SWIFT network of the 20th—shows that lasting rails are those that balance speed with assurance. DeFi's rails are no different.

The forward test, then, is diagnostic. When a remittance clears in seconds, ask not how fast it was, but *who absorbed the risk* while it moved. When a stablecoin holds its peg, ask *whose reserves anchor it* and *which jurisdiction enforces them*. When friction reappears at the edge, ask whether it signals failure—or simply the next layer awaiting redesign. Stablecoins have proven that money can move at the speed of code. What remains is proving that trust can keep up.

Small-Business Treasury

In February 2023, a logistics startup in Warsaw called CargoLink faced a familiar problem with a new tool. The company held customer payments in euros but paid drivers in zloty. Their bank required two days to settle cross-currency transfers, and the fees eroded margins on each contract. Searching for efficiency, the finance director, Anna Kowalska, trialled a treasury model using euro-backed stablecoins and decentralised liquidity pools for near-instant conversions. Within three months, payment lags dropped from forty-eight hours to fifteen minutes. Yet the firm didn't chase yield; it built guardrails. Multi-signature controls limited access, stablecoin exposure capped at 25% of working capital, and liquidity pools were vetted by external auditors. The project's success lay not in speculation but in discipline. DeFi entered the company not as revolution, but as process.

The motif of this subchapter is *control*. It threads through every small-business encounter with decentralised finance. For individuals, DeFi offers empowerment; for firms, it introduces governance risk in disguise. The architecture of corporate finance—approvals, reporting, fiduciary duty—meets code designed for permissionless action. The challenge is not whether DeFi works, but whether it can behave like a professional counterparty. Small businesses sit at that intersection. They have the agility to adopt, but not the capital to recover from mistakes. That makes them the real proving ground for what decentralised treasury management can become.

Show → name → explain → implication. Show: in April 2022, *Monerium,* an Iceland-based fintech regulated under the European Economic Area's e-money framework, issued euro-denominated stablecoins directly onto the blockchain. Name: *regulated stablecoin as settlement medium*. Explain: Monerium bridged on-chain payments with legal guarantees equivalent to traditional e-money accounts. Implication: companies using such tokens could automate treasury flows—payroll, vendor invoices, tax obligations—while remaining compliant with existing accounting standards. This development marked a structural shift. The language of compliance was finally written into code.

For a small enterprise, treasury is not an abstract function; it is survival. Cash flow, not profit, keeps the lights on. DeFi's promise lies in its ability to compress reconciliation cycles and extend access to liquidity. A company that can settle invoices in minutes gains not glamour but breathing room. Yet the path from promise to prudence is narrow. The same autonomy that eliminates banking delays also removes circuit breakers. Without governance, efficiency becomes fragility.

One early example of professional integration came from **Request Finance**, a platform launched in Singapore in 2020, now serving over 3,000 companies across 180 countries. It enables businesses to invoice and pay using stablecoins while automatically generating accounting records. In 2023, it reported over $300 million in transactions, mainly from Web3 firms paying contractors and service providers. The lesson was practical: stablecoins were not speculative assets, but operational currencies. Firms that used them saved time on reconciliation and foreign exchange. Yet even Request Finance learned to implement layered permissions—ensuring no single employee could initiate a transfer above a threshold without co-signers. The speed of code demanded the patience of governance.

A contrasting limitation appeared in the 2022 collapse of *TerraUSD*. Some SMEs, drawn by high returns on Anchor Protocol, treated their treasuries as yield engines rather than liquidity reserves. When the stablecoin de-pegged, their cash equivalents evaporated. The event was not merely a cautionary tale; it was a diagnostic test. It showed that risk frameworks, not software, determine resilience. Firms that treated DeFi as an extension of treasury policy rather than a substitute for it survived. The reconciliation is straightforward: decentralised tools do not replace governance; they make it measurable.

Treasury management in small firms has historically been constrained by access. A multinational can hedge currencies, sweep idle balances, or invest overnight. A small company cannot. DeFi lowers those thresholds. Automated market makers allow efficient swaps between fiat-backed stablecoins, while lending protocols such as Aave and Maple Finance (both launched in 2020) enable short-term financing secured by digital collateral. The practical result:

a logistics firm in Lagos or Tallinn can manage liquidity with a sophistication once reserved for corporates. Yet prudence remains the anchor. In April 2023, Maple suffered temporary loan defaults after counterparties overextended exposure to volatile assets. Its swift restructuring and improved risk parameters demonstrated an important truth: decentralisation evolves faster than governance, but governance always catches up.

The motif of control reappears here. Each design choice reflects an attitude to control. A single-signature wallet is control without accountability; a multisig is accountability shared. A timelock on protocol withdrawals enforces deliberation under pressure. A transparent on-chain audit trail substitutes paperwork with data, but only if teams actually review it. The visible behaviour of a mature DeFi treasury is not yield farming—it is scheduled review, defined policy, and post-trade verification. Stability is not coded; it is cultivated.

To show the operational side, consider **Kraken Ventures'** 2023 investment report on corporate DeFi adoption. It noted that firms allocating even 10–20% of treasury liquidity to stablecoins gained meaningful efficiency in cross-border settlement, particularly those in industries with volatile payment cycles. A design pattern emerged: segregate operational wallets by function (payroll, supplier, reserves); automate recurring transactions; and keep transparent logs accessible to auditors. Each step transformed opacity into traceability. The metrics were concrete: reduced settlement time, lower FX slippage, and faster working-capital turnover. The conclusion, though implicit, was behavioural—firms that treated DeFi as infrastructure thrived; those that treated it as investment stumbled.

A credible counterpoint comes from Japan's small-business sector. Despite regulatory clarity, adoption has lagged. Surveys by the Japan Blockchain Association (2023) found that fewer than 4% of SMEs held digital assets for operational use. The causes were cultural as much as legal: a high trust in banking institutions, low tolerance for volatility, and conservative accounting practices. Reconciliation: DeFi does not spread by evangelism but by necessity. Where legacy systems already deliver stability and efficiency, the marginal benefit of new rails shrinks. But where capital controls, cross-border friction, or inflation erode predictability, adoption becomes rational, not ideological.

The interplay between governance and autonomy defines DeFi's fit within small-business treasuries. In a traditional setting, control arises from hierarchy and documentation. In DeFi, it arises from architecture. A multi-signature wallet is a boardroom vote rendered executable. A timelock is a compliance policy without paperwork. A public ledger is an audit file that cannot be shredded. Governance migrates from paper to protocol, and accountability becomes transparent by default. Yet transparency also carries exposure: one careless transaction, and payroll data may become visible on-chain. The art lies in selective disclosure—showing enough to prove integrity, not so much as to invite risk.

A practical synthesis can be seen in Estonia, whose e-governance infrastructure has quietly normalised cryptographic trust. Several Estonian SMEs now use tokenised treasury tools linked to e-residency accounts, blending DeFi settlement with state-verified identity. The result is strikingly unglamorous: invoices paid, accounts closed, audits passed. The value proposition is not speculation; it is *boring correctness*. In treasury, boredom is the highest compliment.

The enduring image of DeFi as speculative chaos dissolves when viewed through the lens of small enterprises. These firms reveal what decentralisation looks like when it grows up: slow, procedural, cautious. It is less about overthrowing institutions than about right-sizing them. A small business using stablecoins to pay suppliers in two jurisdictions is not chasing ideology—it is managing float. That modest practicality is precisely what gives the movement longevity.

The unresolved tension lies in scale. As adoption widens, the same features that protect small firms—multi-signature access, manual review, conservative exposure limits—may impede speed at higher volumes. Will automation erode prudence, or will prudence reshape automation? Can DeFi treasuries preserve human judgment within programmable processes? The forward test is simple but profound: when every transaction can be executed instantly, what mechanisms ensure that it *should* be?

The companies that answer that question well will define the next decade of digital finance. Their advantage will not come from code alone, but from the oldest corporate virtue there is—control exercised with care.

Identity, Reputation, and Credit

In November 2022, amid the contagion that followed FTX's collapse, a single borrower—Orthogonal Trading in Melbourne—defaulted on roughly $36 million of loans issued via Maple Finance, an uncollateralised lending marketplace. Lenders were pseudonymous pools; underwriters were whitelisted delegates; the loans sat transparently on-chain. When the borrower failed, the protocol did not break, but a premise did: that public ledgers alone could replace judgement. Credit is a handshake, not a hash. Maple survived, reformed its risk process, and resumed issuance in 2023. The episode remains a hard teacher. If reputation is to stand in for collateral, the *handshake* must be made legible, portable, and enforceable. Otherwise, it is performance art.

This subchapter asks how on-chain identity and reputation can unlock unsecured credit without importing the worst habits of off-chain scoring. The proposition is simple to state. It is harder to earn. Blockchains specialise in *what happened*; they struggle with *who did it* and *what they will do next*. Identity, therefore, is not a box to tick; it is a vector through which risk travels. Get the vector wrong, and elegant mathematics merely speeds up disappointment. Get it right, and access expands for those whom legacy systems overlook. This is about precision. And patience.

Show → name → explain → implication. Show: a freelancer in Nairobi has three years of flawless repayment history on on-chain microloans, visible in her wallet's transaction graph, plus verifiable invoices settled by known enterprises. Name: *reputation collateral*. Explain: rather than posting volatile tokens, she presents a bundle of signed attestations—repayment streaks, employer receipts, DAO payouts—proven through verifiable credentials and zero-knowledge proofs. A lender prices risk from behaviour, not balance. Implication: access widens without diluting discipline. The handshake is preserved, but it is recorded.

Two named, checkable examples show this ambition in motion. **Gitcoin Passport** (launched 2022, maintained by Gitcoin in Colorado and remote) aggregates "stamps" attesting to facets of personhood—unique humanity, social accounts, tenure in open-source grants. Lenders and dApps can use a Passport score as a Sybil-resistance proxy, reducing the chance that one actor splits into many to farm incentives or drain credit lines. **Sismo** (founded 2022, Paris) issues privacy-preserving badges—ZK attestations—that let a wallet prove, for instance, "I have contributed to protocol X for Y months" without exposing addresses. Both systems shift the burden from raw identity to *verifiable history*. The handshake begins to leave a trail.

A credible counter-example keeps us honest. **Worldcoin** (public launch July 2023), built by Tools for Humanity, sought to solve Sybil resistance with biometrics—the infamous orb. Proof-of-personhood is valuable for credit, because one human should map to one reputation. Yet Kenya suspended operations in August 2023; European regulators raised GDPR concerns; critics questioned data custody and governance. The reconciliation is operational, not ideological: personhood proofs that rely on sensitive biometrics create attack surfaces and political liabilities that may outweigh their credit utility. The design lesson is blunt. Prefer *verifiable behaviour* over *irrevocable traits*. A lost private key can be rotated; a scanned iris cannot.

What, then, are the prerequisites for reputation-backed credit that works? Four, at minimum, each observable as behaviour rather than rhetoric. First, *attestation quality*. A repayment claim must be signed by a party with skin in the game, and revocable when new facts emerge. W3C verifiable credentials (2019) and BBS+ signatures support exactly this: issuers sign structured statements; holders present privacy-preserving proofs; relying parties verify cryptographically. Second, *Sybil resistance*. Without it, the same actor can borrow, default, and reappear endlessly. Tools range from low-stakes KYC to ZK membership proofs like Semaphore; whichever path is chosen must be measurable in false positive and false negative rates, not vibes. Third, *recourse*. Credit without consequence collapses into grants. Even in DeFi, recourse exists—legal contracts tied to off-chain assets, social slashing of staking rewards, or on-chain liens over future cashflows (e.g., streaming payments via Superfluid). Fourth, *data minimisation.* The system must prove enough to price risk, and no more. That is not piety; it is attack-surface management.

Lest we drift into abstraction, consider **Aave's Credit Delegation** (introduced mid-2020). A depositor can delegate borrowing power to a known counterparty without the borrower posting collateral to the protocol. The real collateral is a legal agreement between them—often off-chain. This arrangement is not unsecured in the wild; it is secured by contract and reputation rather than by token. The implication is instructive: even when credit appears "unsecured," it is only unsecured *to the protocol.* Someone somewhere holds a promise they can enforce. Reputation lives within that promise.

Next, **Spectral Finance** (2021, New York) attempted a "credit score" from on-chain signals, clustering wallets by repayment patterns, DeFi sophistication, and asset volatility to produce a number. It was honest in acknowledging limits. Early users could game the metric by staging "good" transactions in small size; correlations broke during market stress; overfitting lurked. Spectral iterated, adding resistance to wash behaviour. The lesson is methodological humility. A score can compress information without distorting it only if the training objective matches actual loss. Beauty in dashboards does not repay loans. Measure defaults, not decorum.

We also have cautionary chapters. In 2021–2022, **TrueFi** and **Maple** expanded uncollateralised lending to market-makers and funds. Many loans performed; several did not (TrueFi's Blockwater default in October 2022; Maple's Orthogonal default in November 2022). Where did reputation fail? Not in concept, but in perimeter. Underwriting sometimes relied on off-chain financial statements that proved stale within weeks; concentration risk to a few borrowers crept in; covenants were weak on events of cross-default. The reconciliation is plain: reputation cannot be a veneer over traditional credit. It must be integrated with continuous, machine-verifiable performance data and hard-coded diversification limits. Then the handshake is policed by code.

The motif returns: the handshake. Credit begins with a promise and ends with a payment. Between promise and payment lives *prediction*. On-chain reputation offers better inputs to that prediction by rendering history tamper-evident and portable. Portability matters. A contractor who repays a DAO advance in Seoul should be able to present that success to a London protocol without re-proving their entire life. That is what makes reputation valuable capital rather than local chatter. The wallet, if you like, becomes a CV.

What about bias? Off-chain credit bureaus have been accused, with evidence, of baking socio-economic bias into their models. On-chain designs are not born pure. If reputation accrues primarily to users who can afford gas fees, or to those embedded in Western DAOs, it will replicate old exclusions in new code. The antidote is deliberate pluralism in attesters and attributes. Include micro–repayment histories from emerging-market wallets; weight long-tail signals like timely streaming-payroll completions; accept proofs from community lenders with audited track records. Publish model cards—descriptions of features and their weights—and commit to external audits. Bias is not avoided by silence; it is managed by exposure.

We must speak about privacy without euphemism. Reputation that cannot be forgotten becomes surveillance. The technical way through is *selective disclosure*. **Polygon ID** (GA March 2023) and similar systems allow a wallet to prove "I have repaid X on time for Y months" without exposing addresses or counterparties, using zero-knowledge circuits. Pair this with expiry: proofs should time out; old mistakes should not brand forever. The operational way through is governance: protocols ought to publish data retention and revocation policies, name stewards who can be held to account, and instrument their systems so that every access request leaves a log. Privacy is not a vibe. It is routine.

There is also the problem of *attribution*. Whose reputation accrues when multiple people share control of a wallet (a multisig), or when an enterprise uses a smart-contract wallet? ENS names, decentralised identifiers, and contract-based accounts complicate naive scoring, but they also offer an opportunity: attribute reputation to *entities*, not only to keys. The precondition is a canonical link—an attestation that this multisig represents Company X, signed by its directors and, ideally, by a corporate registry offering a verifiable credential. Then repayment performance flows to the entity, not to whichever signer happened to push the button that week. This mirrors conventional credit while preserving cryptographic assurance.

A subtle pitfall lies in incentives. If a protocol distributes tokens to borrowers who perform, scores will be gamed. If, instead, it offers interest rebates conditional on verified performance and external attestations, gaming becomes costlier. If, further, it slashes stakers who vouch for bad actors, community incentives align. **Goldfinch** (2021, San Francisco) experimented with backers who underwrote real-world lenders; defaults in 2023 revealed how quickly optimistic staking can turn into silent risk transfer when diligence is thin. The correction came by tightening audits, diversifying borrower sets, and raising underwriter requirements. Incentives are not decoration. They are the risk engine.

Turn abstractions into metrics. A reputation system that works publishes its *Gini coefficient* of reputation distribution (to detect concentration), its *population coverage* by region (to detect bias), its *false-accept and false-reject rates* (to detect calibration), and its *loss given default* by score bucket (to detect economic meaning). It commits to versioning: when a scoring model changes, historical decisions are marked with the model version to avoid retrospective confusion. It defines appeals: a user can challenge an attestation, present new proofs, and seek score correction within a stated SLA. A handshake deserves an appeals desk.

Where does regulation fit? Carefully. The **EU's MiCA** sets disclosure rules for service providers but does not yet define standards for reputation scoring; the **FATF** recommendations shape KYC perimeters; national credit laws govern explainability and fairness. Reputation systems that aspire to longevity will adopt *explainable-by-design* criteria even before compelled: "Loan denied because your last three streaming repayments were late; present an employer attestation to upgrade." If a system cannot say this plainly, it will fail in courts, then in markets.

Finally, a forward-looking note on *receivables and streaming income*. Protocols such as Superfluid or Sablier make cashflows granular. A borrower can pledge a portion of future streams to a pool; default detection becomes instantaneous rather than monthly. Pair that with verifiable credentials from payroll providers, and unsecured credit becomes a misnomer. It is secured by *continuity of income*, visible in real time. This is not science fiction; it is a rearrangement of primitives we already have. The handshake is continuous, not episodic.

The unresolved test is practical and sharp. Suppose a graduate in Lagos, with no traditional credit history, can present twelve months of on-chain proof: timely rent streams, repaid microloans, invoices from a verified DAO, and a humanhood proof that respects privacy. Should a protocol extend a modest credit line at a rate that reflects history rather than geography? If your instinct is "yes," the next question is tougher: what specific attestations, recourse mechanisms, and model audits make that "yes" defensible when a default hits? Reputation can unlock unsecured credit. It can also excuse wishful lending. The difference is whether the handshake is just a gesture—or a contract that both sides can name, measure, and, if necessary, enforce.

What Will Probably Endure

On 11 March 2023, Circle confirmed that $3.3 billion of USDC's reserves were stuck at Silicon Valley Bank in Santa Clara after the bank's failure the day before. Across that weekend, the dollar-pegged stablecoin—long treated as a paragon of predictability—traded at a discount as deep as 88 cents on several venues before snapping back when U.S. authorities guaranteed deposits. Nothing changed in the smart contract. Everything changed in the context. The lesson was not that stablecoins fail; it was that *designs* matter and *linkages* matter more. The primitives that survive are those whose wiring makes their behaviour legible when stress arrives. These core primitives are load-bearing.

Survival in finance is rarely about glamour. It is about structure. The architecture that endures tends to look unremarkable from the outside: stable settlement media, automated liquidity provision, collateralised credit, and a commitment—sometimes contested—to credible neutrality. Each of these has been tested in public, in dates and events one can verify. Each persists because, even when wounded, it explains itself. What follows is not a prediction; it is a reading of what has already survived.

Begin with the most prosaic: **fiat-referenced stablecoins**. They move wages, pay vendors, and terminate remittance routes. Their virtue is not yield but *certainty*. USDC, USDT, and regulated e-money tokens like Monerium's EUR-denominated issuance (EEA, 2022) work because their liability structure is simple enough to audit and sufficiently conservative to model. Their fragility appears when off-chain linkages wobble—bank counterparties, cash-like instruments, legal enforceability. The March 2023 wobble showed both sides. On-chain, the token contracts were fine; off-chain, deposit concentration at a single institution created a short, sharp crisis of confidence. The implication is operational: fiat-backed stablecoins endure if their reserve disclosures are routine, counterparties diversified, and redemption rights enforceable in court. The visible behaviour is boring: monthly attestations, granular asset ladders, and fast, predictable redemptions. Without that, the peg is not a promise; it is a wish.

This clarity is precisely why **algorithmic stablecoins**—untethered to audited reserves—have fared poorly. TerraUSD's collapse in May 2022 is the canonical case. Its peg relied on reflexive mint-burn dynamics with LUNA rather than on redeemable dollars. It scaled until it didn't. When sell pressure rose, the algorithm's confidence loop inverted. A design that assumed mean reversion met a market that demanded collateral. The counter-example does not refute stablecoins as a category; it refines it. Endurance requires redeemability with minimal narrative. "What backs this?" needs a one-line answer anyone can verify.

Turn to **automated market makers** (AMMs). Uniswap's first deployment in November 2018 replaced order books with curves, making liquidity *continuous* and *permissionless*. The mechanism worked in quiet markets, then learned to cope with busy ones. With Uniswap v3 (May 2021, New York-based Uniswap Labs), concentrated liquidity made capital efficient enough to rival professional market-makers, while keeping settlement atomically on-chain. The surviving trait here is not fashion; it is composability. AMMs became the price engine for dozens of other protocols because their behaviour under stress is observable, and arbitrage closes gaps without appeals to human intermediaries. During the USDC depeg weekend in March 2023, AMM pools repriced in seconds; arbitrageurs, not committees, stitched the system back together once the off-chain news clarified reserves. Endurance, in this corner, looks like this: simple invariant, clean fee paths, and enough surface area for arbitrage to do its job. Curves, not committees.

There are limits. AMMs can be sandwiched; poorly set fees can attract toxic order flow; long-tail pairs can be ghost towns. Yet the pattern remains: they degrade gracefully. A thin pool widens slippage; it does not invent fake liquidity. A fee change transmits instantly; it does not languish in a queue. The implication is sobering and practical. AMMs endure because they fail visibly before they fail catastrophically, and because they invite repair by anyone who sees the gap.

Next, **over-collateralised lending.** Aave's launch in January 2020 and Maker's earlier DAI engine (2017 onward; "Black Thursday", 12–13 March 2020) forged a credit culture that reverses the usual temptation. Instead of stretching collateral thin, they make you post more than you borrow. The protocols run on *health factors, liquidation thresholds,* and fee curves that lift rates when utilisation is high. The tests have been public. On Black Thursday, oracles lagged while ETH crashed; auctions jammed; MakerDAO had to patch governance and collateral parameters in the open. It survived, and its parameter discipline hardened. Aave's liquidations during violent drawdowns in 2021–2023 displayed the same trait: the valve opens, penalties bite, positions reset. Painful, but *mechanical.* Over-collateralisation is not ideology. It is a design that keeps short-term liquidity crises from becoming long-term insolvency.

This does not make unsecured protocols impossible; it makes them narrow. Maple Finance's 2022 defaults, and TrueFi's contemporaneous borrower failures, taught that underwriting cannot be crowdsourced to dashboards. Where unsecured credit persists, it does so with old-fashioned scaffolding: legal contracts, audited borrowers, diversification limits, and continuously monitored cashflow data. In on-chain terms, that reads as segregated pools, delegate accountability with skin in the game, and fast loss recognition. The category that endures is not "unsecured lending" as a vibe, but *disciplined credit* expressed in code with ex-ante governance, not ex-post improvisation.

A fourth primitive sits less in any one protocol than in a posture: **credible neutrality**. The term, borrowed from political philosophy and sharpened by Ethereum research, describes infrastructure that does not discriminate among lawful users and cannot be co-opted by narrow interests without visible cost. The Merge (15 September 2022) made neutrality more pressing, not less: proof-of-stake made censorship risks more salient because validators are identifiable entities. The OFAC sanctions against Tornado Cash (Washington, 10 August 2022) tested the edges: some staking providers adopted partial censorship of blocks to avoid relaying flagged transactions; others engineered inclusion lists and relay diversity to resist soft pressure. The neutral posture that endures is not a slogan; it is a set of *choices*: diverse relays, MEV smoothing without capture, permissionless client diversity, and governance that prizes procedure over personality.

Neutrality has commercial impact. Protocols that embed strong neutrality assumptions—transparent rules, minimal admin keys, clear timelocks—attract integrators, insurers, and auditors because predictability is bankable. The behaviour is countable: number of independent clients in production; percentage of blocks built by non-censoring relays; timelock duration on critical parameters; proportion of fees that flow automatically without discretionary routing. These are the tell-tales of a keel that holds. Keel, not sail.

If these are the likely survivors, what do they *do* under stress? Stablecoins preserve purchasing power across interfaces; AMMs clear trades when humans hesitate; collateralised lending liquidates rather than litigates; neutrality keeps optionality open when politics intrudes. Each primitive earns its keep by performing a boring duty precisely when drama peaks. That is the quiet criterion for endurance: a duty performed *at* the limit is worth three performed in calm.

Two named examples show this endurance in the wild, beyond crisis weekends. First, **Brazil's Pix plus stablecoins** (São Paulo, 2023): regulated instant payments integrated with regulated on/off-ramps, with USDC acting as the cross-border settlement leg. Here, stablecoins did not replace banks; they shortened a path banks already walked. The primitive endured because it subordinated itself to a system that already worked for millions. Second, **Uniswap v3 in traditional FX pairs** on permissioned deployments (London/New York pilots through 2022–2023): AMM logic ran inside compliance perimeters to provide intra-day liquidity for tokenised fiat. The primitive endured because it wore a suit when needed and kept its invariants regardless.

Now, a counter-example that clarifies boundaries. **Proof-of-personhood** via biometric oracles (Worldcoin, July–August

2023; Nairobi, Berlin, San Francisco) promises Sybil resistance for voting and credit. The primitive—identity-as-a-service—has utility. Yet its path to endurance is blocked by governance opacity, data custody debate, and jurisdictional resistance. The reconciliation points to our earlier shortlist: enduring primitives reduce *irreversible* externalities. A scanned iris is irreversible. A zero-knowledge proof of unique membership is not. The design that lasts will prove "one human" without creating a stockpile of sensitive data. The keel must not be made of glass.

Abstractions demand measures. If you want to distinguish survivors from fads, do not count followers; count **invariants**. For stablecoins: average redemption time and haircut, reserve concentration limits, frequency and granularity of attestations. For AMMs: percentage of volume routed through open pools versus captive venues, slippage at defined sizes across volatility regimes, arbitrage time-to-close for one-standard-deviation price shocks. For collateralised lending: average health-factor buffer, liquidation throughput per block during stress, realised loss rate by collateral type over rolling quarters. For neutrality: validator/relay concentration, client diversity (by implementation) above a threshold, proportion of blocks including transactions flagged elsewhere. Numbers civilise narratives.

The motif returns. Keel, not sail. Fashionable tokenomics will continue to appear, then vanish. Incentive programmes can conjure TVL for a quarter; they do not confer purpose. What does is *fit*: protocols that slot into how value already moves while making that motion more auditable, more programmable, and less hostage to single points of failure. The survivals will be those that accept humility—subsystems, not empires.

A word on *governance minimalism*. Enduring systems keep their sharpest tools behind glass. Admin keys wrapped in timelocks; parameter ranges bounded; emergency powers documented, scarce, and expensive to use. This is not only for security; it is for legitimacy. When the March 2023 USDC scare landed, the protocols most trusted to hold composure were those least able to panic. That constraint is a feature. Restraint is an asset.

Where does this leave unsecured credit, synthetic assets, restaking, cross-chain abstraction? Some pieces will persist, but as specialised services that borrow credibility from the four beams described here. Unsecured credit will live within pockets where legal recourse and rich data make it prudent. Synthetics will thrive when backed by oracles and collateral systems that have already endured. Restaking will professionalise where slashing conditions are clear and correlated risk is bounded. Bridges will hide behind standards when proofs of finality become portable. Survival will be conditional on anchoring to the primitives that have already survived.

The forward test is not complicated. When you evaluate a bright new construct, ask four dry questions. What settles it? Who makes its market when screens go blank? What collateral stands between error and ruin? What political wind can turn it off, and how loudly would that switch click? If the answers rhyme with *reserves, curves, buffers,* and *neutral relays,* you are looking at a keel worth trusting. If the answers look like marketing, you are looking at weather.

Chapter 9 Conclusion
The Discipline of Open Finance

In September 2023, a small software firm in Berlin called its first "digital fire drill." At noon, all employees were asked to freeze operations and simulate a complete loss of access to their crypto wallets and cloud accounts. The finance lead timed how long it took to recover access using backups, paper keys, and multisignature approvals. Thirty-seven minutes later, the company resumed normal function. No funds lost, no panic, no improvisation. Afterwards, the team printed a short report titled *Failing Gracefully*. Its first line read: *we are not defined by what we build, but by how we withstand what breaks.* That, distilled, is the ethos of this closing chapter.

Discipline, not enthusiasm, sustains the craft of open finance. Curiosity invites us in; process keeps us from harm. The decentralised world seduces with novelty—new tokens, protocols, and rewards that flash faster than most people can research them. Yet the point of mastery is not speed; it is selectivity. What you refuse to touch often protects more value than what you embrace. This chapter, therefore, is not about finding the next thing. It is about *building the reflexes that outlast the next thing*.

Every mature system—aviation, medicine, cybersecurity—translates curiosity into discipline through routine. Pilots run pre-flight checklists not because they expect failure but because they accept it as natural. The same holds true in open finance. A prudent participant conducts periodic reviews: confirming that wallet permissions still make sense, that recovery phrases are stored separately, that exposure to algorithmic assets remains deliberate, not habitual. These rituals do not announce brilliance; they confirm competence. They mark the difference between someone dabbling in technology and someone practising a profession.

The motif here is the *drill*. It surfaces throughout this chapter because drills transform theory into instinct. A red-team exercise—imagining an adversary who knows your setup better than you do—is not paranoia; it is pedagogy. It teaches humility without humiliation. The same logic applies to a "kill switch for FOMO": a predefined act of restraint, such as waiting twenty-four hours before executing a trade that excites you. This is not moralising; it is cognitive design. The smartest investors and developers alike know that emotion is faster than reason, and that slowing oneself is an act of power, not weakness.

Show → name → explain → implication. Show: an individual trader in Mumbai reviews her portfolio every quarter, logs decisions, and deletes obsolete smart-contract approvals. Name: operational hygiene. Explain: by systematising attention, she lowers both technical and psychological debt. Implication: over time, the routine compounds—fewer errors, calmer reactions, clearer records. Risk management ceases to be a chore; it becomes a form of self-respect.

The deeper lesson is that decentralisation magnifies personal responsibility. Where intermediaries vanish, habits must replace them. Traditional finance externalised discipline: compliance teams, auditors, customer service. Open finance internalises it. You are the compliance department of your own life. That transfer of agency can feel exhilarating or exhausting depending on temperament. But there is no way around it. Self-custody without self-scrutiny is theatre.

The discipline of open finance also requires an appreciation for refusal. To decline participation is not cowardice; it is calibration. The investor who holds no exposure during mania is practising finance in its purest form—valuation by omission. The developer who decides not to ship a smart contract until the audit is finished is protecting not only users but also the credibility of the ecosystem itself. Saying "no" is part of the choreography of durability.

There is a quiet parallel between DeFi and mountaineering. Both attract those who love the frontier; both punish those who treat preparation as optional. Every climber learns the ritual of checking ropes, harnesses, weather. Most climbs fail not because of the mountain, but because of impatience. Likewise, most financial missteps do not arise from code bugs; they arise from human ones—greed, fatigue, the desire to match someone else's screenshot. The antidote is practice. Not theory, not enthusiasm—practice.

Within this frame, security becomes a living discipline, not a static configuration. The red-team exercise introduced earlier is one expression. Another is the *periodic review*, a self-audit conducted at fixed intervals—an accounting of what you hold, why you hold it, and how you would unwind it if required. The purpose is not perfection but visibility. Every pilot knows: you cannot correct what you cannot see. In finance, as in flight, blindness kills more surely than turbulence.

The next layer is social. Discipline is not isolation. True resilience comes from shared norms—small teams agreeing to accountability routines, communities publishing post-mortems when things go wrong, protocols disclosing not just returns but recovery procedures. The best of open finance, paradoxically, looks like an old-fashioned guild: knowledge codified, errors recorded, apprentices trained to spot the same traps their mentors survived. Craft is communal memory formalised.

To reach this level, curiosity must mature into craft. Curiosity asks, "How does this protocol work?" Craft asks, "How could this fail, and what would I do then?" The transition sounds subtle; it is not. Curiosity is episodic; craft is continuous. Curiosity consumes information; craft distils it. The experienced participant reads white papers not to be dazzled but to locate fault lines. They treat hype as data about psychology, not as evidence of quality.

The motif of the drill returns once more. Imagine a periodic simulation: you lose every key, every connection, every credential. How do you restart? Who do you notify? How long before you can transact again? If your answer depends on luck, your system depends on luck. That is the uncomfortable honesty this chapter insists on. Security rehearsed in calm saves reputations under fire.

A further habit—less technical, more philosophical—is *recording refusals*. Keep a simple ledger of what you chose not to do, and why. Over years, this log becomes a mirror of judgment. It reveals patterns of caution, perhaps even wisdom. When markets roar, it reminds you that restraint has a track record too. The compounding of safety and skill begins there—in memory managed as carefully as capital.

The final paragraphs of this chapter will not celebrate winners or warn sinners. They will describe routines, because routines are where knowledge matures into habit. Finance, open or closed, will always involve risk, but discipline transforms risk from hazard into teacher. Those who practise it become less reactive, more analytical, and, perhaps most importantly, more at peace.

The forward tension, then, is this: Can the culture of open finance evolve from one of constant experimentation to one of measured mastery—without losing its creative spark? Can curiosity coexist with procedure, autonomy with audit, speed with deliberation? Each reader must answer in their own practice. The discipline of open finance is not a doctrine to memorise. It is a rhythm to live by: review, test, pause, decide, repeat. Those who internalise that rhythm will find that freedom and safety, far from being opposites, are in fact the same skill performed well.

From Curiosity to Craft

In May 2021, the team behind bZx, a decentralised lending protocol based in Chicago, discovered that an attacker had drained over $55 million in digital assets. The breach was not a code exploit but a lapse in operational discipline: a phishing email had tricked one developer into exposing private keys. The smart contracts remained sound; the humans faltered. Within weeks, the incident became a case study in the difference between *building technology* and *practising security*. The aftermath—emergency recovery, compensation debates, regulatory scrutiny—forced a truth most enthusiasts resist: curiosity may open the door to open finance, but only craft keeps it standing.

The transition from curiosity to craft begins when excitement gives way to ritual. It is the moment a participant stops asking *what can I try?* and begins asking *what must I rehearse?* In aviation, routine drills make flight possible. In finance, the same logic applies. Mastery here is not about predicting prices or discovering the next protocol; it is about designing systems that survive surprise. The habit of structured review—backups tested, permissions audited, exposures capped—turns speculation into practice. One five-word sentence captures the difference: *discipline protects more than talent.*

Show → name → explain → implication. Show: an independent developer in Lisbon stores private keys in a single encrypted file on her laptop. The device fails; backups are months old. The loss is irreversible. Name: single-point fragility. Explain: decentralisation removes intermediaries but not human error; absent procedures, every user becomes their own weakest link. Implication: resilience demands more than curiosity; it requires choreography. The routines that save time under stress are rehearsed long before stress arrives.

The first principle of craft is *periodic review*. In September 2022, a London-based DAO treasurer ran a quarterly audit of smart-contract approvals and discovered dormant permissions granting obsolete apps access to treasury funds. Revoking them prevented potential misuse. This behaviour—documented, routine, repeatable—is what separates a hobbyist from an operator. The visible habit is boring: calendars, spreadsheets, checklists. Yet boredom is precisely the point. What professionals call *hygiene* is the institutionalisation of prudence. Systems that live long enough to matter evolve their own hygiene.

The second principle is *simulation*. Red-team exercises—controlled attempts to break your own defences—translate curiosity into competence. In cybersecurity, red-teaming is standard practice; in open finance, it remains rare. In March 2023, an Ethereum infrastructure firm in Amsterdam ran an internal "crisis weekend," testing responses to oracle failure, liquidity shock, and smart-contract pauses. The goal was not zero errors but measurable recovery time. That metric—*mean time to coordination*—proved more valuable than theoretical uptime. Every serious protocol could borrow the same metric and apply it to governance: how long before a diverse community can make a coherent decision under pressure? Craft begins when performance is measured in minutes, not moods.

A credible counter-example sharpens the argument. During the FTX collapse in November 2022, numerous DeFi projects faced indirect contagion: liquidity vanished, prices slumped, fear spread. Some teams reacted within hours, pausing markets and communicating openly. Others waited, paralysed by uncertainty. The contrast was not technical; it was procedural. Projects that had practised coordination—tested governance calls, scripted fallback measures—contained risk. Those that hadn't wrote post-mortems about "communication gaps." The reconciliation is unromantic but real: culture is part of control. Systems inherit their operators' reflexes.

The third principle, subtle but essential, is the *kill switch for FOMO*. Curiosity, unchecked, becomes compulsion. In markets where incentives change hourly, the ability to *do nothing* is strategic. The best traders and developers construct rituals of delay: time locks before large commitments, pre-declared cooling-off periods, or automated scripts that require multi-signature confirmation after a waiting interval. The philosopher Seneca wrote that no man is free who is a slave to impulse. The digital analogue is clear: no one is secure who acts faster than they can think.

Visible behaviours anchor this restraint. Some professionals impose a "24-hour rule": no trade, deployment, or upgrade may occur less than a day after proposal. Others maintain written rationales—short memos recording why a decision was made and under what assumptions. A year later, these notes read like mirrors. They reveal whether reasoning improved or degenerated into mimicry. The cumulative effect is what behavioural economists call *meta-awareness*: seeing oneself as part of the system rather than above it.

The quiet motif throughout this subchapter is *the drill*. Drills turn competence into habit. They strip glamour from the act of defence and reveal the beauty of repetition. A periodic key-rotation exercise, a scheduled test of recovery protocols, a simulated phishing campaign within a DAO—these are the equivalent of a craftsman sharpening tools before they dull. The act may appear mundane, but it embodies an ethic: *we prepare not because we expect failure, but because we respect entropy.*

Yet discipline, taken too far, can ossify into paranoia. There is a limit where prudence becomes inhibition. A credible limitation: overly cautious teams may reject all innovation, missing opportunities that careful iteration could have secured. Consider Compound's 2021 upgrade from v2 to v3. The team staged months of audits and community tests, delaying release by a quarter. Critics called it excessive. But when the deployment succeeded with zero critical incidents, the delay became a data point for patience as performance. The reconciliation is measured, not rhetorical: tempo must match complexity. The higher the stakes, the slower the beat.

Refusal—what one *chooses not to do*—is the final sign of mastery. In May 2021, as "DeFi 2.0" projects promised unsustainable yields, a few long-standing protocols, including MakerDAO and Aave, refused to chase. Their forums debated participation and declined. They prioritised solvency over spectacle. That abstention looked dull at the time. By January 2022, when those yield experiments imploded, it looked like wisdom. In open finance, refusal is not the absence of action; it is an assertion of standards.

The measure of craft, then, is rhythm. Professionals establish cycles—weekly exposure reviews, quarterly backups, annual policy rewrites—so that diligence compounds like interest. Over months, these habits become muscle memory. Curiosity alone produces movement; craft produces direction. It is the same difference that separates a novice pianist experimenting with keys from a concert musician rehearsing scales daily. The notes are identical; the discipline is not.

One might ask whether such discipline can coexist with the spontaneity that drew people to decentralised finance in the first place. Can rules preserve freedom without ossifying it? The answer lies in the distinction between *structure* and *control*. A red-team exercise, a review checklist, or a FOMO kill switch does not suppress curiosity; it channels it. The structure provides a rhythm against which improvisation can occur safely. Jazz, not bureaucracy.

Metrics make this real. A skilled operator can quote their mean recovery time for lost access, the number of revoked approvals in the last audit, or the ratio of hot to cold wallet funds. These are not abstractions; they are instruments of feedback. They turn slogans about "risk awareness" into dashboards. More importantly, they permit conversation: two professionals can compare notes on procedures the way athletes compare training regimes. Craft is collective.

The motif of the drill returns one last time. A protocol that rehearses governance votes for emergencies, a team that rotates roles in crisis simulations, an individual who schedules a quarterly "digital fire drill" for personal finances—all practise the same underlying discipline. They transform anxiety into preparedness. They treat foresight not as paranoia but as respect for reality. The measure of success is uneventful continuity.

There remains one final paradox. The same curiosity that launches exploration also fuels overreach. The same discipline that prevents disaster can, if misapplied, smother invention. Between the two lies the craft of judgment. Each participant must decide where their threshold lies: how much uncertainty they can bear, how much routine they can sustain. There is no formula, only iteration.

The forward test is simple, though never easy: could you walk away for a month, return, and find your systems intact? If not, what processes would make that possible? To ask that question—and to act on the answer—is to cross the line from curiosity to craft. In open finance, the mark of mastery is not how much you chase, but how little you need to.

About the Author

Avery Grant writes about money as if it were a technology we teach ourselves to use with care. Raised between spreadsheets and second-hand paperbacks, Avery's work treats decentralised finance not as a revolution to cheer or fear, but as an apprenticeship in autonomy. The essays and guides are known for plain language, careful scepticism, and an insistence on habits that outlast hype. Drawing quietly on the long arc from tally sticks to cryptography, Avery writes for readers who want to participate without self-deception, pairing practical checklists with humane counsel: sometimes the smartest trade is the one you do not place. The aim is simple and serious — help ordinary people handle new tools with old virtues.

www.ingramcontent.com/pod-product-compliance
Lightning Source LLC
Chambersburg PA
CBHW031338230926
51848CB00002B/283
* 9 7 8 9 3 7 4 5 9 9 6 0 0 *